Airports for people

Airports for people

Proceedings of the 8th World Airports Conference organized by the Institution of Civil Engineers and held in London on 2 – 5 June 1987

Thomas Telford, London

Conference organized and sponsored by the Institution of Civil Engineers, and co-sponsored by the Royal Institute of British Architects, the Royal Town Planning Institute, the Royal Aeronautical Society and the Chartered Institute of Transport.

Organizing Committee:
G. M. Crook (Chairman), D. Y. Davies, K. Gilham, M. G. Hudson, D. N. Miller, E. Bryan Tutty, A. A. Wood

re'd 10/13/88

First published 1988

British Library Cataloguing in Publication Data

   Airports for people: proceedings of a
     conference organized by the Institution
     of Civil Engineers, and held in London
     on 2 – 5 June 1987.
     1. Airports
     I. Institution of Civil Engineers
     387.7'36

ISBN 0 7277 1327 2

Published for the Institution of Civil Engineers by Thomas Telford Ltd, Thomas Telford House, 1 Heron Quay, London E14 9XF.

Printed in England by Hartnolls Ltd, Bodmin, Cornwall.

Contents

Workshop 1.   Detailed terminal design and refurbishment of existing terminals

Workshop 2.   Commercial applications

Workshop 3.   Airport and environment

Workshop 4.   New technology

1 A consumer's view of world air transport

M. DONNE, Aerospace correspondent, Financial Times, London

The basic requirements of the consumers of world air transport - that is, the passengers - are analysed, and suggestions for improvements in the overall quality of air service are made. The fundamental thesis is that while the air transport industry has made considerable strides in recent years, in improving the service that is offered to passengers, there is still a considerable way to go.

1.   My qualifications for addressing you as a 'consumer' of world air transport, if indeed there is such a description, are that over the past 34 years as an aviation writer (and even before that as an air passenger) I have travelled well over three million miles by air, and that there is now hardly an airline in the world that I have not flown in. I have also experienced my share of aviation mishaps, and the fact that I am still here to tell the tale is, or should be, evidence enough of my conviction that air transport is here to stay. There are also few of the world's airports that I have not been through, from a grass shack in the Seychelles to the latest monsters of steel, plate glass and concrete that litter the landscapes as far afield as Singapore, the UK and the USA.

2.   Anyone commenting upon airports with the critical eye of a consumer must stress at the outset that the views expressed will inevitably be highly personal and subjective. According to the ICAO, there were over 938 million scheduled air travellers throughout the world in 1986, including the Soviet Union and China, and probably well over one billion such travellers if non-scheduled and charter travellers are included. As a result, there are probably well over one billion different opinions as to the qualities and capabilities of the air transport system, so that, at best, any one analyst's opinions must be general in tone, although perhaps one may be permitted to be specific about individual airlines or airports.

3.   It is also essential to establish at the outset just what this basic individual - the consumer - is that we are about to discuss. While it is undeniable that much has been done over the past forty years to smooth the expanding flow of world air travellers, it is nevertheless my experience that the consumer's interests have often become lost in public analyses of air transport. The consumer has become a mere 'pax' (horrible word!), a unit regarded as being of a basic standard, usually miniscule in size, somewhat lacking in both intelligence and general ability to find his way about (especially if he is a holiday traveller on a package tour), and all too frequently an individual to be treated

with disdain, and even with contempt, and with his special desires all too often being ignored, or at best treated with reluctance. If this seems to be a harsh judgement, I suggest that all those of you who are either airline or airport employees, benefitting perhaps from special treatment, should put yourselves into the position of a mere 'pax', at a foreign airport late at night, tired, bewildered and even perhaps ill, to get just some flavour of what millions of air travellers have to put up with. You will then find that my judgement is not so harsh, after all.

4.   And yet, all is not lost. For at the other end of the scale, I have often found courtesy, kindness and consideration, that have made me feel that air transport is not so bad after all, and that somebody within the system does recognise me as a human being.

5.   So, the first parameter we must consider is that the consumer, the air passenger, is the sole reason for the existence of everybody, without exception, who works in air transport. The passenger is their livelihood, their income, and their profit, and, as such, is not an interruption of their daily lives. As soon as everybody, high and low, in world air transport recognises the fact, the sooner the system will improve. It is miraculous how recognition of this fact by British Airways rescued the airline from the brink of bankruptcy, restored its profitability, and put it on the way to a most successful privatisation. It is as simple as that.

6.   However, in any analysis of what more needs to be done to improve the overall condition of the average air traveller, it is essential to determine what he requires. In all that I am about to say, I must stress at the outset that I take safety to be a <u>sine qua non</u>, and so do not intend to devote time to any discussion of it. My basic concerns are with more mundane matters of physical and mental welfare.

7.   Similarly, with airport security, I must stress that, regrettable though it may be, every air traveller must now accept that it is here to stay, and that the likelihood is that it will get tougher as time goes on. However, I suggest that

Airports for people. Thomas Telford Limited, London, 1988

we should all be careful to ensure that this need for more security is not allowed to become, as is already the case in many airports, a recipe for delays, and an excuse to cloak other inefficiencies that have been endemic in the system for so long.

8. Firstly, may I suggest that what any air traveller really needs above all - allowing, as I have said, for safety and security - is convenience: the ability to pass through any airport smoothly, with maximum speed and minimum disruption, no matter whether the latter be caused by airport and airline staffs, the design of the terminal itself, or the desire of others, such as duty-free goods salesmen, to take advantage of the traveller's captive presence for even a few minutes. Ideally, any airport should be a place in which one spends as little time as possible: it is, after all, only a gateway at the beginning or end of an air journey.

9. Nevertheless, despite this need for convenience, the average air traveller still needs a reasonable level of comfort. Contrary to the view of some planners, the traveller is less interested in how a particular terminal is designed, or how many architectural awards it may have won, as in how easy it is to use, and how comfortable and convenient the passage through it may be.

10. Secondly, as part of this overall requirement of convenience, the air traveller seeks a minimum of imposed controls, again stemming either from airline inadequacies or from Government regulations. Insufficiency of check-in desks (a common failing at many airports), and of staff to man those that are available (again an endemic disease of the system - why have them if you cannot staff them?) represent the start of the traveller's woes. Inadequate staffing of Customs and Immigration formalities, and especially the latter, also contribute to the overall irritation factor. All these are built-in factors to make or mar the start or finish of an air journey, and also can make or mar the image of the particular country visited or of the airline with which our passenger has travelled. When will officialdom really begin to understand these few quite simple truths, and do something about them?

11. Thirdly, our traveller wants an intelligent level of information, conveyed discreetly, to help him in his passage, inbound or outbound, which can be interpreted as clearly readable signs, adequate voice information, coupled if necessary with a sufficiency of clearly recognisable (i.e.) uniformed staff, able to speak a variety of languages and trained to be helpful and courteous. It has always been a matter of astonishment to me how poor this latter facility is at many major so-called 'international' airports.

12. Virtually everything else relating to the consumer in airports - the availability of duty-free concessions and other shopping facilities, refreshments, rest-rooms, banks, nurseries, and other facilities - all come under one or another of these basic parameters. The existing position can be summarised by saying that very few major airports, even some of the most modern, meet all of these requirements to the satisfaction of all, or even perhaps a majority of travellers.

13. This is because although billions of dollars have been spent on the development of new airports over the past forty years or so, airport design and construction itself has changed, both under pressures of rising numbers of passengers and because tastes in architectural styles have changed. Probably also it is because airport authorities themselves cannot agree precisely upon what it is that the average air traveller needs. Some take the trouble to find out, but many others do not, and the result has been a curious pot-pourri of designs that vary widely from the totally unsatisfactory, and at congested periods almost unworkable circular Terminal One at Charles de Gaulle in Paris, to the vast labyrinth of Kennedy, New York, and those monsters spreading over the landscape at Dallas/Fort Worth and Atlanta, Georgia.

14. If anything good can be said about the latter, it is that at least their planners have shown a readiness to accept that air travel is inexorably expanding, and that it is better to design spaciously in the first instance rather than to be obliged to add piecemeal to the concept later.

15. In the UK, we have been, it seems to me, especially remiss in this matter, subordinating the long-term interests of travellers to the short-term expedients of the airlines. The long and controversial saga of the London airports situation is a case in point. Every time that an intelligent solution is proposed, there are voices raised against it, from within and outside the industry. I recall vividly that many years ago, when it was first built, Gatwick airport was described as a 'white elephant', and for years it was difficult to get any airline to use it. Today, it is a vital element in the London airport pattern, growing fast and requiring almost constant updating and expansion. Similarly, when an even more intelligent solution was proposed to build an airport on reclaimed land at Maplin off the Essex coast, environmental objections of a limited nature exploded, much noise was made by a small minority, and the venture was abandoned. The result has been that for many years, the UK has been bedevilled with the London airports' problem, involving long and acrimonious controversy. Had Maplin been pursued, we would never have needed either Terminal Four at Heathrow, the second terminal at Gatwick or the further development of Stansted, and we would into the bargain have gained a massive opportunity for the economic regeneration of much of South-Eastern England along the route of the Thames from London to the sea. As it stands, we still have to spend much more money on ad hoc developments that could have been avoided. So much for airport planning in the UK.

16. However, I do not wish to dwell further on the mistakes of the past, because some of them (but not the Maplin error) were made in a genuine desire to meet what were thought to be the consumer demands of the day in a rapidly changing air transport climate that is still evolving today.

17. When many current airports were built, even Jumbo jets had not been envisaged, let alone supersonic air transport. Government regulators, airlines and airport authorities did not quite comprehend what was actually happening in air

transport, and were so busy trying to keep up with the rate of growth that they had little or no time to sit back and think of the future.

18. Today, we are reliably informed that over another $100 billion is likely to be spent between now and the end of the century on the design, development and construction of many new airports, and the reconstruction and refurbishment of existing ones, to fit them for the task of handling double the present volume of traffic by the end of the century, provided that a period of sustained economic stability enables sociological development to proceed, especially in those countries of the Third World where air transport is still in its comparative infancy.

19. Forecasting methods have improved, and we have a clearer idea of what may lie ahead. As a result, we have perhaps a better opportunity to plan ahead than we have had for some time past.

20. Therefore, in order to provide some idea of what the average air traveller may require to facilitate his passage, I will attempt to outline my ideas of an 'ideal airport' of the year 2000. I am a realistic air traveller, and although I am willing to accept that over the next thirteen years there may be some further changes in the pattern of air transport – the development of new air services and the introduction of new types of aircraft such as the much publicised 'prop-fan' – and that some methods of doing things may well be revolutionised – for example, by some advances in computerisation and in information technology – I do not believe that fundamental patterns of human behaviour will change very much, if at all. What the average traveller requires today, he will still require in the year 2000, and he will still tend to do many of the things he does today in much the same kind of way.

21. So my ideas for an 'ideal airport' from the consumer's viewpoint will <u>not</u> involve flights of fancy, costing many billions of dollars. I will base my concepts upon what I believe to be entirely capable of achievement, within the current state of the art of airport design, development and operation, and within entirely achievable reach of average airline and airport managements, given a willingness to accept changes in attitude of mind – probably the most vital ingredient of all.

22. Firstly, getting to the airport. Here, much more needs to be done at most major airports throughout the world, even at those where there have been some considerable advances in recent years. Getting to Heathrow is a joy compared to, say, Kennedy, New York, for with Heathrow one does have the rail link into the underground system, although even there I feel that carriages with more luggage space are desirable, and once again, as with check-in desks in terminals, London Transport could well ensure that all their ticket windows are staffed and all their ticket machines working, at peak hours especially. For Heathrow, I would strongly recommend the early re-instatement of the helicopter link with Gatwick, the cessation of which was a quite inexcusable surrender to a limited but vocal environmental lobby that still complains today about the noise from non-existent aircraft on a link that has halted. Also, there is a need for a helicopter link between Central London, and Heathrow and Gatwick, either from the City

Stolport or from some river-based helistop conveniently sited. Also, I would like to see another rail link directly connecting with British Rail services so that trains from all over the South East could get into Heathrow.

23. For those arriving by road, apart from improvements to existing motorway systems, I would like to see more adequate parking facilities, linked directly into airport terminals by some type of unmanned 'people mover' vehicles operating on fixed circular routes every few minutes, to replace those inadequate, tedious, and uncomfortable buses that now form an unpleasant start and finish to an air journey. This would, I admit, entail some expense, but would in the long run be far more cost-effective than the pesent system. The 'people movers' would be free of charge, the cost being incorporated into the overall car parking charge if required. Also, for payment of such charges, a machine capable of reading the number on any one of half a dozen major credit cards would be speedier and more efficient than the present laborious systems of payment. In an era that promises cashless shopping, cashless car parks should not be difficult to achieve.

24. Once inside the airport, an adequate supply of either hand-pushed or electrically propelled luggage carts is desirable. BAA plc is very good in this respect, especially at Heathrow and Gatwick, and other airports could well follow suit throughout the world.

25. The passengers' real problems, however, begin at check in, which, no matter how hard airlines may try, always seems to generate bottle-necks. These stem either from an inadequacy of such check-in devices, or from the fact that they are frequently never fully manned (British Airways, take note, this is a recurrent problem in Terminal One at Heathrow). Whilst recognising the problems of staffing levels, surely it is axiomatic that if one has a certain number of check-in desks, they should be manned at all times – why else does one have them? Also, is it not possible for airlines to introduce a system of 'late check-in facilities', for those idiots or unfortunates, and there are always some, who come late enough to risk losing their flights if there are big queues at check-in desks. One facility at Heathrow that I find advantageous is the separation of check in between classes of traveller. This works well, and it could be adopted with benefit at many other airports world-wide.

26. I recognise that the problem of increased security checks has severely complicated the whole check-in process. I do not see any alleviation of this situation for many years to come, and it is up to individual airlines and airports to devise their own methods of coping with it. But need additional security checks be quite so time consuming as some airports and airlines make them? Surely, once again, a sufficiency of adequately trained staff could work wonders, but in the meantime, it seems to me that all future airport designs will have to have built into them from the start adequate space for security activities. One of the major problems of today is that in most airports, the need fo extensive security has been loaded on to the top of existing handling facilities on an ad hoc

basis, with the result that overcrowding and chaos often ensue, especially at peak periods. Just as Customs and Immigration facilities are designed into airports now, so must security facilities be for the future.

27. Where Government passport and immigration controls are concerned, the introduction of machine readable passports, already being considered, will do much to speed passenger flows. Where for political reasons such controls are especially strict, innovative methods may not be possible for some time to come, but they should always be thought of as essential in the long term.

28. Similarly with Customs, the introduction of 'green' and 'red' channels has done much to speed passenger flows, but there are still many airports where this principle is not employed, and could be, with benefit.

29. Here, too, with special reference to inbound traffic, authorities at airports could perhaps devise some more stringent methods of dealing with the 'meeters and greeters'. They can be a boon to many travellers, but they can also clog up arrivals concourses - as anyone arriving at Gatwick at peak hours will readily recognise, causing delays that can have a tail-back into the Customs hall. BAA has for long had a slogan - 'say your good-byes at the garden gate' - which has worked wonders in cutting the congestion at the entrance to the departure hall at Heathrow's Terminal Three. Cannot some similar policy be devised for the arrivals hall?

30. Once airside, the question of such facilities as shops, banks, restaurants and duty-free shops is wide open. One could dwell for hours on the lack of such facilities at some airports, the expense of some of them at others (and especially bank charges at the Heathrow and Gatwick banks), and the widely varying qualities of food service at most airports. The introduction of competitive concessions can do much to improve prices and quality, even where the local airport authority itself plainly derives much of is annual income from such concessions.

31. This, in turn, gives rise to that much aired topic of whether duty-free goods should be sold only to outbound travellers, or also to inbound traffic. I have no fixed opinions on the matter one way or another. I recognise the force of the arguments both ways, and if asked to come down on one side or another am obliged to say that I do not overmuch care, since I am not by habit a duty-free goods purchaser. But I do recognise that at some airports, the overall ambience of waiting is largely improved by having at least a number of duty-free shops, and I see no real reason why they cannot be concentrated in one vast area through which both inbound and outbound passengers pass. The influences of local and national laws and Customs attitudes, of course, have a part to play in all this, and all that I would ask on behalf of all air travellers is that the competition is fierce, the quality kept high, the prices low, and the surroundings pleasant. Travellers may then take the situation, or leave it, as they wish. The debate on this issue will no doubt be continued for a long time to come.

32. For my own part, once airside, I would like to see far more attention paid to a traveller's more vital needs. Why is it that, once airside, and out of the main departures hall, there is always an inadequacy of toilets? Why are there never enough telephones, and almost invariably no automatic change-giving machines in the relevant currencies? Time and again one finds oneself in a foreign airport, well equipped with credit-cards and paper money, but not enough coins for phones. Of course, the self-righteous will say one should equip oneself for such situations in advance. One does, but there is always the time when one gets caught out - what traveller can honestly say he never has? (In this respect, I must congratulate BAA plc once again for an innovative move, namely the provision of machines in multi-storey car parks at Heathrow that give change for paper money to enable one to pay one's parking fee swiftly. It is an idea that many airports world-wide could adopt with benefit to passengers, and possibly profit to themselves).

33. My major criticism of virtually all airports is the amount of time spent waiting, once airside, in gate lounges prior to boarding. This seems to me to be compounded of a variety of problems, some of which are perhaps occasionally beyond an airline's control, but which more often than not stem from a too slack approach to the problem. I am often surprised that airlines are so slack in their passenger handling techniques. Many times I have sat in an airside lounge, with the aircraft in clear view, waiting to board, often until well past the advertised time of departure. Then, when boarding has begun, it has taken so long that the pilot has had to confess that the take-off slot had been missed; then there is further delay whilst another slot is allocated by air traffic control. All kinds of other problems are thereby created, which probably could have been avoided. Now, I recognise that there are many reasons involved - late arrivals from overseas, bad weather, technical faults, slackness of cleaning and other staffs. Some of these are avoidable, some not, but all of them require a far higher degree of efficiency in handling than they appear to be given at present. All transport undertakings have such problems, but that is no reason for accepting them in air transport with a shrug of the shoulders. A considerable slickening up of the ground handling procedures at all airports seems to me to be an essential ingredient of the overall improvement of passenger handling per se that I am seeking. There can never be any excuse for poor handling and especially for lack of information for the passenger. It all comes back to the point I have previously made, the need for a total change of attitudes on the part of all in air transport.

34. Another factor here that causes me considerable concern is the increasing use by individual airlines of 'handling agents', rather than their own staff. Now, I recognise that this is probably a more cost-effective method of handling passengers, and possibly is also an imperative at foreign airports where Governments, seeking to protect their own flag airlines' positions, insist upon it. However, it has an in-built defect in that handling agents can never really be as enthusiastic or as understanding of the problems of a traveller of just one out of perhaps a dozen airlines they are working for. I

have suffered horrendous experiences from handling agents world-wide over the years, ranging from the brusque and couldn't-care-less attitude through to outright hostility and ill-concealed rudeness - and some of my worst experiences have been in the UK! In my own country where I speak the language and am more than capable of making my views known forcefully, it is bad enough, but overseas, with other languages and habits to contend with, the problem can be made even more fearsome, especially for the shy, timid, disabled or ill travellers. other languages and habits to contend with, the problem can be made even more fearsome, especially for the shy, timid, disabled or ill travellers. There is only one answer to this problem: more competition among handling agents, so that they can be fired if they do not come up to scratch, but more importantly, at least the availability of the airline's own staff to deal with particularly severe problems.

35. Much of what I have said about the problems and difficulties facing air travellers outbound also relates to the inbound situation, for every air journey has two ends. Undeniably, most airlines strive to do what they can, but are often constrained by local laws and customs, and the often also quite open indifference on the part of the national air transport authorities to take the necessary corrective actions once problems have been identified.

36. To this end, I want to make one basic point before concluding. And that is that in far too few countries, anywhere in the world, is it possible for an air traveller to get any redress for the wrongs that may sometimes be done to him, whether it be lost baggage, ill manners, even physical harm, or just plain, simple laziness on the part of airport and airline staffs. Here in the UK, we have an organisation called the Air Transport Users' Committee, or AUC, which exists to listen to such complaints, and act upon them where it can. It does a massive amount of useful work, following up complaints, as I do know from my own experience. However, it is almost on its own world-wide: few other bodies like it exist, and in my view it is about time that all Governments took note of the AUC, and followed the UK's example. Some people in the UK air transport industry may regard it as a nuisance that should go away. I applaud its existence, and support it wholeheartedly, for the more it is a thorn in the side of the airport authorities and airlines, the more consideration they will pay to the travellers' needs. I have been in this business for long enough to remember what the British air transport system was like in the late 1940s, the 1950s and 1960s, when there were two monopolies, BOAC and BEA, arrogant, powerful and oblivious to genuine complaints. In those days, the differences in handling standards between those giants and the few struggling independent airlines was enormous: the latter, obliged to compete, struggled hard and built up enviable reputations for courteous service. Today, with the advent of increased and still growing competition, and with a continued blurring of those out-dated distinctions between scheduled and charter operation, the overall situation is much better, and I do not ever want to see a

return to the attitudes of those early years. But that there are still many problems is indicated by the fact that the UK Government and Civil Aviation Authority regard it as necessary to have an Air Transport Users' Committee at all, and by the fact that the AUC's annual report is invariably filled with first-class comment and discussion on the wide-ranging problems that still beset air travellers, both in the air and on the ground. If I have any regret at all about the AUC, it is that the latter has not been given by law any punitive powers against offenders, either airports or airlines, but can only in effect be admonitory. And I do know of one or two operators who dismiss its admonitions as being of little account. It is rather like the Press Council in my own field of newspaper journalism. Complaints made to the Press Council are painstakingly studied and ultimate adjudications pronounced. But they are in no way punitive, beyond the value of bad publicity, and no-one gets the sack. Similarly, with the AUC. If it had powers of punishment - say, by fines against transgressors - it might be able to play an even more effective role in keeping the standards of UK air transport up to the highest levels. The suggestion is worthy of much further study.

37. In conclusion, I would stress that everything I have said relates solely to the ground experiences of air travellers, and in no way deals with their experiences once airborne. That is the subject of a different address and for a different conference. What I have been endeavouring to outline is that while many airports and airlines world-wide do work quite hard, and do think out their policies towards air travellers very carefully, and spend very large sums in implementing them, and indeed very frequently do succeed, there are still some who neither think nor act in these ways. The results are at best poor quality handling on the ground, and at worst, chaos. Furthermore what I have said does not relate only to the smaller airports in many poorer or developing countries where perhaps the basic understanding of an air transport infrastructure is lost beneath the euphoria generated by having a flag airline at all. There are some major airports in parts of the world where conditions are little removed from those of airports in the poorer nations, where indifference reigns, and the air passenger is openly regarded solely as a means of providing much needed foreign exchange to a cash-starved exchequer. On the other hand, many of the problems and difficulties that I have mentioned do not exist in some smaller airports, because they are still sufficiently small to have been able to retain that atmosphere of friendly intimacy that the bigger airports have long since lost under the sheer weight of their expansion.

38. But throughout the world airline and airport industry, the one thing which I consider is needed more than anything else is a change in attitudes, a change in the whole mental approach to the air traveller. As I mentioned much earlier, the air traveller is the reason for the existence of the industry as a whole, and not an interruption of the daily lives of those who work in it. In many cases, this change of

attitudes can be instilled simply by an awareness on the part of management as to its necessity, and a willingness to go out and achieve it. In this regard, it is fruitful to study the quite astonishing turn-round in British Airways, over just a few years, from a titularly bankrupt airline into one not only earning big profits but also capable of being successfully privatised. This metamorphosis has been achieved by just the requirements I have outlined - an alert, willing and vigorous management, recognising the problems and sparing no-one in their efforts to achieve their desired goals.

39. So, it can be done. In a few cases, it will require the outlay of some money, but in reality very little compared with the billions of dollars already being spent on airport growth and refurbishment world-wide. But in all cases, all it needs is for more thought to be given in the initial stages of airport design, development and construction to the air travellers' needs; more co-operation from all involved in air transport to see those ideas translated into effective action; and more energy devoted on a daily basis to ensure that the new found improvements in standards are maintained. If it seems that throughout this address I have been especially critical, I make no apologies. I am a consumer of air transport, and perhaps by the nature of my occupation, I can speak on behalf of my fellow consumers more forcefully and effectively than they can. Some in the air transport industry may disagree with my thesis, but I doubt if many of my fellow consumers would argue with it. They would be more likely to claim that I have not gone far enough. For, as I said at the outset, there are well over one billion of us, taking into account both scheduled and non-scheduled activities, and that means over one billion opinions. Within such a wide field, there is room for wide discrepancies of view.

2 Review of passenger service issues at airports

G.F. DOUGHTY, Director of Aviation, Stapleton International Airport, Denver, USA

Passenger service issues take many forms and require a variety of approaches to assure that the passenger experience in the airport is satisfying and problem-free. Service issues are a major focus of the airport proprietor.

INTRODUCTION

1. When focusing on the needs of the airline passenger in the airport environment, it is necessary to consider the fact that none of the ultimate users of the airport really wish to be there; they are in the airport only for the purpose of getting somewhere else. It has been demonstrated that passengers are normally under fairly high emotional stress in the airport environment and, as such, have needs that are unique to that situation.

2. The needs of the passenger are the principal focus of the airport operator. While the airport operator has obligations and commitments to the businesses operating on the airport and to the public-at-large, passenger needs must come first. Regrettably, as aviation has expanded into a mass transportation business, the airport operator is increasingly in a position of eliminating negatives rather than enhancing positives.

3. At the major airports of the world, particularly in the top 20 or so airports in the United States, the most serious passenger issue is that of delays. The passenger, it seems, is willing to accept almost any indignity and inconvenience as long as he or she can move through the terminal onto the aircraft and to his destination as scheduled.

Reducing delays

4. Much of the delay problem at major airports throughout the world is not within the control of the airport operator but rests with the air traffic control system. But increasingly, the lack of adequate numbers of runways and other airfield facilities appropriately placed to accommodate the demands of an ever-increasing number of airline aircraft is a major contributor to the delay problem.

5. The airport operator has the responsibility to attempt to meet this demand by providing additional facilities. Unfortunately, political and community interests are, at times, in conflict with the provision of such facilities. Despite better technology, major land acquisitions, land-use controls, and other programs, noise remains a critical issue severely limiting or, in some cases, totally preventing additional capacity from being provided.

6. At Denver, for example, additional airfield capacity—although badly needed in the face of average passenger growth in excess of 10% per year—was essentially halted between 1975 and 1986. Some additional capacity has recently been provided, but only after major concessions were granted to airport neighbors. A new airport for Denver, which is now making progress, is still several years in the future. Little or no hope exists for additional aviation facilities in major aviation markets such as New York, Los Angeles, Chicago, and Boston.

7. Delays will remain a major unresolved issue for the traveling public in the foreseeable future. Short of providing major new facilities, airport operators can, at times, take certain steps to minimize airfield delays. In cooperation with the airlines and the air traffic control tower, it is possible to identify minor improvements and operating changes that can improve the delay situation. These can include such things as better utilization of displaced thresholds, additional high-speed exits from runways, and greater flexibilty with additional taxiway and ramp areas. Operationally improved snow removal and better scheduling of airfield maintenance activities can also help to keep facilities available to the maximum extent possible. Efforts such as these can be helpful but may only scratch the surface of the problem. Action is required by the government and the airlines to deal with the delay problem in a strategic way. Changes in air traffic rules and procedures dealing with spacing of runways, in-trail separation, and other issues need to be addressed quickly.

8. Long-term airport capacity issues can be resolved if the source of community complaints is reduced or eliminated. Airlines must transition as soon as possible, either voluntarily or through governmental requirement, from 1960's technology aircraft to present-generation Stage 3 aircraft like the

British Aerospace 146 and the Boeing 737-300. Those aircraft still make noise but they affect a much smaller land area and population. The more limited problem can then effectively be dealt with through land acquisition, land-use controls, and special programs such as sound insulation. Currently the noise problem is unmanageable and will continue to prevent additional airport capacity from being realized in the near future.

Access and ground travel time

9. Travel time to the airport may be less important than air delay to the traveler but, nevertheless, is a significant issue. Passengers have some very specific ideas about how far or about how long that travel should be. In Denver, a ground access time in excess of 40 minutes is not considered acceptable by the traveling public. A recent survey of Denver metro area residents indicates this attitude.

10. The survey question was asked how individuals feel about the driving time to the proposed location of the new airport which would add an additional ten minutes from the downtown area. The responses were as follows:

	Very Convenient	Reasonably Convenient	Very Inconvenient	Too Far
15-20 min	75%	22%	1%	1%
25-30 min	28	46	11	4
35-40 min	8	44	32	15
45-50 min	2	16	46	37
60 minutes	1	6	32	62
1 to 1.5 hrs.	0	2	14	84
Over 2 hours	0	0	9	91

11. Obviously such travel time perceptions would vary from community to community. They will, nevertheless, impact the passengers' perception of the services provided by an airport and ultimately, if options are available, would affect the decision as to which airport is to be used. The most significant example of airport location acceptance problems is probably the Washington, D.C. airport situation. The convenience of National Airport to the Washington metropolitan area and the relatively high travel time to Dulles Airport from the same population centers has kept traffic levels, until just recently, from growing dramatically at Dulles where far more capacity is available. While the reasonableness of access time pulls the airport as close as possible to the metropolitan area, the NIMBY (not in my back yard) syndrome begins to push the airport location further away. These two issues begin to interact with technical issues such as flight departure corridors, runway alignments, and method of operation of the facility. Siting a new airport raises many complex issues needing resolution early in the planning process.

12. Again, the results of a recent survey in Denver indicate the new airport planning work is apparently reflecting community desires with regard to such a location. The question was posed as to whether the proposed loca-

tion--which is about 15 miles northeast of the present location--is too close to houses in the area. The responses were as follows:

Too close to houses	12%
About right	42
No opinion	39
Too far to commute	6

Ground access modes

13. The passenger has essentially three principal options for accessing the airport landside:

   (1) by personal vehicle over the road access system;
   (2) by public transportation vehicles over the road access system; and
   (3) by a fixed rail or other dedicated mass transit system to the airport.

14. In most airport facilities in the U.S., the traveling public votes very heavily for the private vehicle, either his personal vehicle or one rented while visiting the community. In excess of the 65% of the passengers arriving or departing Denver's Stapleton International Airport, for example, do so by private vehicle. Therefore, the airport administration places great emphasis on the accessibility of the personal vehicle to the airport, often at the expense of other modes.

15. While airport limousines and buses transport a large number of passengers, they are clearly a secondary option. Where fixed rail has been provided, it has not been able to attract a ridership. One of the most convenient systems, for example, is operated at Cleveland, Ohio, with direct access from the lower level of the terminal building to the heart of downtown and several other suburban locations within 25 minutes. Yet less than 3% of the passengers at Cleveland utilize this system.

16. In most cases, airport design in the U.S. has favored the automobile as the principal means of accessing the airport. Overuse of this mode, in relation to available facilities, has resulted in roadway congestion aggravated by airline-supplied curbside check-in facilities that are traditionally ill-equipped and undermanned to handle the traffic volume. It is unlikely, however, that major changes in ground access patterns are likely to occur in the next 10 years. Innovative solutions to the curbside congestion problems are badly needed.

Parking

17. Despite these congestion problems, there is little reason for airport operators to provide incentives for passengers to use modes of transportation other than the automobile since airport parking normally represents the single largest non-airline revenue source to the operation of an airport. Most major airports find it difficult to provide adequate parking facilities within a reasonable walking distance of terminal locations. This has resulted in low-cost, remote parking which has become fairly popular with the traveling public. Remote parking, however, is expensive

to operate requiring an extensive bus system to transport passengers from the remote lot to the terminal. These lots are often only marginally profitable, whereas close-in structured parking located directly adjacent to the terminal building nets substantial profit. Remote lots provide an option to the passengers who are more concerned about cost than convenience. In addition, the remote lots provide a relatively inexpensive overflow solution for holiday travel periods.

18. Passenger complaints with regard to parking focus primarily around the availability of spaces, courtesy of employees, and delays in exiting the parking facility. The use of management contracts by airport operators in lieu of concession agreements has provided the necessary management control to assure that service problems are kept to the minimum. Strategic pricing of the close-in parking facilities, which forces price-conscious consumers to the remote lots, has been an effective way to assure availability of spaces.

Check-in facilities

19. Moving from curbside and parking facilities into the terminal building--another area of concern to passengers--is the speed and convenience with which they may check in either at the ticket counter or the boarding area. There has been little change in the design of facilities to accommodate passengers with ticketing and check-in during the past 50 years. Innovations have occurred, of course, in the data processing area which have allowed airlines to handle greater volumes of passengers, but long queues at peak times are the rule rather than the exception. Other than to provide larger facilities to accommodate more check-in positions, the airport operator is normally unable to deal with these issues which are principally airline responsibilities. While some attempts may be made by the airport operator to influence the manner and staffing of these functions, airline economics dictated by regulation, or in the case of the U.S., a free-market approach, result in a waiting time and level of service equal to what the passenger will probably tolerate prior to taking his business elsewhere. While these conditions are infamous as they relate to some of the recent operations by low-cost carriers in the U.S., even major carriers catering to the business traveler will permit check-in waiting time approaching 20 minutes without adding additional staffing to deal with the problem. Some airlines are beginning to look at various options to reduce ticket queues including flow-thru ticket counters and automatic ticketing machines. It remains to be seen whether these advancements will, in fact, result in improved passenger service or simply further reduce the amount of staff required to provide service at the current levels.

Walking distance to gates

20. The walking distance from curbside or check-in facilities to departure gates has become a significant issue as airports or size of airports increase. The Dallas/Ft. Worth and Kansas City concepts attempted to solve the problem for airports designed as origin/destination facilities. But as hubbing became a more frequent practice, particularly in the U.S., these linear concepts were not adaptable and airports looked toward people-mover systems to attempt to resolve the walking distance issue. While reducing the walking distance, people-mover systems did little to reduce the time required to cover the distance. In general, however, passenger acceptance of people-mover systems has been good. Such facilities are in use on a daily basis in Tampa, Orlando, Atlanta, and Seattle. The most significant disadvantage of such systems is the high cost of construction and operation, but as airports continue to grow, such systems will become much more common, and improved design should help reduce transit time.

Shopping as specialized services

21. As the passenger moves through the terminal he has one or more opportunities to take advantage of retail services. Retail facilities are currently one of the most active areas of change in the airport facility. Various innovations with product and design concepts are being tried. Products are no longer limited to typical newsstand and fast-food items. Gourmet dining, up-scale apparel shops, and specialty foods such as cookies, ice cream, dried fruit, and yogurt are becoming commonplace.

22. The airport operators must balance the desire for increased concession revenue with a commitment to high-quality retail facilities providing adequate variety to the traveling public. The price for services and goods in airports is a major source of complaints from passengers. In order to deal with this problem, many airports have imposed strict price controls on basic items such as food and sundries. Pricing is normally tied to a survey of local food establishments of comparable quality or to local convenience stores. Unfortunately, where the system is in place, public perception of "high prices" remains.

23. Certain specialized services are now being requested by today's travelers. Health and fitness centers and business centers are two recent innovations which appear to be popular with travelers. The revenue per square foot on such facilities is in many cases significantly below what the same space may command for office use, but a few airports are experimenting with these services to see if they result in greater customer satisfaction and become popular enough to begin to pay their way on an equal footing with other retail space.

Bag claim

24. Baggage claim is a service that receives less than its deserved attention. It is the last opportunity for the airport to disappoint the traveler. The handling of bags from the aircraft to the claim device remains a challenge for the airport operator and the airline. Overcrowding of many airports has resulted in bag claim areas that are extremely congested and impose serious delays on the passenger. Even at the most modern facilities, the significant distance between the aircraft gate and the bag claim device has meant

unacceptable waiting times. Major innovations are needed in the handling of the bag from the aircraft to the claim device, particularly at these larger facilities. This particular issue could be the most challenging technical problem to be faced as new terminals are developed. Passenger dissatisfaction with the bag-handling process is evidenced by the ever-increasing volume of carry-on bags.

Cleanliness

25. Not always viewed as a service, the overall cleanliness of terminal facilities is a matter of importance to travelers. In many instances airports have attempted to upgrade custodial services. The new standard appears to be the theme park. It is not unusual for an airport operator to receive a complaint letter regarding cleanliness from someone who just returned from Walt Disney World.

26. Cost to maintain high standards in this area are increasing and represent a major portion of the airport operating budget. For example, in 1986, Stapleton Airport spent $3,594,826 just to keep terminal facilities clean.

Overview

26. The preceding represents a review of some, but not all, passenger service issues as viewed from the perspective of an airport operator. Passenger satisfaction is a daily focus for airports and persistent emphasis on these and other issues will continue. Innovations in solving passenger service problems are badly needed in some areas; others can best be resolved by more attention to detail and an active management approach. Full cooperation of airports, airlines, and government will also be required if passenger experience with airports is to be pleasant and trouble-free.

3 Seamless service: aided or hindered by airports?

C.M. MARSHALL, Chief Executive, British Airways plc, Heathrow Airport, UK

1. An Airport is apparently all things to all men and all women . For the airlines, it is hopefully the smooth running conveyor by which the airline can funnel the delivery of services and products to its customers, whether as animate passengers or inanimate boxes, crates and containers. For the people running the airport, it is a business, a service business to be sure, but one which is required to show a profit and a satisfactory return on investment just as must any other self-respecting business. If it is owned and operated by a government entity, these rules may vary to a degree from normal business practice.

2. Then there is the customer, whether as a passenger in the shape of a person or as cargo in the form of something somebody wants sent somewhere in a hurry. Both see airports simplistically: As a place to get in and out of in a hurry. The airport operator may be happier if he or she lingers. The airline may wish to use the airport as a mode of decanting, of persuading the passenger or the cargo not to go directly from A to B, but to pass through C. This will give the passenger a better service as well as perhaps more frequent flights. It may also lengthen his time of travel as well as his trouble---but many times, it does give the airline more efficient use of its equipment.

3. You may begin to see that the concept of "airport" is not as simple as many would have you believe. It may be all things to all persons---but in so doing, it may leave large bodies of them very dissatisfied. For example, we have not even mentioned those people who live right in the landing or takeoff patterns and see the airport as the bane as well as the banshee of their existence.

4. Then there are the various localities near an airport who wish to have all the advantages of the financial pump priming derived from having an airport near by, but feel that there must be some way to avoid such problems as road networks, water supplies, upheavals in labour rates and all the other economic elements which always seem to infest even the most carefully planned arrangement.

5. Thus "airport", an apparently quite simple straightforward noun, seems to rouse large numbers of people to impressively high decibel levels in almost any conversation.

6. Even worse, many airports are finding that not only are they unapproachable by land or by sea, but they are beginning to present the same crowded aspect from the air. To put it bluntly, there are many times of the day when a great many airports throughout the world are not approachable for their customers in the air and those seeking to get there on the ground.

7. Simple solutions, you say: Build more. Well you have to have much finance available, at least ten years in time, the patience to work with so many committees that you cannot even keep track of all the deliberations and finally the willingness to accept that no matter what you do, the airport in its final garb will probably look little like what all the stake-holders hoped for when it started.

8. In short, an airport is never simple. It is always a long tangled story of the often desperate attempt to get scenarios which are almost diametrically opposed in objectives to match and mesh. There are days when I am sure that the Mole, the Water Rat and even Toad could perhaps do better...

9. The conflict of interests, the disparity of end goals, the inability to focus on clear objectives and programmes is not the result of any illwill or any conscious ineptitude on the part of the airlines, the airport operators or all the people who work with them in an ancillary capacity. It is the result of the fact that the airport itself becomes the focal point of divergent needs and interests.

10. As has been noted many times, almost every change suggested for airports anywhere in the world starts with a statement about the need to do something for the good of either the ultimate customer or perhaps those living in the nearby surroundings. These statements of goodwill often have to conflict with some of the real needs:
   i) Airports have to operate as going entities. They do not have unlimited resources, nor can they avoid the

political pressures and the foibles of
either their owning bodies or those which
regulate them.

ii) Airlines increasingly have competitors
from all over the world. They are in one
of the few industries in the world which
is both highly capital and labour
intensive at the same time.

iii) Political authorities are constantly
heckled by environmentalists and by those
who have special concerns or interests in
preventing or altering airport
activities, whether with regard to sleep,
noise, access or many other elements.

iv) Different categories of passengers take
very dim views of the needs and
activities of other passengers. The
business traveller does not wish to be
held up by the long straggling lines of
people dealing with luggage on their
departure to or return from holidays.
The vacationer resents any special
priority given to the business traveller
while attitudes towards babies would
often seem to encourage an immediate zero
population growth rate.

11. Thus the airport, as an operation and a
business, finds itself tossed back and forth
between demands and requirements which are
almost impossible to satisfy, even given the
greatest desire and empathy with compromise.

12. When the surrounding neighbourhoods quite
understandably want to preserve their sleeping
hours (especially when the airport was built
after established communities were already
there), the airport and the airlines serving
it find themselves in a schedule squeeze.
Modern aircraft are very expensive, costing as
much as one hundred million pounds apiece.
When adding their owner's other overheads,
every minute they are idle on the ground costs
hundreds of pounds which results in either
higher charges to the passengers and cargo
shippers or in relatively less money to pay
salaries and other expenses.

13. The whole question of scheduling flights
becomes a tug of war between the needs of
those living around airports, those passengers
and shippers using the aircraft and the
airlines operating them. Inept resolution can
result in legal tangles that go on for years
or even more abruptly in the bankruptcy and
disappearance of an airline.

14. Take another problem---the glut of airline
traffic in and out of airports in the 8AM and
5PM periods. There have been many articles
written about how stupid it is to overtax
airport facilities, the airways in and out of
airports as well as the road and
transportation links. The obvious commonsense
solution is to spread the traffic out, earlier
in the morning, later at night and during the
middle of the day.

15. Unfortunately Europeans, unlike their
American counterparts, take badly to early
morning travel. The airlines by using cutrate

fares try constantly to persuade travellers to
move towards the middle of the day. The
effort is largely unsuccessful with the
business traveller. Even Aunt Esther, going
to visit her new grand-daughter, is not the
ideal candidate one might think. She depends
on being picked up by a son or a daughter who
can do it only at the beginning or the end of
the day or as an add-on to some other travel
mission. Therefore she tends to join the mass
of people travelling at the peak. Thus all
the fulminating by the regulatory authorities
as well as the travel pundits against the
stupidity of the airlines and the airports,
the former for bunching their flights, the
latter for not having bigger facilities,
simply takes no account of the fact that we
all are somewhat helpless, given the wishes
and desires of our customers. Could we all do
somewhat better to alleviate the situation?
Perhaps---and I will come to that a little
later on in this paper.

16. There is a constant outcry from all of us,
whether as people inside or outside the
service businesses of travel transportation
and tourism, that methods of getting in and
out of airports are a scandal. The clogged
roads, the crowded buses, the jammed terminals
are seen as the result of the greed and
stupidity of Them---the pronoun being
qualified by the vantage point of the speaker.

17. As we have seen over time, if airports are
located in areas where there is enough space
to permit accommodation of all the needed
services, they inevitably are located so far
from the dwelling areas of the customers that
the journey there becomes overlong,
overtedious and one which many people reject.

18. Numerous answers are supplied to this
aspect of the problem ranging from the use of
underground extensions to rail links and
expansion of helicopter facilities. The
obvious problems here run from objections to
the construction costs to factors of added
noise and need for environmental protection.

19. From my own experience, I can tell you
there is another factor having particular
application to leisure travel: the person
flying is often not the problem---it is the
wellwishers arriving from miles around to see
them off or to welcome them home who create
the difficulty.

20. Flying for many people is still an
occasion of concern. Any experienced cabin
staff can tell you that at least 25% of the
passengers on any flight display white
knuckles during takeoff and landing in the
calmest of weathers. This is especially true
of the leisure traveller who tends to fly only
once or twice a year. He or she therefore
welcomes the support and reassurance of
friends and relatives before departing. The
best planned rail, underground and air links
simply cannot service these additional flows.
Therefore extensive road networks, bus and
parking facilities become essential, and very

quickly one finds oneself back in the same problems which the change was supposed to alleviate.

21. I know of one American city which formerly had an airport on an island just four minutes from the heart of the business centre. It became overwhelmed some 12 years ago and moved to a rather elaborate facility some 45 minutes out in the country. It too is now overwhelmed. What do you say to the bondholders who financed the move?

22. It is very easy to get haughty about the ineptitudes of the planners who constantly underestimate how traffic will grow and therefore permit this kind of congestion to occur almost "unnecessarily"! But we are dealing with periods of 30 years---a whole generation---stemming from the time an airport is planned to the time it can be expected to approach a reasonable point of payoff. Those planners who created the M25 around London working within a far shorter span of time found their assumptions in some controversy even before the highway was opened let alone after 20 years, so I think we have to be kinder in recognising the burdens carried by airport planners.

23. There is another factor which everyone seems to forget: if airports are built with adequate capacity in terms of land and all the other physical facilities to allow for future traffic growth, who is going to pay for the unused facilities while they are lying fallow? Unused land can become an expensive burden for the airport operation.

24. I would not wish you to believe that I think that airports as institutions are totally blameless. As a passenger and as Chief Executive of a world airline, I have done more than my share of fulminating at the things which occur, sometimes without any apparent reason at all. Airports are very large, very complex bundles of service entities, and since we operate one terminal ourselves, I know how helpless you can be at spotting the small foibles which can create major faults in service delivery when least expected.

25. My point is that there are no easy solutions, given the present state of technology. With the growth of airline traffic and the limit on the number of slots for departure and arrival at airports, inevitably one answer was to try to limit the number of flights and use larger and larger aircraft as replacements. This places burdens upon baggage handling, immigration, customs, passenger service, road networks and all the rest of it---to everyone's sweaty displeasure. There do not seem to be that many easy alternatives.

26. Obviously if someone would quickly create quasi-vertol aircraft, a civilian but greatly enlarged version of Britain's very successful Harrier jump jet, we could solve some of the air traffic problems. That is a long time away, if ever---and it would not meet all the areas of passenger concern in the airports themselves

27. The principal problem is that the airport customer whether passenger or cargoshipper, wants what we at British Airways call Seamless Service: the ability to go from one place to another effortlessly and without obstacles or hitches of any kind for any reason. In effect, to take the travail out of travel. As I have noted earlier, this runs right into the differing needs of the airport operators, the regulatory authorities, those living around the airport, the airlines as well as all the other stakeholders in the complex equation of getting large masses of objects and people from one place to another on a regular and timely basis.

28. One suggestion has been made that there should be no private airports, no private airlines, nothing but one smoothly running government agency devoted to customer satisfaction. Marvellous theory, but for some quaint reason it does not seem to work in practice. Having recently emerged from the tender ministrations of government ownership, I can assure you that ragged and rugged as some of the aspects of the present modus operandi may seem to you, they are far better than they would be as part of one huge government agency.

29. The reason is that government involvement of this type is determined by values quite different from those of customer service. It has to be responsive to conflicting political demands, questions of special interest, satisfaction and, perhaps most difficult of all, the arcane feuds and fights which arise when large groups of people are forced to live together in situations where accommodation rather than productive output is the index of value. Big Brother, no matter how benificent its compulsion, is never the way to arrive at better output in a service industry.

30. Then to complicate a resolution of all this, there is the question of Who Is To Blame. For example, British Airways does not run its terminals at its home base of Heathrow. They are run by the BAA. As you can imagine, the staffs of both organisations from time to time have harsh things to say about each other's perceived inadequacies. One of our people was seen to turn almost apoplectic recently trying to restrain himself when a Concorde passenger was inveighing mightily against the stupidity of British Airways for flying people across the Atlantic in a little over three hours and then letting them sit for 30 minutes while the problem was solved of a jetway which malfunctioned. It was too far away to permit disembarkation but too near to permit any other method to be used. The jetway of course belonged to the BAA, not BA--but the passenger did not know this, and blamed the airline. I well appreciate that BAA people will just as

vociferously claim that they carry the can for the mistakes of the airlines using the airport, and get tagged for mistakes which are not theirs.

31. May I say in passing that any of us who work around airports have become collectors of exotic examples of invective, since our morning post often has liberal scatterings of these. One of my associates recently suggested a series of form letter answers. Included and addressed to Dear Sir or Madam were:

> "Thank you for your letter. I shall lose no time in reading it" (cribbed I suspect from Disraeli)
>
> "I am obliged by your opinions, but will endeavour to retain my own."
>
> "We are indeed sorry that our meal service was not as good as your own. Have you thought perhaps of pleasuring yourself more?"

32. Obviously these are form letters we would never send, but there are times when our staff dream of sending them. Just last week, a gentleman called from Heathrow Airport demanding that my office find immediately a passenger who was travelling to the Far East. We made strenuous efforts to find the lady concerned without much success and with many calls back and forth between ourselves and the irate gentleman who felt that airport security was no reason to keep him from personally searching the lounges in question. Finally in desperation, my staff member offered to pass on the information to the lady in question when she boarded the flight. The message was: "Have a good trip".

33. One learns when working in service businesses that one's view of what is important may differ considerably from that of the customer---and that you must learn to suspend judgement and try your best to fill the need, answer the query or perform whatever service may be requested even if it does not always seem appropriate to you. The continuing quixotic nature of people is what makes this occupation so fascinating as well as occasionally mind-boggling. It is also why we try to give our staff changes in types of work during the day to reduce the stress and preserve their sense of humour. Passengers delayed through no-one's fault but perhaps the Great Scheduler In The Sky can after the first dozen cases represent a somewhat formidable burden even to the most resilient and best trained person.

34. All of this brings us back to the second problem in operating airports effectively: not only are the output needs very often conflicting, but airports have to deal with people under all kinds of stress:
Unease about flying
Concern about what one faces at the end of the trip
The terrible day which preceded the journey
The changes in schedule for any one of a myriad of reasons which may make the trip even more difficult than it seemed at first
Unfamiliar food
Strange venues
Officials of one kind or another who are being officials
Overheated surroundings
Underheated surroundings
Friends who do not show up for departure
Friends who do not show up for arrival

The list is endless---but it results in people under real stress who find coping with the hustle, bustle and rustle of an airport more than they had bargained for.

35. Part of the trouble is that most airports are built to engineering needs, safety needs, security needs and operating requirements---but they very often were not subjected to the ultimate requirement: what is essential for the passenger who is often under conditions of stress of one kind or another.

36. For us in the airlines, it is a serious problem. We spend very large sums of money trying to create an ambience in the air which will make the passenger feel wanted, well-treated and well turned out---only to have them descend into a welter of discomfort when they arrive at the airport of their destination. All we can do is try to deliver their luggage quickly and accurately---but often we do not have anything to say about the ways in which it is delivered or the signage which tells the passenger what to do and where to go.

37. Since each of the elements involved is trying to satisfy some segment of passengers to the best of its ability, coming up with an overall compromise which will give maximum satisfaction to the greatest number is almost impossible.

38. Take for example the problems of the cargo shipper. This may seem like an also-ran, a mere ancillary factor which supplies extra profit to the airlines. I assure you this is not the case. Without the cargo carried in their holds, most aircraft flying long distances on anything but the most popular routes would be operated at a loss. Cargo literally is the difference between red and black ink on many of the longhaul routes everywhere in the world.

39. As congestion in airports has increased, as the need for better security has become omnipresent, it has become more and more difficult for the cargo operators to work efficiently out of many of the world's largest and most passenger-popular airports. They have tended to move to airports where the strain on facilities is not so great, labour costs are lower, and their ability to get vans and lorries in and out of cargo areas can be expedited.

40. As a result, the airlines find themselves in a continuing quandary: how to continue important cargo operations in airports which increasingly involve higher costs and longer periods of turnaround time, at the same time competing with other operators working in more favourable environments?

41. Having clean, quiet places to rest while awaiting boarding is a key concern for any passenger under stress---but just as necessary for cargo is having secure, convenient, efficient places from which cargo can be moved to aircraft. Without both as samples, any airport is not serving its customers properly, and sooner or later it is going to lose business.

42. It becomes obvious that the operation of an airport is a case of continuing trade off analysis---where there is never any totally satisfactory answer, but where compromises have to be found which can stand up over considerable periods of time and take into account the large sums of money which are required to bring them about.

43. I have avoided larding this paper with depictions of the intricate array of services an airline must perform through the various tentacles of the airport before it can get just one group of passengers into the air. For example, just to get one jumbo jet up and away, we have to:
- Load as many as 28,000 separate articles into the aircraft
- Supply a fully trained and equipped flight deck crew
- Put together a cabin crew depending upon the destinations, the languages and the numbers of passengers who may be involved.
- Assemble all the luggage and baggage in the appropriate containers, while making sure that there are enough vehicles to carry them to and fro at both arriving and departing airports
- Provide the incredible array of clearance papers, transit documents, flight plans, weather analyses and all the other paperwork needed.
- Assemble the food and drink with an array of choices which each of three or four classes of passengers may require, along with all the special requests which may be made for a particular flight
- Make sure that there is adequate service to check passengers in, handle their pre-flight telephone requests and to traffic anything they may need before or after the trip
- Soothe and care for unaccompanied children

44. These and literally hundreds of other activities having to do with the departure of an aircraft must interface with all the activities at an airport and avoid being hampered by any shift in the airport's own operations. At Heathrow, the key entrance to a major part of the airport's operation is through one two lane tunnel. If there is a van or bus breakdown, we can lose whole flight

or cabin crews, not to speak of passenger loads with the resulting disruption of service, much to the mystification of passengers sitting and waiting for departure. Airports are finely tuned watches which perform admirably so long as every element involved does exactly what it is supposed to. Unfortunately Mr Murphy and his Book of Laws is always available to cause trouble.

45. The people in charge of airline activities as well as those working for the airports quite often perform major feats of improvisation which the passengers never see or hear of to make sure that aircraft get away on schedule and in total safety. Sometimes we fail, either because we are human beings or because the complexity of the airport mechanism is so intricate that as one factor is adjusted, others fall out of sync and soon a situation sets in which makes the Tower of Babel seem like a church social. All any of us can do under those conditions is grit our teeth, try to keep our sense of humour and do everything we can to help our customers, recognising that they are going to be very displeased with us.

46. I take exception to the remark of one very well known writer who is justifiably considered a world expert on air travel. He said quite recently, that "the long term interests of passengers are subordinated to the short term interest of the airlines," I do not know about which airlines he was writing---but at British Airways, we try desperately hard to think about what passengers will want and need now and ten years or more from now---because if we do not, we will not supply a successful service and they will most surely vote with their feet.

47. That ability for passengers to vote with their feet and the need of any airline servicing them to take account of it and respond effectively is why I believe so strongly that private competition is the only mechanism in the long run which will ensure improving standards of service for everyone. The most well-intentioned of bureaucracies are just that---bureaucracies, and sooner or later become immobilised by their patterns and procedures.

48. The short term interests of the airlines have to be the same as the long term interests of their passengers simply because the time and money frames involved are so large. An airline which is shortsighted will be shortlived.

49. This same writer noted that BA was doing a bad job at Heathrow since it did not always have all its check-in desks manned, pointing out that it is silly to construct check-in desks if one does not keep them manned at all times. I disagree. We construct check-in desks just as we do aircraft fleets, to handle peak periods, since we do not yet have self check-in (though it may be coming) nor can we supply the odd extra passenger with wings and

tell him to cope for himself. It seems to me that our proper concern must be queue length: to have a standard which says that we will have queues such that in either slack or peak periods, the passenger should not have to stand in a queue more than say eight minutes, thereby adjusting our personnel and manned desks to make sure that this standard is maintained.

50. Actually, we hope that over time we can meet the problem of airport congestion on queueing differently: to take large groups of our passengers, ticket and check them in remotely so that we can avoid the physical bottleneck of the airport itself. There are obvious problems of security, traffic, transport and other factors which make this difficult. The systems technologies are already here which should permit us to do this and we are working on it now. We would like to see the day coming when the check-in desks in the terminals would be for the last minute arrival or the person who has decided to travel at the very last minute. If we can accomplish this kind of transition, then we will be on the way to what I think the airport must be: a facilitator rather than an inhibiter of travel service. Again, I would wish to say that I am speaking of the average airport as a physical entity rather than something which results from the lack of focus of the operators themselves.

51. There can be no question that the only solution to the airport problems near and longterm is to find a more effective way to get the concerned stakeholders together in practical working units which will put together the kinds of compromises which can create the best possible outcome for all concerned.

52. This is very easy to say and very difficult to do. Who would speak for the passengers? Which segments? Living where? Flying how? How would the airlines sort themselves out so that the often quite directly opposed interests of domestic and international flights as well as those of UK-versus foreign carriers could be properly compromised and put into effective modes of operation?

53. The traditional answer of the inter-interest study group or working party is not good enough. It only creates more paper to be read and disagreed with as well as internecine conversations which have more to do with ego than output.

54. There has to be something better. It seems to me that each airport needs to have a small permanent body with an expert staff and policy members designated and delegated for periods of three years from the following stakeholders:
a) The airport itself
b) The airlines serving it (one representative each for the three or four

major categories of service
c) The cargo shippers (represented as in the case of the airlines)
d) Neighbourhood Community members
e) Six or seven passenger representatives

55. The work of this group would be to turn out as skilfully as possible simple expedient but thoughtful suggestions for service improvement which could be used to persuade all the elements involved that their best interests lay in following the recommendations. The body could have no regulatory power and could not issue fiats. What it could do is learn how to use the media skilfully enough so as to be a source of real pressure for good.

56. This would mean that its members must learn how to sort out their partisan interests from those which are for the overall good of the airport and its interested parties in whatever time frame is required.

57. In no way is this meant to replace any of the regulatory or industry planning bodies, each of which has much to say about whatever particular hobby horse it may be riding. Rather it is meant to be a forum where policy differences can be met and confronted in a useful and compromising fashion, where the stakes are on the table and visible for all to see.

58. It would be a difficult body for its members, as well as the companies and organisations which supply them. It implies that fairly specific interests are going to be explored in open debate, not always the happiest forum for organisations which find a backroom more comfortable. In my opinion it is perhaps the only way in which a forum can be created which will respond to the needs of ALL the stakeholders, rather than just a chunk of that particular element which for the moment may be able to command more attention.

59. As we have all learned to our sorrow, airports and airport policy is not something which can be dealt with either on a short term or a narrowly focussed basis. The interplay of all the viewpoints is needed, but on a basis which is concerned with output, rather than position or political accommodation.

60. A group such as this, manned by people who do not work for it, but who are detailed to it for a sufficient period of time, and who have been picked from their respective companies and organisations as being doers rather than time servers, should be the beginnings of a combined point of view towards creating effective policy to which airports can then become more responsive.

61. It obviously will not be perfect; it will obviously make mistakes, but it will make them in public where they can be seen, weighed and changed. Further it supplies a means for a unified point of view rather than having

government bodies hearing evidence from conflicting special interests while they themselves have conflicting special interests which never emerge in the light of day.

62. Obviously something is necessary. In the United States they are already talking about government fiat to restrict airport traffic, even to setting limits to the numbers of aircraft which may be admitted to any one airport. Cargo interests are already shifting some of their movements to airports such as Maastricht which can handle packages far more quickly, more inexpensively with less customs and paper problems than some of the major airports. Twenty-two airports in the US are being looked at for traffic limitation. We already have some in the UK which are moving towards the same category of problems. We have to find ways and forums which can come up with suggested solutions before the problems themselves become archaic.

63. There can be no question that air travel and airport use is going to increase steadily in the next twenty years, notwithstanding the plateaus caused by economic cycles. The ways in which business and leisure time are being accommodated make travel, both short and long haul, an increasing need. The suitable space for airport expansion is very limited. Therefore we have to find better ways to use what we have, better ways to deliver passenger service or we will find ourselves pushed aside sooner or later.

64. Let me point out as a technological aside that the recent discovery of superconductivity materials which can be created at convenient temperatures on thin films which can carry 100 times the currents ever thought possible previously is one of the great technical revolutions of our time. The electric aircraft, the magnetic train, power generated in one place and used 4000 miles away---all of these are clearly within practical possibility. It is just one thing which will change the way we operate in and use airports and which should make them sources of considerably less harried activity than they are at present.

65. I report this to you since I was solemnly assured at a technical meeting just last year that any discoveries which would affect this industry for the next decade had already been made. At the rate the super conductivity field is moving, I am not sure this is a safe assumption.

66. What this says is that with airports as well as everything else, the only thing which is unchanging is that there is always change---and laterally, its rate seems to be changing itself---which means that if we do not create ways of being more flexibly effective, we will find ourselves in difficult business straits.

67. Change is the one thing we all support as long as it impacts everyone but ourselves.

The expense of being efficiently rigid will be more than most of us will be able to sustain over the short and long range futures with which we have to contend.

68. To return to the title of this paper: "Seamless Service--Aided or Hindered by Airports?"--the answer is obviously that at this point, both conditions prevail at every airport in the world. There is no such thing as any airport whose physical apparatus or policies are flawlessly designed to give the ultimate in service. On the other hand, each airport I know of seems to have some things it does very well.

69. If we are truly to move toward Seamless Service, the ideal of giving a passenger a super-conductive trip: one which is accomplished with an absolute minimum of resistance to an effective outcome, then we must think and function quite differently within the industry than we do. All of the components of the industries and stakeholders which surround the airports will have to bury the knives they have carefully honed over some decades, and arrive at a new modus vivendi which will allow them to be of more effective combined service to the ultimate consumer than they have ever been before.
None of the elements, whether they be airport authorities, airlines, regulators, consumer groups or environmental interest groups can accomplish it by themselves. The only hope is to find an effective, non-lethargic way of combining the interests to create a policy-articulator which can be of genuine utility to all the stakeholders.

70. Cynics will of course say that very quickly this will become just another do-gooder effort which will be given lipservice and no more. It does not have to be that. Equipped with good people delegated from the various interests and staffed by a small group of experts really concerned with airport efficiency as well as airport responsiveness over a variety of time frames, it could become the launching pad for effective combined policy suggestions which could be used to lobby the industry and regulatory bodies concerned.

71. If we do not do this, then the potential for Seamless Service will be more limited than it needs be. We at British Airways believe in the idea. Meanwhile we are working on a variety of experiments to answer the problems noted so that our own customers, passenger and cargo alike, will be assured that we are doing everything we can to expand the limitations of the airport wherever we find them.

72. The Airport should be a site for service choice rather than one for service constraint. Speaking for a major airline, we want to do our part in making this happen.

4 Airports for people — a passenger viewpoint

G.H. LIPMAN, Executive Director, International Foundation of Airline Passengers Associations, Geneva, Switzerland

This paper examines passenger influence on decision-making by airports. It looks at passenger needs, consumer views and the role of surveys. It examines specific practices and procedures at airports affecting passengers. It focuses on those areas where passengers might reasonably expect improvement in the years ahead.

CONSUMER NEEDS AND AIRPORT DECISIONS

1. Passenger requirements from the aviation system have been a principal consideration of airlines, airports, aircraft manufacturers and governments since the dawn of commercial flying.

2. No policy statement is ever written without the words: "In the public interest" at the head of the preamble. No airline advertisement is complete without subliminal emphasis on "satisfying customers". We have "passenger pleasing planes" and "user friendly airports".

3. However, the requirements of users are as diverse as the users themselves and they can change rapidly depending on exposure to new experiences and ideas.

4. In the final analysis, even with the best of intentions, producers and regulators have so many other considerations to take into account in their planning and decision-making that consumer needs are only one of a myriad of competing priorities. The realities of politics and economics are all too often the final determinants of international aviation decisions.

5. In moving to the specifics of airport decisions there are a number of overriding factors to take into consideration. The traditional issues. The difficulty of finding space for new airports or for runway and terminal expansion. The enormous capital costs involved and lead times required. The problems of local community and environmentalist concerns in the industrialized world or of resource availability in the developing. All underlining the need for long-term planning.

6. The newer issues. The dramatic escalation in terrorist attacks at airports in the recent past which has forced a major re-think of screening, terminal flow patterns, border control, airport access and even basic design concepts. The consequences of more competitive aviation policies and practices spreading around the world disrupting airport development plans, terminal conditions.

Privatization and commercialization at airports, changing the attitudes and actions of airport management. All underlining the need for rapid adaptation.

7. It is against this background that consumer requirements have to be taken into consideration.

THE VOICE OF THE CONSUMER ?

8. Some airports, have "consultative committees" to comment on aspects of their decision-making. Passenger representation may be by individuals, organized user groups, Chambers of Commerce etc. Other airports have no such process. Similarly, some government bodies making decisions on airport-related issues provide the opportunity for direct public input.

9. Some consumer groups have established policy positions on different aspects of airport operations. For example, the Airline Users Committee in the UK has taken positions in recent years on such issues as airport privatization, new runway capacity, establishment of regional airports, night curfews, surface access and intra-airport helilinks. The UK National Consumer Council has focused on a number of issues including slot allocation, baggage, competition in provision of services (including duty-free) and the strengthening of consultative procedures. The Federation of Air Transport Users in the European Community has campaigned for the purchase of duty-free on arrival. The International Foundation of Airline Passengers Associations has also argued the case for duty-free on arrival, opposed the suppression of the London-Gatwick heli-link and argues that decisions on airport siting and expansion should take greater account of passenger and community needs in relation to historical environmental restrictions.

10. From the above, it is evident that there is an emerging passenger representation, taking a growing interest in airport matters.

11. Passenger surveys represent another important source of information on attitudes towards airports. Individual airports throughout the world routinely undertake surveys of the public passing through their terminals. A typical survey might seek information on the use of different forms of transport to and from the airport, parking, lounges, restaurants and duty-free shops. It may also assess attitudes to check-in, terminals flow, baggage claim and other services. The resultant data gives an indication of reaction to airport facilities and can also be taken into account in planning. Consumer groups have surveyed duty-free prices at major European airports. Interestingly enough, their conclusions suggest great discrepancy in prices and that in some locations, despite the tax-free status, spirits can be purchased more cheaply from local supermarkets.

12. Since the mid-70s the International Airline Passengers Association has conducted a regular survey of its worldwide membership of more than 100,000 frequent business flyers. This survey has inter alia included an evaluation of airport services/facilities and an assessment of a need for improvement. The results of the survey for 1984, broken down separately for North America and the rest of the world, revealed a predominant interest in speedy baggage claim, quick and easy check-in, rapid customs clearance, ease of changing planes, short walking distances and comfortable waiting areas. Respondents also feel that these are the areas where airports should concentrate their improvements. The responses have, of course, to be seen within the context of the questions that were asked, the nature of the sample and also of the timing of the survey. In 1984, for example, when the last such survey was conducted, security was considered a critical factor by some 10% of respondents only, compared with 60% who viewed quick baggage claim as critical. A similar point might be made in respect of airport delays and congestion which have only emerged as a serious problem in the United States in 1986 and '87. In correlating attitudes with specific airports, the IAPA survey concludes that Amsterdam, Singapore, Zurich and Frankfurt are the most popular non-US airports whereas Tampa, Atlanta and Dallas are the most popular in the United States.

13. Passenger polls are conducted annually by specialist travel magazines amongst their readership. The same airports emerge (with the addition of London). The reasons cited for selection are similar.

14. IFAPA has now taken over the IAPA survey and, in the process, has significantly expanded and adapted it to ensure that it is properly representative of passenger preferences. The sample size has been increased to 250,000 frequent flyers. Information has been sought on use of some 180 airports worldwide for both business and leisure purposes. Attitudes to 14 different features of airport operation are being queried in the following categories – flight information, duty-free, border controls,

inter-terminal transport, parking, aircraft transfers, restaurants, lounges, access to planes, security, waiting areas, check-in and baggage claim. Views on the relative importance of these features and the need for improvement are being canvassed. In addition, passengers are asked to specify the airports they prefer generally as well as specifically in relation to security, border controls and duty-free shops. Views on duty-free purchase on arrival are being sought. Passengers are also asked for their assessment of US deregulation and liberalization in their regions on airport conditions. Finally, a number of specific questions are posed concerning airport security.

15. The objective of this survey – of which airports are just one element – is to quantify opinions of frequent travellers in as accurate a way as possible. It has been designed by professionals according to generally accepted market research standards. The responses will be reviewed against public travel data and the findings weighted to ensure that they are as representative as possible for each major travel market.

16. The survey is in circulation at the time of preparation of this paper but preliminary results will be incorporated at the time of presentation.

FUTURE TREND ASSUMPTIONS

17. The assessment of passenger requirements contained in this paper are based on the following assumptions concerning trends in air travel over the next 10 to 15 years. There will be generally positive, but moderate, world economic growth. Beneficial operating cost trends can be anticipated due to comparatively low real fuel prices and labour/equipment based productivity improvement. Traffic is foreseen to increase at close to 7% per annum with Pacific markets showing the highest increase. Fares are expected to decline in real terms but profitability for more successful companies is expected to improve. Less regulation is foreseen with more competition, particularly in Europe and Asian markets. Consolidation of the industry in the United States will continue with retained regulation for airport slots, computer reservation systems, mergers and safety standards. There will be continued fleet expansion, particularly in short/medium range mid-sized aircraft and longer range larger aircraft. There will be increased privatization of airlines and of airports, which will enhance competition and productivity. Mergers and cooperative links between major carriers will evolve on a regional and even trans-regional basis in the '90s. Increasingly sophisticated computer equipment will lead to widespread use of yield/inventory control and automated airport flow procedures. Security will continue as a high priority item as terrorist activity against civil aviation continues to flare. Few new land-based airport developments will be initiated, but there will be increased terminal expansion projects and new dedicated short-haul projects. Environmental pressures will

continue, limiting airport expansion, but countervailing pressures resulting from frustrated travellers in overcrowded facilities will have some political effect in more industrialized nations.

CHANGING PASSENGER PROFILES AND HABITS

18. Air transport consumers are not a homogenous group. For the purpose of this paper they can be considered to fall into two broad categories: business passengers, who make up about 30% of the total; and leisure travellers who account for some 70%. Some 25% of all international travellers are women and this is increasing rapidly. There are also more "yuppies" - young, fast rising executives, and "golden oldies" - earlier, more mobile retirees. Passengers are taking to the air when they are younger, and they are travelling more frequently.

19. Business passengers have always looked for speed, convenience, schedule, ease of making or changing travel plans and on-board comfort as the main priorities. Leisure travellers have looked for price - flight price or total package price - and timing to fit in with holiday plans. All travellers have tended to look to such matters as safety and security as well as airport arrangements as "standard" - taken care of by the airline within the price of the ticket.

20. Times are changing. For both categories of passenger time spent at airports is on the increase, perceptions of airport services and airport efficiency are becoming more important determinants of whether it was a "good trip" or a bad one. Airports are conscious of this - they are advertising their advantages directly to the passenger - "the lowest duty-free prices", "the best connections to Asia", "the world's number one passenger pleasing airport", and they are enhancing their terminals to reflect such features. Airlines are also conscious of the fact, focusing attention on check-in facilities, providing more lounges, improving duty-free shops where they are the concessionaires.

21. Habits are changing. Pre- and post-flight airport facilitation is becoming a more important factor in passenger choice. Technology is playing an ever-increasing role. In the '90s, in the major generating markets, the passenger will be able to plan itineraries on home and office computers and pay for a ticket with a smart card. Carrier selection may take into account frequent flyer programmes, corporate discounts and any other form of brand loyalty scheme the ingenious marketeers devise. Hotels and rental car companies will be a part of these schemes, and who is to say that airports will not? Comparison of price and quality options for travel will be easier by computer, even though tariffs will be more complex. The passenger will be able to select branded or neutral offerings according to how his travel advisor holds himself out. He will be courted for custom by credit card companies, banks, department stores and others as the distribution system becomes more diversified.

He will be offered an increasing range of flight-related services from hotels, airports and even cities anxious to attract his business.

22. Safety and security have forced themselves onto everyone's agenda as high priority/no compromise items. He will have become used to heavy security protection at airports, even though he may well object to the hassle or the price he is asked to pay for what he sees as a basic State obligation.

23. The continued growth of low fare mass transport largely, but not exclusively for leisure travel, will place continuing strains on airport facilities. The leisure traveller will not be content with continually crowded terminals and will expect ample and comfortable waiting space with entertainment sections, nurseries, shops, restaurants and bars.

24. The business passenger will expect lounges with business centres, automated check-in with possibly staggered security controls to minimize waiting time. On board, he will expect separate cabins to reflect differences in products offered and at destination, speedy deplanement and rapid airport to city centre connections. It is foreseeable that special business flow patterns will be established by airlines and airports to attract passengers. Expanded regional services in Europe, a city airport in London and successful STOL services in North America may even lead to some airports being virtually dedicated to business passengers with the premium on speed of passage through the terminal and provision of extensive business amenities.

WHAT PASSENGERS WANT FROM AIRPORTS

25. Every airport is unique - facilities and flow patterns differ depending on such factors as size, nature of traffic (passenger compared to cargo, domestic compared to international, vacation compared to business), single terminal or multi-terminal, hub or non hub and the socio-economic conditions of the country in which the airport is located. Many airports have made great efforts to become "passenger responsive"; others have done less.

26. Generally speaking, the larger the airport and the greater the number of terminals the more likely the potential for passenger confusion and dissatisfaction. International airports, with the need to cater to diverse cultures and languages as well as the added border control security and check-in procedures, clearly have more work to become "passenger pleasing" than domestic airports. Many of them accomplish this exceptionally well and consistently emerge high in passenger polls. Much of this is due to exceptional planning, but a large measure is also due to the fact that the responsible authority places a very high priority on passenger attraction and satisfaction. It might also be noticed that in those locations where airport management, local authorities, airlines and national government work in harmony, the synergism involved is probably an important factor in increasing passenger appeal.

Advertising of airport qualities by national tourist boards, for example, or special prize promotions for passengers transiting airports offered by national airlines, all contribute to the concept of passenger appeal.

27. Single terminals are no doubt an important factor - particularly where interline journeys are concerned. It is particularly important in the trend to hub and spoke operations. With the rapid traffic expansion of recent years and anticipated for the future it is inevitable that fewer and fewer major airports will be able to operate on a single terminal basis. It is to be expected nevertheless that those airports which have made one terminal operation a feature of their appeal will endeavour to ensure the highest quality of connection with newly developed terminals.

28. But it is not only interlining which is important to passengers, such items as airport access, check-in facilities, border control procedures, lounges, shopping and baggage check-in and collection are all factors which contribute to a passenger's attitude towards a particular airport.

29. The requirements drawn out below concerning airport facilities are covered at many of the world's major airports, but by no means all of them. Taking into account survey results and press articles the "requirements" are an attempt to catalogue the most important needs and attitudes of passengers.

Airport Access

30. Airports located as close as possible to city centres have always been popular with passengers. However, even where located some distance from the city, efficient transport links can enhance appeal significantly. This means adequate well signposted road connections with easy access to major national arteries; integrated rail networks and preferably dedicated high speed rail connections. Executive Travel Magazine, in an article in September 1986 identified over 20 rapid rail links at airports around the world with a half a dozen more on the drawing board with mainline stations directly under the airports.

31. The worst situation for passengers tends to occur where airports are primarily accessed through main suburban road connections and where traffic peaks with normal rush hour peaks. This is regrettably the situation at many of the world's major airports.

32. Where there is more than one airport in a system, then good connections are needed for interlining purposes. Helicopters or rapid train connections are the optimum because they don't depend on the vagaries of road traffic flow. In this context passengers interlining between London's Gatwick and Heathrow airports on the already overcrowded new M25 must lament the continued refusal of the government to allow the helicopter service to recommence operations.

33. Taxi and bus services should be clearly signposted inside terminals and an indication of the fares to city centres should be posted. As far as taxis are concerned, intelligent

methods of flow control need to be established. It is frustrating, however, for passengers at the end of a long journey to find themselves caught up in something as down to earth as an inefficient taxi despatch system.

34. As for buses, clear distinction should be made between bus stops for city centre operations and those providing intra-airport links. For the latter there should preferably be no charge as interlining foreign passengers may well not be equipped with local currency.

Car Parking

35. Airports should make available reasonably priced long and short term parking, signposted clearly and in a timely fashion on access roads. Parking should preferably be within easy walking distance of terminals - where this is not possible there should be moving pavements or frequent shuttle bus services and a system for baggage trolley pick up/drop off. Parking charges should be clearly indicated at point of entry. Parking facilities should be made available for disabled passengers as close as possible to entry with ramps and adequately sized lifts to facilitate their movements. Adequate space is needed in front of terminals for passenger pick up and drop off and appropriate procedures to prevent traffic congestion.

Check-in/Baggage Collection

36. Regardless of purpose of travel or size of airports, passengers look for speedy check-in facilities with enough desks and staff to handle the traffic. Given the peaks and troughs of daily and seasonal demand, airlines have by and large responded well to this requirement. Certain airports, however, have developed a reputation for crowded check-in facilities - this may be the result of inadequate planning, slow adaptation, or simply dynamic traffic growth as in the case of Newark during the heyday of People's Express's operation or Gatwick when the number of Sky Train standby's eventually led to off airport check-in. Rapid increase in the number of airlines using a terminal can lead to congestion and passenger delays. In a different context, developing nations' airports often suffer from check-in problems due to lack of trained staff or large numbers of checked baggage or inadequate facilities to handle wide-bodied aircraft.

37. The increasing use of separate check-in facilities for first and business class travellers as well as the use of special desks for passengers with hand baggage only helps to keep the flow moving. It also helps those passengers who are time sensitive and pay higher prices to receive faster check-in service and value for their money. This can be envisaged to become a more important service feature in the future. The trends point towards check-in at hotels (SAS full service concept) or at rent-a-car facilities (Allegis Corporation's Hertz subsidiary). In addition, some airlines are already providing for special accelerated check-in for premium passengers.

(Pan Am is advertising a "private terminal" at Kennedy and British Airways/Air France offer such a facility for Concorde passengers). One feature which is likely to disappear in the years ahead, however, is US curbside check-in. Increased security concerns have pinpointed this practice as a dangerous one.

38. Automated ticket issue and check-in facilities are already in widespread use on shuttle services in the United States and at other airports on an experimental basis (including in Europe). Facilities of this type which allow passengers to bypass normal check-in desks and proceed directly to the gate can be expected to increase in the future to allow airlines to cope with anticipated traffic growth.

39. Baggage rules can be expected to change with the two piece concept gaining widespread acceptance over time. This will be largely of interest to leisure travellers. Aircraft with additional space and better storage for "hand baggage" will, however, allow business travellers to check-in more easily. This is an important service feature for the business traveller and one where increased attention can be expected. Quick baggage claim is the number one item passengers cite in surveys both as a positive feature at favourite airports and an item to be improved at less favoured. Airlines and airports need to work together to improve deplaning techniques and terminal handling – a requirement which becomes more important in easing passenger frustrations when they have been subject to earlier arrival times and intensified checks for security purposes. In a similar context, an adequate supply of baggage trolleys is essential, with procedures and people to ensure the supply is maintained. There is a growing trend towards the use of fee or deposit dispensed trolleys at certain airports. This undoubtedly helps to ensure return of trolleys and therefore continuing availability. It is, however, frustrating for passengers at international terminals who invariably do not have the small change required (exchange facilities inside the baggage collection area would make sense).

40. Porters are still needed by many older or disabled passengers as well as by those who prefer not to carry their own baggage. Porterage rates should be clearly marked in baggage collection areas. This is particularly important in developing countries where cheap labour supplies and absence of baggage trolleys increases the likely use of porters and where bartering practices and unfamiliarity with local custom leaves the traveller open to potential abuse.

41. Finally, there should be clearly signposted depositaries for left baggage and procedures established to move such items through detection machines as a routine matter.

Security

42. All signs point to a continued increase in airport controls. Controls will differ from airport to airport. Some will insist on earlier check-in times, others may restrict

hand baggage, some have more stringent searches. Controls may be stepped up or down depending on government assessment of specific risks at different times. Spot newspaper polls indicate passengers expect and accept this. The likely features include guards in airport terminals, improved surveillance procedures, tighter border control (see paras. 45–47 below). And more efficient scanning of people and baggage. Higher levels of training for security staff and more sensitive detectors can be expected. This is another area where passenger frustration can easily be created – scanners out of service or simply not used, undermanned facilities or overmanned facilities with staff not contributing to efficient flow through are all features which airports and airlines need to work at. Airports are perceived by passengers to generally do a good job but with increased flights, more travellers homing in on hubs and tighter security procedures, the potential for congestion and frustration also increases. In some cases the answer simply means more staff or machines or better coordination with flight schedules.

43. The costs of security should not be passed automatically to passengers. States have obligations to provide for the wellbeing of their citizens and airports and airlines should seek government support for enhanced security measures to deal with terrorists. This may run counter to new market based economic theory. The question is where do States responsibilities begin and end? Railway, port and automobile passengers aren't charged directly for security and nor should airline passengers be. Some airlines have introduced surcharges on certain routes to cover security protection but it's a vague, virtually unaccountable charge. It is not clear if all the monies collected are applied to security controls or whether airlines are paying for procedures which should properly be paid for by States and not simply be passed on to passengers. Some States have begun to introduce security levies. But terrorist actions are not aimed at passengers, their objective is to destabilize States. The costs incurred to deal with this should be taken out of general funds for security police or national defense. It's simply too easy to impose a small surcharge which gradually increases and never goes away.

44. Passengers also have real obligations to help themselves in respect to new security measures – to be alert, not to leave bags unattended in terminals and to report suspicious activities to the appropriate authority. Passengers may need improved briefings and more regular security announcements in terminals (many airports already make such announcements about unattended luggage for example) and in pre-flight hand out materials.

Border Controls

45. Immigration, health, passport and customs controls are integral features of international airports. Obviously the passenger's interest lies in the minimum degree of control necessary for entry and security

formalities, the most streamlined features and the most efficient operation. At many airports these controls, which are in the hands of States and not airport authorities, have been subject to heavy bureaucratic dictate, poor flow methodology and inadequate utilization. At airports in developing nations passengers too often find themselves enmeshed in red tape (compounded by stringent health regulations and tough exchange control provisions). Although labour supply is not a problem in such countries, shortage of adequately trained staff often is. In industrialized States, where the red tape may be looser, the shortage of resources or deployment uncoordinated with aircraft arrival peaks and troughs may equally mean significant delays.

46. Efforts to streamline border control procedures include segregation of immigrants, visitors and returning residents; the use of red and green channels for custom clearance and even pre-flight clearance; improved staff training and resources; more use of computers to check documents and down line, machine-readable passports.

47. Two current trends merit attention.

i. The increase in terrorist activity at airports means additional border checks; this is a regrettable but necessary development. Some States are introducing visas for foreign visitors and, at some airports, passports are being photographed or electronically checked for tampering. Governments need to keep these intensified procedures under close review to see that they impede passenger flow to the minimum extent possible. In this context it is very important that adequate numbers of staff are on duty – taking into account peaks and troughs of demand. Passengers by and large recognize the need for exceptional measures to deal with terrorism; however, their tolerance is tried when inadequate resources are deployed to efficiently handle the tasks.

ii. The pace-setting United States under the twin pressures of budget deficits and the new economics has devised its own unique approach to charging for border control facilities – namely to run these monopoly public services activities as profit-making entreprises, milking captive consumers. Passengers are now paying for the customs service to the tune of $5 per journey. To add insult to injury the customs service is cutting back on staff. The immigration agency, not to be outdone, also charges $5. The agricultural department has jumped on the bandwagon with a proposed $2 fee for inspection services, and the tourism and travel administration (ironically the body responsible for promoting travel to the USA) is asking for a more modest $1 per passenger. This trend, which may prove attractive to other governments, has to be nipped in the bud before it spreads. Before passengers begin to

pay for basic services at various points on their journeys. New international charging principles are needed to safeguard passenger interests in this area. The International Civil Aviation Organization (ICAO), which has succeeded in keeping down the charges levied on airlines over the years, could perhaps perform the equally valuable role in controlling passenger add-ons.

Access to Flights and Inter-Terminal Connections

48. Rapid boarding and deplaning is a highly valued feature for all travellers. It is particularly important for business flyers, for whom time is a premium. Many airports have been forced to expand their terminal facilities by adding extra sections or fingers and, where this has been done without adding moving walkways, it means long walks for passengers. At other airports where gate space is limited transfer is made by bus or people mover. Some airports such as Montreal's Mirabel and Washington's Dulles have had this feature built in at the design stage. Today, terminals are increasingly designed with short walking distances from check-in to gate.

49. The hubbing phenomena in the US has given a new meaning to quick access. With banks of arrivals and departures timed to coincide (subject only to the vagaries of air traffic control) at airports like Atlanta, O'Hare and Dallas/Ft. Worth. In these circumstances, it becomes essential to provide for rapid transfer between gates. The ideal situation for a hubbing passenger is to find his connection at a nearby gate (which is more likely when he is transferring on the services of the same airline). Terminal transfers at hub airports are much less desirable; where they are necessary, rapid transit systems or moving walkways are the optimum. Hubbing makes the bus and the plane mate even less popular.

Communications

50. Good clear signs using universally accepted pictograms are vitally important for international travellers. Information centres staffed by multilingual employees with centrally held information on arrivals and departures are another sine qua non. Increased use of remote electronic message terminals can be envisaged for announcements other than flight information.

51. As airports become larger with many terminals and where connecting times are tight, good communications can mean the difference between making the connection or not.

Seating and Meeting Areas

52. Adequate space is needed not only for passengers but for meeters and greeters. At many airports the scene outside customs control for deplaning and arriving passengers often resembles a football crowd. It seems that no reasonable procedures have yet been developed to deal with this situation.

53. Passengers need seating space in central

terminal areas and at gates. Flight
information data should be close at hand.
Telephones are needed preferably including
machines which use credit cards and those which
provide increased audibility for hard of
hearing passengers.

54. Airport lounges are proliferating
providing both an exclusive segregation for
higher fare paying passengers as well as a
status symbol. Specialized businessmen's
lounges are foreseen as increasing with meeting
facilities, secretarial services, computers,
modems, photocopiers, telexes and fax
machines.

Car Rental

55. Many passengers are looking for rental
cars at the end of their air journey - both for
business and leisure. Most airports offer car
rental facilities although an increasing number
of pick up and drop off points are located off
airport. In the 1984 IAPA survey "on airport
location" was the most important feature for
60% of respondents - well ahead of price and
condition of cars. However, the off airport
trend is a consequence of increased needs of
car rental firms, reduced available space at
increased prices and tighter security
procedures. Integration of the travel industry
is likely to change the reasons for rental car
hiring with a greater emphasis on car selection
as simply a part of a total package, driven by
frequent flyer type bonus points and packaged
via one or another computer reservation
network.

Shopping

56. A good range of shops and restaurants is
also important to passengers. It is even more
important to airports, who are well aware of
the money that can be obtained from
concessions. Quality stores offering high
fashion brand names have discovered the
willingness of passengers to pay for their
projects when transiting airports. Whether
it's the "duty-free" aspect or the glamour or
simply the fact that the passenger profile
contains a very high proportion of upper
quartile income people, sales at airport shops
have boomed in recent years. Transit
passengers are a captive market. In many parts
of the world the airport is the ideal outlet
for local industry to market its wares to high
flying businessmen and affluent tourists. Some
airports such as Schiphol, Changi, Dubai
advertise strongly their range of duty-free
goods and their prices. However, whether the
keen prices stem from the duty-free aspect or
simply the massive turnover is not clear.
Airports do well out of this business and in
many instances so do airlines who are involved
in the duty-free concessions in many
countries.

57. Finally in this context, there is the
important question of whether passengers could
and should be able to buy duty-free on arrival
rather than on departure. It is a question
that is more relevant with the expansion of
duty-free sales at airports and the growing
concern over the quantity of carry-on baggage.

IFAPA maintains that from a passenger safety
and convenience viewpoint, the arguments for
purchase on arrival are very strong. Airline
pilots are of the same opinion. Even some
aircraft manufacturers suggest that the
carriage of duty-free alcohol impedes the
performance and range possibilities of certain
aircraft. Airports, on the other hand, argue
that terminals would have to be redesigned,
that important revenue may be lost and that the
customs authorities are opposed to the concept.
Airlines who see both sides of the argument
(given their interest in duty-free sales) seem
unwilling to take a position. Yet some 15-20
airports do offer purchase on arrival and
others, such as Brussels - where both arriving
and departing passengers pass the duty-free
shops - could easily make the switch.

CONCLUSION

58. Historically, when airports talked about
their users they were invariably referring to
airlines. Today there is a growing recognition
that passengers are also important direct
clients. It is likely that in the future this
relationship of provider and consumer of
airport services will become even clearer. In
many respects passengers will continue to have
to take basic services to meet their needs and
luxuries to meet their wants as the airport
determines. However, there will be increasing
competition between airports to attract
passengers to their terminals. With the
information explosion accelerating into the
90's - computer, TV, video and
telecommunication networks - consumers will be
better informed as to the positive and negative
features of airports they intend to use, just as
they will be in respect of airlines. They will
be able to access data banks easily to ensure up-
to-date information on airport facilities. In
this world the airport which meets passenger
needs in the most efficient and competent
manner and appeals to his wants in the most
imaginative and original way is the airport
that is likely to attract his custom whenever
he has a choice of routing.

59. There is, of course, no ideal airport
but if one can be envisaged it might well have
the following features: easy access to city
centre by public and private transport; ample
parking; clean, spacious, well connected
terminals; well positioned, clear signs;
adequate fast check-in facilities; tight,
unobtrusive security; fast efficient border
controls; comfortable waiting areas with easy
access to essential services; modern business
centres; well located banks and communication
facilities; a range of reasonably priced
restaurants; a good selection of shops
including low priced duty-free (which could be
purchased on arrival); on site hotels and rest
facilities; short distances from check-in to
boarding and very fast baggage collection with
a good supply of trolleys. Such an airport
would take into account the needs of
businessmen, holiday makers, disabled
passengers, the very old and the very young, in
its design. It would undoubtedly routinely be
voted number one in the passenger opinion
polls.

5 The Munich Airport project

Dipl.-Ing. W.O. TOEPEL, Ministerialrat, Bayerisches Staatsministerium für Wirtschaft und Verkehr, Munich, West Germany

The new Munich Airport is one of the few major airport projects in Western Europe, that will be realized within the foreseeable future. This airport will serve as a gateway for long-haul flights to and from the Federal Republic of Germany. The users of the airport will find a most functional passenger building offering short walking distances and providing fast passenger and baggage handling. Careful regional planning will minimize negative environmental impacts to the airport vicinity and will enable people of the surrounding communities to share the benefits of the airport infrastructure.

INTRODUCTION

1.   In 1969 the Bavarian State Government decided to develop a new airport for Munich and Southern Bavaria, Germany's high-technology center and most attractive tourist district. The new airport is supposed to replace the old pre-war airport Munich-Riem which, in spite of many modernization programs, became inadequate for modern air transport due to its proximity to residential areas and its lack of possibility for capacity extension.

Fig. 1.   Existing Munich-Riem Airport

2.   The government's decision was made after a six-year site investigation taking into account more than 20 sites within a 40 km radius around Munich. Following the government decision two administrative procedures for the selected site had been performed from 1969 to 1979 in accordance with the German Aviation Law. The first approval procedure dealt with all planning authorities concerned including communities and counties. It was based upon the airport masterplan and discussed location and size of the airport, environmental impacts to the airport vicinity, safety aspects etc. This first procedure was concluded in 1974 and the approval was issued by the Bavarian State Minister of Economics and Transport giving the airport operator the right to implement and to operate the new airport. But construction work must not start until all problems between the future airport and its neighbours are investigated thoroughly during a second approval procedure. This procedure was based upon the preliminary design of all airport facilities; this documentation was presented to the public, and communities as well as each individual who felt to be affec-

ted by the airport were entitled to submit a statement to the appropriate authority. About 30.000 statements were presented which had to be discussed in more than 100 public inquiries. After careful consideration of all arguments the authority issued a decision in 1979 granting the airport operator the right to commence construction works. This approval became subject of suits filed by some 5000 people in the Administrative Court. Early 1985 the decision of the Higher Bavarian Administrative Court gave green light for construction works, and this court decision was confirmed by the Supreme Federal Administrative Court in December 1986. The airport is supposed to go into operation in 1991.

FACTS AND FIGURES

3.   The site of the new Munich Airport is located 28 km northeast of the City of Munich in a flat rural area at an altitude of 1470 feet. The airport area covers about 1400

Fig. 2.   New Munich Airport site

Airports for people. Thomas Telford Limited, London, 1988

27

hectares (3427 acres). On the site the ground water table is rather high requiring appropriate technical precautions, and several drainage ditches crossing the airport area had to be diverted.

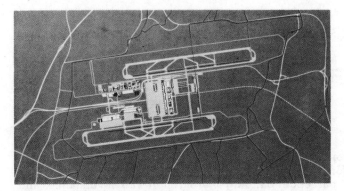

Fig. 3. Drainage of the airport site

4.   The airport will be connected to the traffic generating area by motorways which are integrated into the autobahnsystem around Munich, and by public transport which is part of the Munich Region Rapid Transit System (400 km in total). Access time from Munich downtown to the airport is estimated by 30 min by car as well as by public transport.

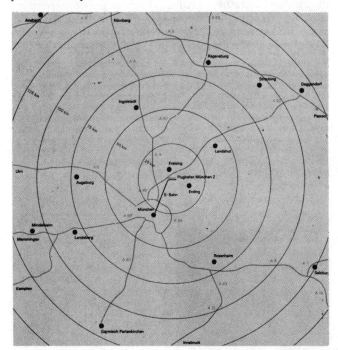

Fig. 4   Munich Airport access system

5.   The runway system will consist of two runways each 4000 m long orientated in east-west direction (082/262). The lateral runway separation of 2300 m will allow independent and simultaneous IFR-operations on both runways. For noise reasons and in order to facilitate aircraft taxiing runways are staggered by 1500 m. All runways will be equipped for all-weather operations CAT III.

6.   The terminal area is located between the runways. A linear passenger building rectangular to the runways is designed for 12 mio annual passengers in the first stage, and on the airside the appropriate apron will provide 20 gate positions plus some 30 remote positions. Multi-storey parking decks on the landside will contain 7900 parking stands for passenger cars. In the center of

the terminal area a public transport underground station is located. The cargo terminal will have a handling capacity of 100.000 t/year in the first stage of construction. A major maintenance base will be developed by Lufthansa and some other airlines. Soon after inauguration at least 10.000 employees are expected to work at the airport.

Fig. 5. Munich Airport layout

7.   The investment costs for the project are estimated by 4.600 mio DM. Investor and operator of the airport is the Munich Airport Co., a public entity in form of a limited liable company with shareholders Federal Republic of Germany (26 %), State of Bavaria (51 %), and City of Munich (23 %).

AIRPORT FOR THE MUNICH REGION

8.   During many public discussions about the new Munich Airport the question was raised whether 11 international airports for the Federal Republic of Germany are justified; opponents against the airport project proposed concentration of international air transportation to one major airport only like in other European Countries. This proposal did not consider the decentralized structure of population and economy in the Federal Republic of Germany, caused by historical development. There are several similar-sized centers of business activity like Düsseldorf, Cologne, Frankfurt, Hamburg, Munich and Stuttgart, contributing each a rather equal share of 4,5 — 8,5 % of total population and of 6,5 — 8,5 % of total gross domestic product; but there is no dominating center like London in UK or Paris in France.

Table 1   Population and Gross Domestic Product (GDP) in German Regions — 1981

Region	Population in mio	GDP in bio ECU
Düsseldorf	5,20 (8,42 %)	57,9 (9,44 %)
Köln	3,92 (6,36 %)	38,0 (6,19 %)
München	3,66 (5,94 %)	42,6 (6,95 %)
Stuttgart	3,49 (5,65 %)	39,2 (6,38 %)
Frankfurt	3,44 (5,57 %	42,8 (6,98 %)
Hamburg	2,81 (4,55 %)	39,0 (6,35 %)

This multi-centralized national structure of economy and population can only adequately be served by an appropriate transportation system. Therefore, in a long-term process the multi-centralized German Airport System was developed which meets the requirements of the country's economy in a suitable way. Munich Airport plays an important role within this multi-centralized airport system.

Table 2   Traffic volume development
of Munich Airport 1960 — 1986

	1960	1970	1980	1986
Passengers	0,79 mio	3,55 mio	6,06 mio	8,40 mio
Cargo	7,500 t	32.000 t	39.100 t	38.400 t
Mail	1.475 t	8.700 t	10.800 t	16.400 t

9.   The Munich Region, an area of 17.500 km² with a population of 3,7 mio inhabitants, is one of the major hubs of economic activities in the Federal Republic of Germany. It is the home of many high-technology industries (aircraft and airspace, electronics, chemical, automobile) having high export rates and requiring extensive international cooperation. Many research institutes and

Fig. 7.   Bavaria, the largest of the German States — and the southernmost

Fig. 6.   Bavarian places of interest

Fig. 8.   Munich in the heart of Europe

scientific centers are located in the Munich Region (e.g. Max-Planck-Institutes, German Aeronautical Research Institutes, Fraunhofer Society). About one quarter of all German banking institutions and numerous important insurance companies have their headquarters in Munich. Here is a German center of international fairs and congresses, and finally, the Munich Region is the most traditional tourist and resort area of Germany with 6,5 mio annual tourist arrivals and 25 mio overnight stays per year.

10.   This most active region, part of Bavaria which is the southernmost state of the Federal Republic of Germany, is located in the center of Middle Europe, but find itself on the periphery of the European Community. In order to offset this geographical disadvantage an effective transportation system by road, rail and air is indispensable for this region. The new Munich Airport will serve the transport demands of the Munich Region, and, likewise, will be a link for traffic flows from Germany to Eastern Europe, to Middle and Far East, and to Africa. Therefore, the Bavarian State Government strongly support the development of the new Munich Airport in the interest of people, trade, and tourism of the Munich Region.

AIRPORTS FOR PEOPLE

AIRPORT FOR THE USERS

11. Developing an airport for the users requires a careful analysis of the user's wishes. The users of an airport are air passengers as well as airlines, authority employees as well as concessionaires; and also taxidrivers and porters are airport users. All these different users have different wishes; they require each specific facilities of certain size and standard, and the sum of all these user's wishes form the planning criteria for an airport.

12. What are for instance the wishes of air passengers? Passengers want short ground handling time, because handling time particularly on short-haul flights is a substantial portion of the total travel time.

Table 3 Time segments on short-haul flights

Route	MUC-FRA (domestic)	MUC-LON (internat.)
Distance	170 nm	520 nm
Flight time	60 min (43%)	110 min (44%)
Handling time	30 min (21%)	60 min (24%)
Access time	50 min (36%)	80 min (32%)
Travel time	140 min (100%)	250 min (100%)

To gain short ground handling times requires
— handling procedures which guarantee minimal waiting time in front of check-in counters and control counters.
— terminal concepts allowing short walking distances from the curbside to the aircraft and vice versa.
— well-developed information systems giving passengers clear and concise guidance.

13. These requirements were taken into account for Munich Airport in the following way:
— The linear terminal consists of four modules each containing one arrival unit and one departure unit.

Fig. 9.   Passenger Terminal — 1. stage

Each module has a handling capacity of 1500 peak-hour passengers offering to passengers two blocks of check-in-counters, one block of immigration/security control, and a huge waiting area with shopping kiosks. Departing passengers are free to select this check-in counter and this control counter having the shortest queue in front by this guaranteeing minimum possible handling time.
— The linear passenger building with curbside along one edge of the building and the apron along the other one allows straight passenger flow in one level only and short walking distances of not more than 50 m for passengers travelling by car to the airport. Passengers using public transport on their way to the airport must accept longer walking distances up to 500 m because they have to be delivered at the airport in one central point where they are distributed to

their particular module by moving sidewalks. They may elect to check-in their baggage either in the central building or in their module.

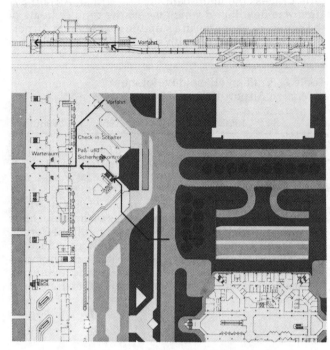

Fig. 10.   Passenger terminal — flow of car passengers

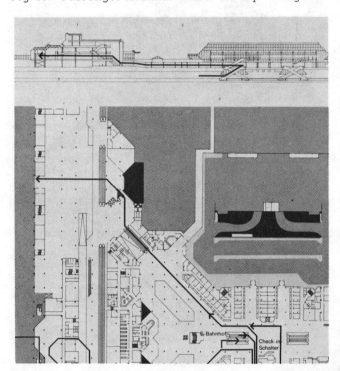

Fig. 11.   Passenger terminal —
flow of public transport passengers

— The four modules will be indicated by letters A-D, and each module will serve special types of flights. Module A will be designated for domestic flights of the national carrier and of local carriers, module B will be used by the national carrier for international flights. Module C is supposed to handle all international flights of foreign airlines, and module D is reserved for charter flights which form a substantial share of 31% of the total air passenger volume at Munich.

14. What are the wishes of the airlines? Airlines want to minimize costs for passenger and baggage handling.

This requires
— handling of passenger and baggage with minimum amount of personnel and equipment,
— providing fast handling procedures in order to maintain on-time arrivals and departures and to guarantee late check-in.

15. The module concept meets these airline requirements in an ideal way. This concept allows to concentrate airline staff and equipment at four central points of the passenger building, and the number of personnel on duty can flexible be adjusted to traffic requirements. Furthermore, check-in and control facilities are located as close as possible to the aircraft on the apron resulting in short transfer time of 35 min only and in acceptance of late-check-in passengers.

16. In similar ways the wishes of all other airport users were analysed. It can be assumed that the facilities of the new Munich Airport will adequately meet the requirements of the different users from the air passenger to the cab-driver.

AIRPORT FOR THE NEIGHBOURS

17. In Middle Europe airports are frequently considered by their neighbours as monsters consuming farm- or woodland and distributing noise and pollution. This negative airport image often obstructs the development of new airports or the extension of existing ones. People speak rather rarely about the positive impacts of an airport to its vicinity such like the airport as an employer or the improvement of local infrastructure caused by the airport.

18. The Bavarian State Government initiated soon after the decision in 1969 with all regional and local authorities a program in order
— to minimize the unavoidable negative impacts of the new airport, and
— to develop an integrated infrastructure for the airport vicinity considering both the requirements of the airport and of the surrounding communities.

19. The most serious problem burdening the relationship between an airport and its vicinity is aircraft noise. The noise problem came up in the past not only by the introduction of jet aircraft but also by the increasing development of residential areas into noise-sensitive zones around airports. Therefore, it must be the policy of all planning agencies to restrict urban development within these noise-exposed zones and likewise to grant to people forced to live in these zones noise protection (e.g. noise-proof windows). This policy was strictly observed by the Bavarian State Government in the case of new Munich Airport. In the seventies already careful investigations were performed what equivalent permanent noise level would be tolerable to people and which communities in the airport vicinity could be accepted to become subject of restrictions in urban development. A noise contour taking into account the long term traffic development of the new airport was defined and formally established beyond which an equivalent permanent noise level of 62 dB (A) shall not be exceeded. Outside this contour urban development is unrestricted as far as noise reasons are concerned; within this contour limitations for residential areas have to be observed by communities. Further contours were established in order to grant noise protection to all people which are exposed to noise exceeding certain levels. It need not to be mentioned that all these contours go far beyond these prescribed by the German Law for Protection against Aircraft Noise.

20. Also the positive impacts of the new Munich Airport were carefully investigated in order to use these benefits for the airport neighbourhood. As already sta-

ted the new airport will have at least 10.000 employees. Another 5000 jobs can be expected in commercial activities outside the airport but caused by the airport. The question was, where to locate these activities — decentralized in many communities or centralized in few locations only. It was found that the second alternative should be favoured. The road and rail access system of the airport will likewise improve the accessibility of

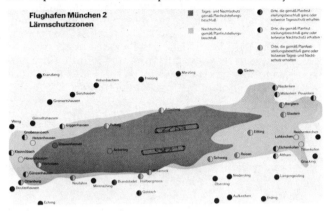

Fig. 12. Contours granting noise-proof measures

most communities surrounding the airport. In this context it is seriously considered to extend the railway line beyond the airport to the next major community in order to improve the attractivity of this community for airport employees as well as for commercial activities. The airport needs a sewage plant. A common facility was built together with several communities which could improve their sewage situation by this project.

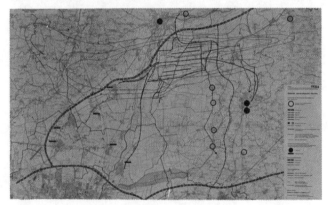

Fig. 13 Infrastructure serving the airport and communities

This positive cooperation between new Munich Airport and surrounding communities was directed and supported by the Bavarian State Government. Hopefully the new airport won't be longer considered as a monster but as a good neighbour.

CONCLUSION

21. Developing an airport is sometimes a painful and time-consuming job — but it is doubtless a great challenge for all to be involved. An airport should not be considered as a monument but as a facility of vital interest for the people. These people formulate opinions and statements, and all these opinions and statements — even negative statements — contribute to the development of an airport. Careful evaluation of all opinions and statements is necessary in order to build an airport for the people. This is what was tried to do in case of new Munich Airport.

6 São Paulo International Airport at Guarulhos

Maj. Brig. Eng. T.P. DA SILVA, Superintendente, Regional de São Paulo, Brazil

This work presents both the philosophy and the concepts that oriented the conception of the airport design, with the observations resulting from daily contact with the operational activities, after two years of operation, since January of 1985. This experience is being assimilated and incorporated into the second phase of construction, presently under way and with its conclusion forecast for 1989. Such interactive is only possible due to the fact that the technical team responsible for the conception, design and construction still participates in the administration, operation, maintenance and commercial exploitation of the airport.

BRAZIL AND AIR TRANSPORTATION

1. Due to its continental dimensions, with 8,500,000 km2 area and 140,000,000 inhabitants, air transportation is one of the vital factors for the progress of Brazil.

2. Despite the economic difficulties inherent to a nation in the stage of development, Brazil already has a network of 170 regular airports which, during the past ten years, has been strengthened by the construction of new airports in the capital cities of the large states, such as Rio de Janeiro, Manaus, Belo Horizonte, Salvador and, finally, São Paulo.

SÃO PAULO AND AIR TRANSPORTATION

3. The city of São Paulo, with its 10,000,000 inhabitants, has the largest population in Brazil and one of the highest growth indices in the whole world. The largest industrial complex as well as the largest export and import market in Brazil are concetrated in this city.

4. In this context, air transportation appears as a vital instrument for the achievement and promulgation of the services and goods generated by the metropolis.

5. The cities of São Paulo and Rio de Janeiro represent 55% of the domestic air traffic and 90% of the international.

6. Until recently, the principal airport of the São Paulo city was Congonhas, attending pratically alone an annual flow of 6,000,000 passengers.

7. This airport started out in 1936 as a simple landing field and then developed to adequately attend São Paulo up to the 1950 decade. However, at that time, which marked the beginning of the modern concept of airports resulting from post-war aeronautical technology, the urban structure of the city was already compromised and no sufficiently large free areas were avaiable for expansion of the Congonhas Airport.

8. Surrounded by the city and without condictions for expansion nor for attending the constantly growing demand, large intercontinental line aircrafts could not operated from this airport. The restraint of air operations during the period beetween 23:00 and 6:00 hours as a form of diminishing city noise caused the majority of brazilian domestic flights to conform to this operational schedule.

CREATION OF AN AIRPORT SYSTEM

9. Due to the fact that in large urban centers the requirements of air transportation can no longer be attended by one sole airport, the terminal area concept was envolved.

10. Thus, in the molds of equivalent complexes in New York, London and Paris, the São Paulo Terminal Area was created, basically comprised of three airports: Guarulhos, Congonhas and Campinas, making use, within the brazilian reality, of the existing resources and rationalizing air traffic distribution.

11. For this purpose, the following activities were carried out:
. restudy of all the air space of the São Paulo Terminal Area;
. creation within the area of eleven new air navigation aid sites;
. preparation of Masters Plans for the Airports System, so as to allow its development in stages and in an integrated manner.

12. Within this working philosophy, priority was given to the implementation of the São Paulo International Airport at Guarulhos.

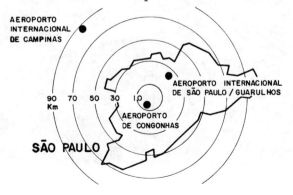

SÃO PAULO INTERNATIONAL AIRPORT AT GUARULHOS

13. The airport occupies an area of 14 km2 and is situated 25 km from the center of the city, close to an efficient highway network comprised by the President Dutra Highway, which connects São Paulo to Rio de Janeiro, and the Workers' Highway, of recent construction. In planning the airport, an area was reserved for the future construction of a station for mass transportation (train or underground) which, it is expected, will connect the airport to the neighboring vicinities.

14. The location of the new airport, as was to be expected, gave rise endless discussion. Its location, although not ideal, was the best feasible alternative found after study of more than 30 sites around greater São Paulo.

Advantages presented by the location:
. proximity to the city;
. making use of the terrain area already belonging to the Cumbica Air Base, owned by the Ministry of Aeronautics and requiring few expropriations for completing the area necessary for the airport.

Disadvantages presented by the location:
. Not very favourable meteorological condictions, requiring the use os ILS Cat II landing aid, still not routinely used in Brazil;

. noise polution of Guarulhos, a city of industrial characteristics, but having a frank demographic explosion with a present population of about 700,000 inhabitants.

15. Expropriation problems did not assume great proportions, due to the small number (about 2,000) and to good negotiation with fair payment of the value of the properties, almost all modest, which, in the majotiry of cases, represented an improvement in the living level of the occupants.

16. The noise pollution problem, more difficult to solve, was the object of noise curve studies and the local city government was encouraged to pass laws restricting the use of the land arround the airport. Only by the application of careful zoning can the noise problems be minimized and, even so, at long term.

17. As regards the part directly under the control of the brazilian aeronautical authorities, studies are being carried out of landing and takeoff procedures for attenuating the air noise, as well as for restricting the operating schedules of the noisier aircrafts.

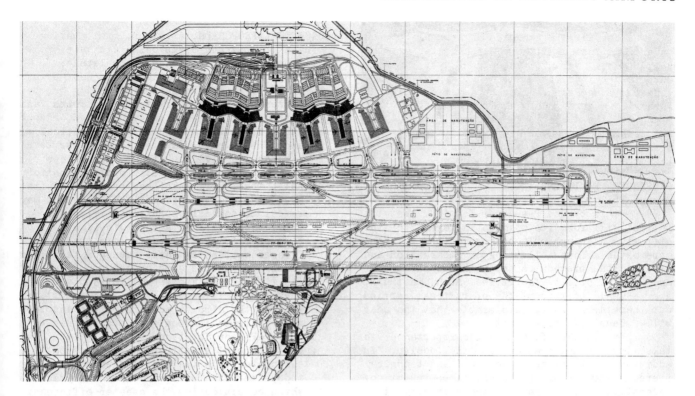

MASTER PLAN

18. The Master Plan for the Airport presents, in its maximum utilization configuration, a system of two proximate (370m) and parallel runways of 3,000 and 3,700m, as well as the forecast for a possible third auxiliary runway of 2,000m length. This system represents a forecast maximum annual capacity of 250,000 aircraft movements.

19. There are four passenger terminals, interconnected two by two in integrated groups. Each terminal has the capacity of handling 7,500,000 passengers/year, making a total of 30,000,000 passengers/year.

20. Aircraft parking in the various areas is thus distributed:

- 44 positions for aircrafts stationed directly at the embarkation bridges of the terminals;
- 39 positions for aircraft at remote position;
- 12 positions for aircraft directly in front of the cargo terminal.

21. For composition of the mix of stationed aircraft, the models Boeing-747, DC-10 and Airbus-A300 were taken into consideration.

22. Vehicle parking areas are distributed throughout the whole airport area, with a total capacity for 10,000 vehicles distributed horizontally, that is, without taking into consideration the possibility of parking buildings.

23. In addition to the elements already described, there are all others necessary for the operation of an international airport, such as:

- cargo sector;
- aircraft maintenance sector;
- utilities sector (electric power, telephones, iced water, drinking water, garbage disposal, sewers, etc.);
- Control Tower and Flight Protection Unit;

CONSTRUCTION PHASES

24. The first phase of construction establishes the construction of the runways and aprons system, passenger terminals 1 and 2 and other elements necessary for the operation of the airport complex. These works were programmed to be carried out gradually, within the requirements of brazilian air traffic.

25. The works were started in 1980 and attained a first partial goal with Terminal 1 entering operation in 1985.

26. The works for Terminal 2 are in process for conclusion in 1989, at which time the start of saturation of Terminal 1 is forecast.

27. Among the principal electronic aids projected and destined for air operations, the following are already in operation:

- Radars;
- ILS Cat II System;
- Automatic Meteorology Station;
- Surface Radar;
- ALS System of approach lights;
- PAPI System at all heads of runways;
- Radio-Apron communications system.

28. Among the principal support installations, the following are already in full operation:

- Control Tower;
- Air Cargo Terminal;
- Electric power substation;
- Telephone exchange;
- Iced water central for the air conditioning system;
- Fire Brigade;
- Fuel Deposit System;
- Sewerage Treatment Station;
- Garbage Incinerator;
- Plant nursery;
- Heliport;
- General aviation terminal;
- Vehicle parking areas.

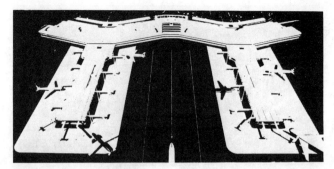

PASSENGER TERMINALS
Design Philosophy

29. It is by the Passenger Terminal that the public will form its opinion in regard to the airport. Although only having contact with the more ostentatious activities of embarkation and debarkation procedures and with the commercial and public utility facilities which, in truth, are a small portion of the operations carried out therein, it is by this sample that the user will "classify" the airport.

30. It is therefore of vital importance to take into consideration in the design, in addition to all of the functional and technical prerequisites, this psycological component of receptivity on the part of the community that is to use the airports.

31. There are no magic formulas for the perfect solution of an airport terminal design.

32. The forms, whether straight or curved, the systems, whether centralized or decentralized, area all valid, so long as well developed and well applied for each particular case.

33. The internationally recommended formulas and standards for attaining an ideal dimensioning are indices that merit analysis in the light of local and temporal condictions.

34. Every project worthy of the name must originate from an idea that gives it body and soul.

35. Thus, the Passenger Terminals of the São Paulo International Airport at Guarulhos originated from an idea consubstantiated on two basic principles that served as guidelines for the design of the whole airport complex:

36. Design a brazilian airport:
  . permiting the user to make use of it with the least number possible of restrictions, due to the strong attraction it represents since, to the brazilian, air transportation is still an attraction far greater than a simple mean of transportation;
  . using natural illumination, so generous in our tropical region.

37. Design a green airport:
  . dispensing with large viaducts or elevated roads, making access to the terminals by mean of grass and flower planted slopes;
  . planning ground movement so as obtain various tree planted planes around the buildings, harmonizing the great volume of concrete they represent with the natural environment of the region;
  . using the landscaping not only for purposes of decoration, but also with defined technical objectives such as the protection of drainage canals, covering the areas between runways and setting up vegetation acoustic barriers.

CONCEPTUAL PROPOSALS

38. Architectonic Division:
  . the terminal have three basic levels:
    ground level - debarkation;
    upper level - embarkation;
    mezzanine - restaurants, VIP rooms and terracces.
  . the terminals are structurally identical and of symetrical design. This symetry permits the division of a terminal into 2 distinct sectors (domestic and internatio nal). Thus, Terminal 1 has one half of its area adapted for international use, but may revert to domestic condition or become fully international, as required;
  . Terminals 1 and 2 are joined by the Interconnection Building having 6 floors on which are located some of the common use facilities (chapel, auditorium, press room, authorities room, AIS room, etc.), as well as the airport administration and the electronic operational centers.

39. Pier-Finger Solution
  . the choice of a semicentralized system associated with the pier-finger concept was made after careful comparative analysis which concluded for the greater efficiency of this system in the particular condictions of terrain and geometry of the runways of the São Paulo airport at Guarulhos;
  . the maximum capacity considered optimum was of 7,500,000 passengers/year for each terminal;
  . the average distance to be convered by a passenger is 250m, considered perfectly reasonable to be covered without the aid of mechanical devices and providing economy and efficiency to the whole complex.

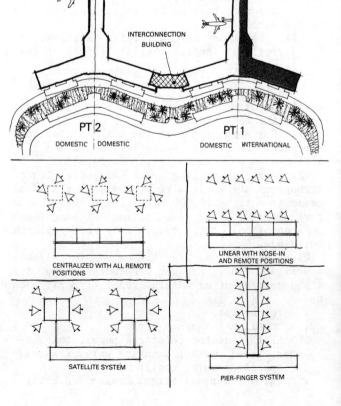

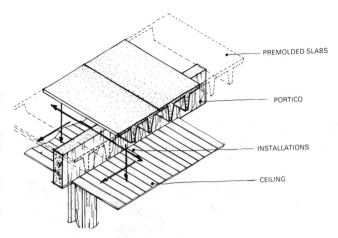

40. Structural System:
- dimensional module: 1.25m;
- columns and main beams molded "in loco" forming rigid porticos;
- Floor slabs of premolded elements of prestressed concrete, supported on the main beams of the porticos;
- this system permits the free passage of the installations in all directions without interfering with the concrete structure.

41. Environmental Integration:
- each terminal has a markedly prominent central point of triple height (15.00m) from which the three floors comprising it may be seen, thus integrating the environments and making it easy for the users to understand them.

ELECTRONICS SYSTEMS
1. ILS - Instrument Landing System
   CAT I, CAT II, capture effect glide slope antenna, monitoring system
2. ASR - Airport Suveillance Radar
   The transmitter/receiver equipment is installed at the Guarulhos Airport with information transmission through microwave link to the Congonhas Airport, and also the TWR at the Guarulhos Airport through a physical line.
3. SSR - Secondary Surveillance Radar, connected to the primary radar
4. ARTS - Automated Radar Terminal System
5. APP Equipment
   07 operator positions, 01 supervisor position, hot-line communication central, 03 radar information displays.
6. VHF - Communication Equipment
   - Guarulhos Airport
     Earth/air transmitter and receiver station, currently with six channels and expandable up to fourteen
   - Congonhas
     Earth/air communication station, with eight channels for the APP
7. ASDE - Airport Surface Detection Equipment installed on the top of the control tower of the Guarulhos Airport, with 03 displays.
8. Airport Lighting System - ALS
   ALS II for 720 meter, inbed runways and taxiway lights and touch zone for CAT II operations, airport identification lights, PAPI System and vertical signalling system.
9. Automatic Surface Meteorological System
   RVR station, ceiling meters, anemometers, telepsicometers and pluviometers.
10. FIDS - Flight Information Display System
    It presents the relevant flight information for airport users and airport workers, through the use of flap-board units and TV monitors which are computer controlled.

ELECTRIC AND ELECTROMECHANICAL SYSTEMS
1. Transmission Devices, Control Keys, Circuit Breakers, Measuring and Protection Transformers for the Main Substation, Shielded and Protected by SF6 Gas
2. Power Transformers for the Main Substation (138/13,8 KV)
   3 transformers, each rated 20/25/30 MVA.
3. Emergency (stand-by) Energy Generation Groups
   Four groups are rated for 3 MVA and 2 are rated 600 KVA.
4. 400 Hz Fixed Power Supply System, Which Supplies Eletrical Power for the Aircraft on the Apron.
5. Emergency (UPS) Power Supply Systems
6. Air Conditioning System Characteristics:
   variable air volume system, with 3500/4000 TR of installed capacity, for the 2 terminal buildings, centrifuges, with unit capacities rated at 1000 TR, multicells refrigerating towers, with concrete built structures, cold water and condensation pumps.
7. Pneumatic Automatic Doors
8. Baggage Conveyors
9. Scalators for Passengers and Public, and Bag
10. Moving Stairways
    capacity rated at 5000/8000 people hour
11. Check-in and Cargo Terminal Scales
12. Frigorific Chambers
13. Pumps for the Fire Combat System
14. Loading Bridges
15. Waste and Sewage Treatment Plants
16. Waste Incinetators
17. Fire Attack Cars
18. Ambulances
19. Aircraft Fuel Supply Hydrant System

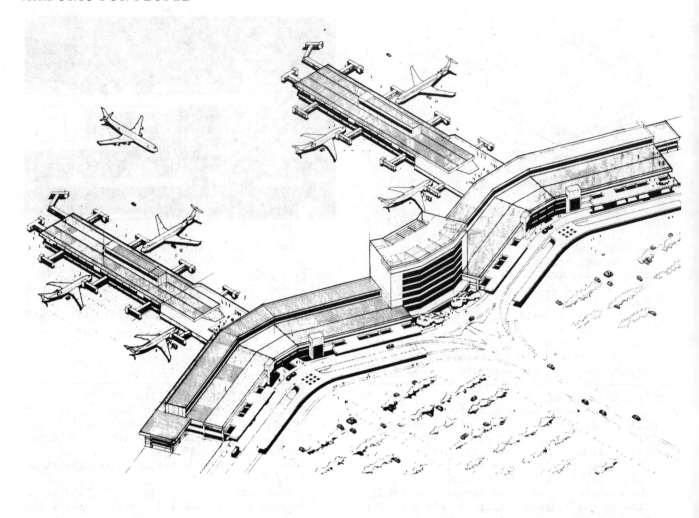

GENERAL COMMENTS

Airport Population

42. All of the theoretical planning, all of the design intentions, are effectively tested when the terminal is handed over to its population, comprised of:

- passengers;
- passengers companions;
- eventual visitors (inhabitants of the region or even of distant areas);
- airline company employees;
- operations employees;
- maintenance employees;
- service company employees (food, medical, cleaning, garbage, etc.);
- commercial concessions employees;
- Government bodies employees;
- press.

43. At the starts of operations of an airport it becomes extremely important for the administrator to evaluate the operational conflicts resulting from the mixture of two factors:

- many details of design conception, when put into practice, are impaired by the dynamic evolution of the airport during the period between its conception and its construction. Proper criteria and knowledge of the basic philosophy of the design are necessary for these adjustements to be made

without prejudice to the complex; frequently, criticisms made as to the performance of the constructed installations are due to the improper use by the operators due to the lack of a more profound knowledge of the basic concepts of the design. These criticisms are generally followed by suggestions for the correction of the supposed errors, causing the situation to become even more disturbed. It is once again the duty of the administrator to teach and train his personnel to act within the proposed objectives.

Passenger Flow

44. Essentially, the efficiency of a terminal is measured by the flow of the embarkation and debarkation operations.

45. In Brazil, air journeys are still, for the great majority, an unusual occurrence, ocasioning commotions due to the large number of accompanying people, as well as to indecision as to normal check-in procedures and the use of the airport facilities.

46. It was attempted to minimize these difficulties by simplifying the course to be taken by the passengers and marking them by different colours and different floor covering and wall covering materials. The escalators are strategically located in the flow current to encourage their use and not overload the elevators. The visual integration of the

different floors allows a restricted use of signalling, since it permits the user to rapidly identify the activities taking place in the interior of the building.

47. For those having locomotion difficulties, there are ramps on all sidewalks and in all elevators, as well as special sanitary facilities scattered throughout the terminal.

48. The finger solution, with individual halls for each flight, brings greater tranquility to the passenger unaccustomed to frequent flying, freeing him more rapidly from the outside commotion.

49. The total length of the finger is 200m, the ideal distance to make it unnecessary to use mechanical transportation devices (conveyer belts). The final 50m of the finger comprise a large embarkation hall of the satellite type with simultaneous access to 5 embarkation bridges. By means of sliding doors, this hall may be connected to the domestic or the international sector. This flexibility is very useful for attending the peak hours.

Commercial Exploitation

50. In Brazil, the commercial exploitation of airport space for shops, services or publicity is a relatively new matter and for such reason has not reached the ideal degree of equilibrium between the economic objectives of profit and the activities of real interest to the passenger.

51. Only essential commercial activities should be located inside the terminal. Others should be housed in independent buildings, always connected to the terminal, in conjuction with shopping centers, public transport stations or garage building.

52. Among the main points are the food service facilities, since they are used not only by the passengers (in an eventual manner), but by the rest of the airport population. Any deficiency, whether in quality or price, immediately results in complaints, discontent and loss to the good working environment.

53. The planning of Terminals 1 and 2 provides for about 20 different food service points, although not fully active at present, with characteristics for serving different categories comprising their population:
. coffee shops for the public and passengers;
. coffee shops private to passengers;
. snack bar for the public and passengers;
. coffee shop and snack bar for the ramp service personnel;
. bars for the public and passengers;
. bars private to the passengers;
. a la carte restaurants for the public and passengers;
. cafeterias for the public and passengers;
. restaurants for the administrative personnel;
. restaurants for the ramp service personnel.

Human Scale

54. During only the 1st phase of construction of the São Paulo International at Guarulhos, about 25 buildings were constructed, totalling 200.000m2, all studied and designed to attend the basic requirements of the sophisticated electrical, mechanical and electronic equipment, as well as the proper functioning the flow of passengers, visitors, employees, air and land vehicles and support services and infra-structure resulting from these activities.

55. In addition to all of theses prerequisites, respect for the human scale was sought throughout the complex by means of:
. the distance between buildings to permit the majority of times, covering it on foot;
. landscaping care in the positioning of the buildings so as to respect adjacent nature and integrate with it;
. intensive use of urban facilities such as sidewalks, marquees, covered passage ways, shelters for bus stops, pedestrian walkways, gardens, etc.;
. Bright, cheerful and easily understood building interiors, coherent with the principle of form in respect to function.

56. Finally, it should be said that despite all of the techniques at our disposal which should be used to confere the human scale to an airport, what is really important is that the human scale be in the heart and mind of its planners, constructors and administrators.

REFERENCES

1. MINISTRY OF AERONAUTICS
   Responsible for brazilian air transportation planning and control.
   Address: Esplanada dos Ministérios - Bloco M
            8o. andar
            70.045 - Brasília - DF
   Telephone: (061) 223-0409

2. INFRAERO - Empresa Brasileira de Infra-Estrutura Aeroportuária
   Reponsible for brazilian commercial airports operation and maintenance.
   Address: Edifício Chams - 6o. andar - Setor Comercial Sul
            70.300 - Brasília - DF
   Telephone: (061) 217-4222

7 Second Sydney Airport site selection program

I.W. WOONTON, Assistant Secretary, Major Airport Projects, Department of Aviation, Canberra, Australia

Sydney (Kingsford Smith) is Australia's busiest passenger airport and last year handled some 191,000 runway movements, and 11,500,000 passenger movements; it is however Australia's smallest major airport in area occupying only some 700ha.

As with many other cities in the world, the saga of the search for a site for a second major airport to serve the city of Sydney gradually unfolded through the late 1960's, 1970's and into the early 1980's. This paper is an account of the fourth major study in the saga, that of the second Sydney airport site selection program which resulted in a Government decision in February 1986 to acquire a site at Badgerys Creek for Sydney's second major airport. The decision has been well received by the community and the aviation industry. The site is some 46km directly west of the CBD. The preliminary master plan for an airport on the site is described in broad terms.

BACKGROUND

1. Following the end of the Second World War, the Government decided to expand Sydney (Kingsford Smith) Airport to serve as the major airline airport in the Sydney Region. The Government also decided, with the agreement of the New South Wales State Government, that a site at Towra Point on the southern foreshore of Botany Bay would be reserved for development as a second major airport should the need arise. This situation continued throughout the 1950's and 1960's. On 1 April 1969 the then Prime Minister announced that Towra Point was no longer to be considered as a second airport site and that he had requested a Committee of Government Officials to make recommendations on a suitable second site.

2. Four major studies ensued. The first study in 1969 by Australian Government Officials recommended a further joint study by Australian and New South Wales Government Officials. The second study committee submitted an interim report in August 1973 recommending that a decision in principal be made to develop a parallel runway at the existing airport. The Government took no action on this recommendation and in 1976 a further Commonwealth State Committee known as the Major Airports Needs for Sydney (MANS) studied the matter again.

3. The Officials of this latter committee were unable to reach agreement and in December 1979 the Commonwealth Committee members recommended amongst others that a contingent site for a curfew free second major airport should be protected through land use planning and acquisition and that Badgerys Creek was the preferred site. No action was taken on this recommendation.

4. Following a change of Government in 1983, the new Minister for Aviation announced in March that year that every effort would be made to identify and reserve the site for Sydney's second major airport.

PROGRAM

5. The second Sydney Airport site selection program was conducted by the Department of Aviation. It commenced in March 1983 and was completed in February 1986 when the Government announced the site for the second airport. The program was undertaken with the assistance of other Commonwealth and State agencies and the environmental impact statement (EIS) was prepared with the assistance of consultants.

6. A call was made in October 1983 for expressions of interest from consultants and 18 consortia from round the world registered with the Department. Six consortia were invited to submit detailed proposals in response to a brief and Kinhill Stearns were engaged in March 1984. Kinhill Stearns were assisted by specialist advisors

   - Professors de Neufville, de Monchaux, Odoni and Simpson from M.I.T.

and subconsultants

   - Greiner Engineering Sciences Inc.

A draft environmental impact statement for public comment was released in June 1985 and a supplement to the draft EIS incorporating public comment was completed in October 1985.

Airports for people. Thomas Telford Limited, London, 1988

Need

7. The requirement to reserve a site for a second major airport has not diminished with the passage of time. Runway movements at Sydney (Kingsford Smith) Airport have increased over the period 1975 to 1986 from 156,000 movements to 191,000 movements.

8. Continued growth in air travel demand is more likely than zero growth. The capacity of KSA is limited and it is forecast that runway capacity at the level of four minutes average delay will be exceeded by demand sometime between 1988 and 2003, depending on rate of future growth.

9. The possibility exists for some traffic rationalisation and there is some limited potential for marginal increases in runway capacity, but these would only defer by a few years and not replace the need for a second airport.

10. In addition the supply of suitable land in the mountain-ringed Sydney Basin is dwindling rapidly due to spreading urbanisation, and regional planning authorities had a need to incorporate a second site into their studies on how best to cope with a 1M population increase by the turn of the century. The current population of Sydney is 3.5M.

THE SITE SELECTION

11. Locations selected to be studied initially were from the voluminous work carried out in the previous three studies, and from locations promoted strongly in the media and by personal representations to Government and the Study Team. The locations comprised:

Badgerys Creek Scheyville	From previous MANS Study short list
Bringelly Londonderry Holsworthy	Other Sydney Region MANS sites
Warnervale Somersby	Mid distance (north) sites
Darkes Forest Wilton	Mid distance (south) sites
Goulburn	Outlying site

Airport Layouts for Site Selection

12. The agreed guidelines for the preparation of the Draft EIS under the Environment Protection (Impact of Proposals) Act required that the environmental assessment be based on the "worst possible case" for each location. Therefore, in order to examine each location for a feasible airport site it was necessary to adopt an airport layout based on the worst case assumptions regarding the future, and to conduct sensitivity tests on the outcome of the

examination for a lower level of airport development.

Assumptions for different activity levels

Factor	Lower Level	Higher Level (worst case)
Pax. p.a.	5M	25M
Runways	SR + crosswind	WSPR + crosswind
Aircraft mix WB/ NB/Comm/GA	10/20/30/40	30/40/20/10
Daily Operations	300	750
% night flights	20	20
% on crosswind	20	20

13. It was found that all locations could offer an airport site capable of accommodating any runway layout including double widely spaced parallel runways.

Shortlisting of locations to be studied indepth

14. The sites at the above ten locations were evaluated against twenty-five factors. Four broad groupings of site selection factors were adopted roughly corresponding with the major concerns of groups in the community. The broadly defined environment included air quality, water quality, flood potential, flora, fauna, archeology, European heritage, agriculture, mineral resources, disruption, existing and potential land use. Factors grouped as accessibility were market share potential, private travel and public transport. Operations factors included airspace, wind coverage, meteorology and site flexibility. The remaining group of costs included acquisition, relocation of facilities and infrastructure, site preparation, access works and new infrastructure.

15. Use was made of a site ranking matrix consisting of these twenty-five factors. For each site each factor was quantified on a common scale. Each factor was then scored on a ratio scale and assigned a relative value or weight when compared with other factors influencing site selection. The total rank for any one site for one set of assumptions, weights and scores could be determined by aggregating the weighted scores. Sensitivity testing was carried out by varying assumptions, factors, scores and weights. One matrix for a WSPR layout at the 25M passenger level is shown at Figure 1. Each location was then reviewed for serious weaknesses and three were found to have fatal flaws. Further evaluation of the remaining seven established that Badgerys Creek was the best inner and Wilton the best mid-distance location.

16. Results of the evaluation can be summarised as follows:

LAYOUT : WSPR ; PAX NO. 25.0 (MILLION)

FACTORS/SUBFACTORS	FACTOR WEIGHT	SUBFACTOR WEIGHT	FACTOR SCORES									
			Badg. Ck.	Bring.	Hols.	Lond.	Schey.	Darkes Forest	Som.	Warn.	Wilt.	Goul.
ENVIRONMENT	31.5											
. Air quality		1.2	3.8	3.5	5.4	0.7	0.0	8.5	8.5	6.5	8.3	10.0
. Water quality		1.3	3.0	3.0	6.0	4.0	5.0	2.0	5.0	7.0	0.0	10.0
. Flood risk		1.3	6.0	6.0	10.0	0.0	0.0	10.0	10.0	4.0	10.0	10.0
. Flora		2.1	9.0	9.0	2.8	0.0	1.2	0.0	3.0	4.4	1.7	10.0
. Fauna		2.1	10.0	9.5	3.7	3.8	7.8	0.0	7.4	1.7	4.0	7.0
. Archaeology		2.7	10.0	10.0	0.0	6.2	3.4	0.2	2.2	5.5	2.0	6.2
. European heritage		2.7	0.6	0.6	10.0	0.0	1.9	10.0	6.6	6.5	7.8	7.0
. Agriculture		1.6	1.1	0.0	7.5	5.3	1.4	10.0	2.0	3.8	7.7	2.1
. Mineral Resources		2.0	4.5	7.3	7.3	2.7	8.6	0.0	6.4	5.0	4.5	10.0
. Population displaced		4.9	6.9	0.0	7.1	6.0	2.6	10.0	8.0	9.1	9.3	10.0
. Existing noise incompatible land use		4.7	2.6	2.0	5.8	1.3	0.0	8.9	7.0	3.0	8.6	10.0
. Future noise incompatible land use		3.6	0.0	2.0	8.7	6.3	2.9	10.0	5.5	4.1	6.2	10.0
ENVIRONMENTAL RANKING			3.7	3.0	4.9	2.7	2.2	5.1	4.8	4.1	5.0	6.9
ACCESS	21.9											
. General aviation market		2.6	1.2	0.0	0.1	4.7	10.0	0.5	0.1	0.0	1.2	0.0
. Private vehicle accessibility		4.3	8.9	8.8	10.0	7.4	8.4	8.0	7.0	6.5	6.7	0.0
. Public transport accessibility		3.7	8.9	9.9	10.0	8.9	9.1	8.3	6.2	4.7	7.6	0.0
ACCESSIBILITY RANKING			5.4	5.4	5.9	5.6	7.0	4.8	3.9	3.3	4.4	0.0
AIRPORT OPERATIONS	31.3											
. Airspace		4.3	6.7	4.4	0.0	7.8	6.7	8.9	10.0	10.0	8.9	10.0
. Wind coverage		3.0	10.0	10.0	5.0	10.0	10.0	5.0	5.0	10.0	5.0	0.0
. Other meteorological conditions		4.7	10.0	10.0	7.8	7.8	6.7	0.0	7.8	7.8	7.8	7.8
. Site flexibility		2.3	8.9	10.0	0.0	6.7	8.9	6.7	1.1	3.3	3.3	6.7
OPERATIONAL RANKING			9.9	9.3	4.0	9.0	8.7	5.4	7.6	9.2	7.6	7.4
VARIABLE CAPITAL COSTS	15.3											
. Present value of savings relative to most expensive site		1.0	5.2	3.8	1.5	5.4	0.0	10.0	6.2	6.1	8.9	2.9
VARIABLE CAPITAL COST RANKING			0.8	0.6	0.2	0.8	0.0	1.5	0.9	0.9	1.4	0.4
AGGREGATED RANKING			19.8	18.3	15.1	18.2	17.8	16.9	17.3	17.5	18.4	14.8

RESULTANT RANKING

SITE	SCORE	RANKING
Badgerys Creek	19.8	1
Wilton	18.4	2
Bringelly	18.3	3
Londonderry	18.2	4
Scheyville	17.8	5
Warnervale	17.5	6
Somersby	17.3	7
Darkes Forest	16.9	8
Holsworthy	15.1	9
Goulburn	14.8	10

Fig. 1. Site ranking matrix

Closer Locations

BADGERYS CREEK
Bringelly	four times people affected
*Holsworthy	topography
Scheyville	three times people affected, topography
Londonderry	two times people affected, flooding, pollution, flora

Mid-distance Locations

*Darkes Forest	meteorology
Somersby	environment, cost
Warnervale	access, cost, land use
WILTON	

Outlying Locations

*Goulburn	access (170 km)

* Locations suffering a "fatal flaw"

Evaluation of Two Shortlisted Sites

17. It was decided, following the evaluation described earlier, to proceed with a detailed assessment of two airport sites, Badgerys Creek and Wilton, and to prepare a draft EIS on each site consisting of a description of the site to be acquired, potential airport development on the site, and the environmental effects arising thereon. The draft EIS concluded with a comparison of the two sites and some comments on the public access program conducted concurrently with the technical evaluation.

Preliminary Master Plans

18. A preliminary airport master plan was prepared for each site in order to:

. define a site boundary for acquisition of property;

. provide a definition for a maximum level of future development at a second Sydney airport in sufficient detail to permit assessment of the potential environmental impacts

. predict noise contours based on this maximum level of development so that appropriate land use planning controls could be implemented to protect potentially noise-affected areas from further incompatible development;

. identify required airspace for a new airport so that this airspace could be reserved and necessary modifications planned in the existing airspace in order to avoid disruptions to the aviation system in the future;

. establish requirements for access to an airport at the site so that long-range planning could be undertaken.

EIS Process

19. The results of the team's efforts on shortlisting and the detailed studies of the two sites were released in the form of the draft EIS on 12 June 1985 by the Minister for Aviation. The draft EIS was placed on exhibition for public comment for ten weeks from 17 June to 26 August 1985. Some 423 submissions were received outlining the concerns of the public, but no major new issues emerged. Submissions were responded to in a supplement to the draft EIS.

THE DECISION

20. This work demonstrated that either Wilton or Badgerys Creek would be capable of providing a major airport.

21. It was also clear that one site was nevertheless superior.

22. On 17 February 1986 the Minister for Aviation announced that Badgerys Creek had been selected as the site for Sydney's next major airport because it was

- closer to the markets it is intended to serve

- would involve a lower development cost

- would have less effect on the natural environment.

23. The site is 1770 ha in area and is currently zoned largely agricultural with minimum 40 ha development but has some pockets of rural residential development. Some 241 properties lie within the site including 207 houses and 750 residents. The properties are being purchased by agreement from the owners and as at end of February 1987 50 properties had been purchased by the Government.

MASTER PLAN FOR AN AIRPORT AT BADGERYS CREEK

24. The following assumptions were adopted for the preparation of the Master Plan

. a second airport would supplement but not replace Sydney (Kingsford Smith) Airport

. a second Sydney airport would be planned to serve all types of aircraft, from small piston-engined general aviation aircraft to large, future wide bodied jet operations

. the operational mix of aircraft activity would be similar to that currently experienced at major airports but with a higher proportion of general aviation.

the future airport would operate without a night curfew, thus requiring careful consideration of potential aircraft noise levels and existing and future land uses in areas surrounding the airport.

25. For planning and evaluation purposes, it was determined that the maximum level of development that could be accommodated within the proposed site would be an airport with a capacity of 275,000 annual aircraft movements and 13 million annual passenger movements on a widely spaced parallel runway layout without a cross-wind runway.

Operational Capacity

26. Table 1 sets out the number of aircraft movements, operational mix, and capacity assumed for the purposes of the preliminary master plan. Utilising this mix of operations, a calculation of passenger activity was made as in Table 2.

Table 1 - Annual Aircraft Movements

Aircraft Type	No. of Movements	Percentage
B747, DC10	37,500	14
A300, B767, B727	87,500	32
F27, Metroliner	60,000	21
General Aviation	90,000	33
Total	**275,000**	**100**

* Business jet, twin and single piston-engined aircraft.

Table 2 - Passenger Activity

Aircraft Type	No. of annual aircraft movements	Average passenger load per aircraft movement	Total annual passenger movement
B747, DC10 A300, B767,	37,500	150	5,625,000
B727 F27,	87,500	75	6,562,500
Metroliner	60,000	15	900,000
Total			13,087,500*

* Does not include passengers carried on general aviation (estimated at less than 5% of the total).

Runway Layout

27. The following range of airfield layouts were examined

- a single runway (SR)

- a set of closely spaced parallel runways (CSPR)

- a set of widely spaced parallel runways (WSPR)

- a double set of widely spaced parallel runways (DWSPR).

28. Airport capacities were calculated for each layout and found to vary from 117,000 annual aircraft movements for the SR layout to over 300,000 annual aircraft movements for the SWSPR layout (without a cross-wind runway).

29. The SR layout was rejected because of its limited potential capacity (117,000-138,000 annual aircraft movements) and the difficulty of providing a wide range of operational mixes on a single runway.

30. The DWSPR layout, which gives a total of four primary runways, was rejected because the theoretical additional gain in capacity over that of a WSPR layout did not justify the additional land needed.

31. The final choice of layouts was thus between the CSPR and the WSPR layouts. Table 3 provides a theoretical comparison between these two layouts based on a hypothetical airfield using minimum dimensional criteria (no allowance for local topography, sub-division of land and severance) and assuming no cross-wind runway.

Table 3 - Capacity and area comparison between CSPR and WSPR layouts

Layout type	Approximate annual aircraft movements (000s)	Minimum land area requirements
CSPR	190	1,070
WSPR	275	1,340
Percentage difference	45%	25%

32. The WSPR layout was selected as it allowed greater operational flexibility for an aircraft mix containing a high proportion of smaller aircraft, and it was more efficient in terms of total runway capacity related to land area requirements.

Cross-wind runway

33. The number of runway directions required at an airport site is influenced by the direction and strength of prevailing winds at that site. Transport category aircraft can manoeuvre in cross-winds as high as 30 knots but other categories of aircraft with lower flying speeds have less cross-wind capability. Nonetheless, 20 knot cross-winds can be tolerated by most general aviation aircraft when landing on dry runways.

34. International airport design criteria with respect to operations with cross-winds allow for such factors as variations in pilot proficiency, wet pavements and a range of runway surface conditions. The International Civil Aviation Organisation recommends that "the number and orientation of runways at an aerodrome should be such that the usability factor of the aerodrome is not less than 95% for the aeroplanes that the aerodrome is intended to serve".

35. It was concluded that the Department of Aviation's even more stringent requirement for wind coverage (99.8% at capital city airports) would be unnecessary when applied to a second Sydney airport, given the presence of Kingsford Smith Airport and several airports within reasonable flying distance of Badgerys Creek. The Department of Aviation's requirement was relaxed to 95% wind coverage for the second airport. When this criterion was applied to the site at Badgerys Creek it was found that there was no need to provide a cross-wind runway.

36. It is estimated from wind data that aircraft certified to operate in cross-winds up to 10 knots would be able to use an airport at Badgerys Creek for 95% of the time, while aircraft certified to operate in 20 knot cross-winds would be able to use it for more than 99.8% of the time.

Master plan dimensional criteria

37. The preliminary master plan is based on dimensional criteria published by the Department of Aviation and used as the basis for planning the new Brisbane International Airport.

38. Accordingly, for the geometric planning of the airport, a maximum size, long range, subsonic design aircraft with the following characteristics was adopted:

- wing span of 95m
- length of 113m
- tail height of 27m
- overall wheel track of 18m
- wheel base of 34m
- gross weight of 1 million kg
- maximum seating capacity of 1,400.

39. Although supersonic aircraft operations are now only a minor part of civil transport aircraft operations in the world and whilst the USA supersonic passenger aircraft proposal has been shelved, there still remains the possibility of future supersonic transport aircraft operations to Australian airports. Therefore, the geometric planning takes into account a Supersonic Design Aircraft with the following characteristics:

- wing span of 45m
- length of 100m.

40. The adoption of maximum size design aircraft is not intended to imply that operations by such aircraft will comprise other than a small proportion of the aircraft operations at the airport. The total aircraft operations at the airport will be composed of operations by numbers of aircraft of different sizes ranging from the smallest to the largest and with the diversity of aircraft types expected to use the airport, not all components needed to be designed to handle such large aircraft, and lesser geometric criteria could therefore be used in certain areas.

41. Table 4 sets out the dimensional criteria that were established for the purpose of the preliminary master plan and Figure 2 shows the criteria in schematic form.

Table 4. Dimensional criteria used for preliminary plan

	Criteria (m)		
	Future aircraft (95m wing-span)	ICAO (60m w-s)	ICAO (36m w-s)
Runway Width	60	60	45
Taxiway Width	30	30	23
Runway/taxiway separation	200	190	168
Taxiway/taxiway separation	122	101	46.5
Taxiway/apron edge separation	107	86	35

Runway Length

42. Examination of performance characteristics of various aircraft showed that the Boeing 747, operating at maximum gross loads over maximum haul lengths, would require a runway of 4,000m. Research of available data on future aircraft trends revealed that this length should also be adequate for any new aircraft likely to be designed in the foreseeable future. A length of 4,000m was therefore used for the primary runway in the preliminary master plan.

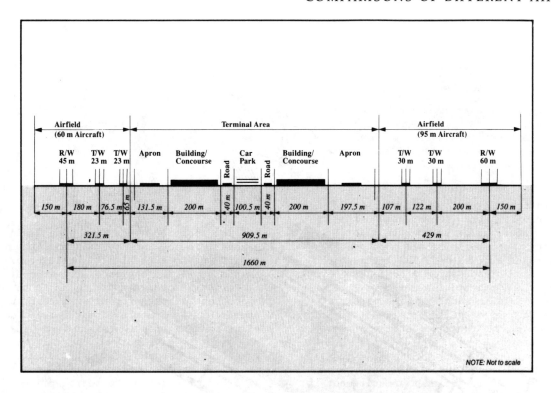

Fig. 2. Typical airfield cross-section for 1660 m runway separation

43. The second runway does not need to be the same length as the primary runway, and it was established that a sufficient length would be 2,500m; the length required for most short and some long haul operations.

Runway separation

44. The International Civil Aviation Organisation standard for the minimum separation required between parallel widely spaced runways to allow independent aircraft movements is 1,500m, while the US Federal Aviation Administration standard minimum separation is 1,300m. However, although these widths may be sufficient for operational purposes, it was considered that they could be restrictive given the need to develop and operate a terminal area between the two runways.

45. Separation distances between parallel runways at other existing or planned airports around the world were reviewed for a variety of terminal layout concepts. It was found that many of the busy airports with activity levels similar to the maximum assumed for a second Sydney airport (275,000 annual aircraft movements) had separations of 1,500 - 1,600m. This separation dimension was reviewed for a

variety of terminal concept configurations and the spatial requirements of large aircraft with 95m wing-spans. It was concluded that a distance of 1,660m would be a minimum but adequate separation which balanced all airfield operational requirements, and ensured that a second Sydney airport did not occupy more land than was needed.

46. The proposed runway layout at Badgerys Creek is based on a set of widely spaced parallel runways designated 05R-23L and 05L-23R, with the terminal area located between them. Runway 05R-23L is 4,000m in length and runway 05L-23R is 2,500m. The distance between the runways is 1,660m. The approach and departure surfaces have a 1.6% gradient, and thus meet the Department of Aviation's criteria. Figure 3 provides some of the detail of the proposed airport layout.

Noise Effects

47. Aircraft noise is consistently identified as the most adverse effect of airport operations. For the draft EIS, examination of noise effects was based on the assumed 'worst case' of 275,000 annual aircraft movements. Table 5 compares Badgerys Creek with existing Australian airports.

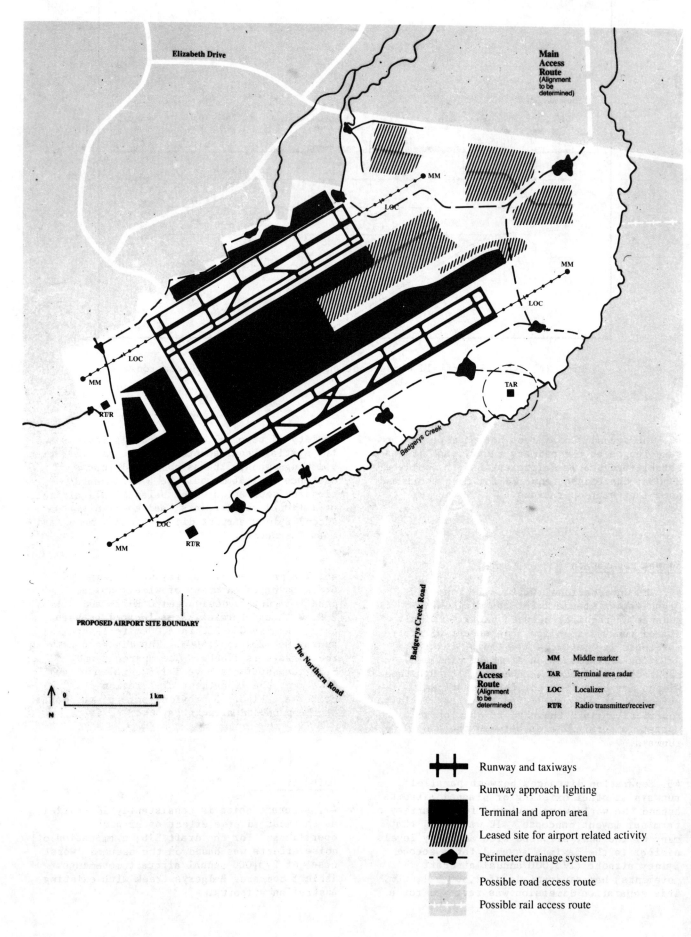

Fig. 3. Preliminary master plan - Badgerys Creek

Table 5. Comparison of populations within the 20 ANEF contour.

	Number of people within 20 ANEF contour			
Airport	Seriously affected by noise	Moderately affected by noise**	Others	Total pop.
Badgerys Creek	364	1,115	836	1,951*
Sydney (Kingsford Smith)	62,198	141,436	67,374	208,810
Melbourne	2,238	8,188	6,374	14,562
Adelaide	10,005	31,586	19,347	50,933
Perth	3,438	9,812	9,234	19,046

* Estimated maximum for full development under existing zoning.
** Includes seriously affected.

CONCLUSION

48. The search for a site has taken 17 years, some frustrating, some exciting, but the site selection program described above has been an extremely satisfying task for the members of the Study Team. The successful outcome is due to the determination of the Government, particularly the Ministers directly responsible, to resolve the issue, to the professional work of the Study Team and in particular the effectiveness of the community access program, and to a changed public perception of airports that admits that airports do benefit the community they serve. At this time there is no commitment as to when construction of the airport on the site might begin. However, the conceptual master planning to date will ensure that a major airport on the site will meet the demands of the twenty first century.

7a   Development of the airline industry in Mexico

A. MARTINEZ DOMINGUEZ, Director General, Aeropuertos y Servicios Auxiliares, Mexico

The instability of the economy world-wide has created a severe crisis in many countries, but it has not stopped development in the aviation industry.

In Mexico, the prime objective of President Miguel de la Madrid's Government is to modernise the country, and as part of this endeavour the national aviation network has grown and has contributed to the expansion of the tourist trade. Today, Mexico's tourist trade is booming. Of the 57 airports in Mexico, 15 have been built under President de la Madrid's administration. This aviation infrastructure, which has put Mexico at the top of all South American countries, has encouraged great investment in the hotel business.

Modern hotels are being built on the most beautiful beaches of the country in Cancun, Puerto Vallarta, Acapulco, Manzanillo, Huatulco, Zihuatanejo, Los Cabos, Cozumel and Mazatlan. We have 35 international airports with jet capacity, and we are supporting regional developments on a national basis.

Some statistics will illustrate the extent to which the development of the aviation industry is linked to the modernisation of the country and the growth in international and domestic traffic: in 1986, 33.4 million passengers passed through Mexican airports against 4.7 million in 1966, an increase of 647%. In 1986, we experienced more than one million take-offs and landings against 363 000 in 1965.

The best and most up-to-date example of tourist development in Mexico is the Port of Cancun in the Yucatan peninsula, where aircraft movements began in 1975 with 305 000 passengers: in 1986, more than 1 800 000 passengers passed through this airport; the number has increased six times in ten years.

The modernisation of the airport structures, the hotel developments, the increase in tourism, the expansion of the mining industry, the industrial transformation, the growth in exports, the foreign investments, the privatisation of companies, the return of wealth and the social stability that guarantees the Mexican political system are very objective elements that show how the President of Mexico is confronting the economic crisis that exists in the country, on account of fluctuating oil prices and the increase in international bank interest rates. Mexico has shown itself to be both imaginatively and creatively united in adversity and, because of a solid political

system, is a country which not only lives in peace but promotes peace. Mexico, convinced that this is the best infrastructure for progress, is a country that internationally generates, gives and receives confidence.

Aeropuertos y Servicios Auxiliares (ASA) of Mexico is a government owned company which is financially sound, has large reserves of cash, receives no subsidies, and has no debts either within the country or abroad; its funds allow it to operate the airport network comfortably while having an annual net surplus of funds.

At the present time, complete remodernisation work is being carried out in eight terminal buildings in main cities, as well as the upgrading of seven runways. Furthermore, the maintenance and operation of the whole system is under way.

At the same time, airports and related services have striven to improve their levels of efficiency and productivity, by attempting to keep themselves up-to-date with the various aspects of an efficient airport operation. Included in this are the technical questions related to the fundamental aspect of security and administration, as well as information and communication work.

In this respect, ASA has maintained a permanent presence and has participated actively in the various international forums on the aviation circuit, particularly at congresses, conferences, special committees and varied meetings of the International Association of Civil Airports (ICCA) and the International Advisory Body of Airport Operators. It has achieved this while in no way prejudicing systematic and institutional relations with other international associate bodies in the aviation industry – for example, ICAO (International Civil Aviation Organisation), IATA, IFALPA (International Airline Pilots Association) and many others.

We are convinced that only through a permanent interchange of ideas, opinions and experiences is it possible to increase the efficiency of the organisations that we represent and to accomplish, each time more efficiently, our objectives.

International meetings, in general, make this interchange and assimilation possible. The high technical level of these meetings and the indisputable quality of the delegates guarantees results that undoubtedly will be of world-wide benefit.

Airports for people. Thomas Telford Limited, London, 1988

7b Design trends in civil transport aircraft development

W.D. WISSEL, Senior Project Engineer, Airport Compatibility, Airbus Industrie, Blagnac, France

INTRODUCTION

New airplane design will often have a significant impact on an airport's infrastructure operation. It may affect the operation on the airside, at the terminal and on the landside.

Many factors influence the design of an aircraft; basically, a new product is determined by two main parameters which are inseparable and should not be seen as a justification for each other: the market demand and the technology supply.

MARKET DEMAND ASPECTS

Generally we, as well as the other aircraft manufacturers, believe that the air transport industry has a healthy future. An average annual 5-6% passenger-km and 7-9% freight ton-km growth promise to translate into a need for roughly 6000 new aircraft to be manufactured by the year 2006, i.e. in 20 years from now.

The basis for this view is the trend, widely recognised within the aircraft and airline industries, that the demand for new aircraft will remain closely related to the state of the world economy; therefore, the forecast is based on a number of assumptions about the global economy and industry (Fig. 1).

World economy: real increase in GNP of the order of 3% per annum although structural problems persist which cannot be solved in the near term, such as:

. unemployment in the industrial world
. development and commodity prices in developing countries
. the risk of international trade being more and more hampered by increasing protectionism, monetary instability and social unrest.

The second influential factor in stimulating demand for air transport is the fares. We believe that increased airline competition and productivity gains should allow for a continued slight decline in real fares of the order of 1% per annum. This appears particularly likely for airlines outside the US where some sort of 'controlled liberalization' as regards fare setting and market entry will gradually change the competitive position between airlines.

It would certainly justify the organization of another conference to elaborate in detail the various elements which our economists believe will show a definite influence on the demand side, such as:

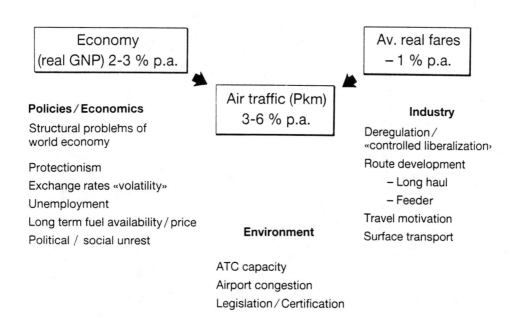

Fig. 1. Demand structure

. fuel price developments and currency exchange rates where forecasts, with an acceptable level of accuracy, are impossible
. new route and network developments
. environmental considerations (noise, infrastructure and so on)
. travel motivation
. legislation (EROPS, crew duty time)
. the whole issue of aircraft financing
. surface transport alternatives over short distances.

Generally, any successful supplier will try to counter the uncertainties of the market place and will contribute to the financial performance of the airline industry by supplying:

. a family of aircraft designed for high competitive efficiency
. a variety of derivative versions which cater for all combinations of layouts for passenger and cargo operation over short/medium and long haul distances (Fig. 2).

When we are talking about the future we have to realize that the traditional airline/supplier relationship has to be enlarged to include other elements which constitute the air transport system. For instance, the crucial point in all forecasts is to find, for a given total traffic, the most likely split between the number of flights (frequency) and the corresponding seat capacity. More flights mean the manufacture of more aircraft, which is exactly what we, the manufacturers, desire. On the other hand, fewer flights mean bigger aircraft, which is exactly what we have.

In light of the uncertainties in the long-term development of factors which affect traffic developments, we have initiated a range of alternative forecasts to enable us to answer the 'What if...?' questions, in order to assess possible program risks better than one single case with fixed parameters.

Our forecasters expect the status of the world's operating jet fleet to develop (as shown in Fig. 3) as a function of different growth scenarios.

A basic assumption in our forecasts is that the growth in frequency will be roughly one-third of the passenger-km growth, which is in line with the historical average.

At the end of 1986, we counted around 6200 passenger jet aircraft in airline service. This fleet will increase to 7800, 8500, 9300 or 9800 aircraft by the year 2006 depending on what growth case you choose. In other words, it is quite reasonable to assume that in 20 years from now there will be 50% more aircraft in operation than there are today. However, it should be remembered that these numbers relate only to jet aircraft, which will have to be augmented by a rapidly growing fleet of feeder and commuter aircraft.

As the traffic growth projections are higher than the expected increases in the number of flights, it is just a matter of arithmetic to conclude that aircraft size will, on average, increase.

Independently from such 'mathematical considerations', well-known <u>operational constraints</u> (in particular, airport and airspace congestion) do not permit unlimited increases in flights. Bigger capacity aircraft seem today to be the only solution to ease congestion problems, at least in the short term.

The 3% and 4% growth cases seem to be manageable from an operational standpoint, whereas in the 5% and 6% cases, growing congestion and delays are almost inevitable in the long term, not only in the US (where they are already happening), but also at major airports in Europe and Asia.

Generally, we can say that small growth

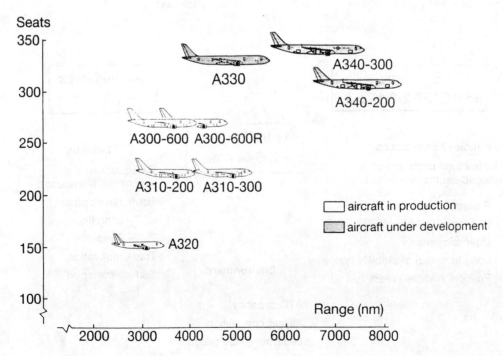

Fig. 2. The airbus product line

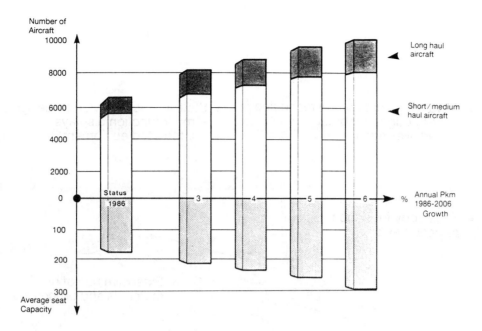

Fig. 3. Jet aircraft fleet status: year 2006

favours smaller (i.e. narrow body) aircraft and high growth favours bigger capacity aircraft (Fig. 4).

We can predict with a high level of confidence that at the beginning of the next century, wide body aircraft will make up around 50% of the world's fleet; assuming a 6% annual traffic expansion, this share can even climb to two-thirds of the total fleet.

TECHNOLOGY SUPPLY
Technology for its own sake is of no great interest. So why do we pursue it? What are our aims? What do we hope to achieve with new technology?

We have three basic objectives in design and each of them must be considered when assessing new technology. The three objectives are:

. safety and reliability
. operational efficiency
. environmental compatibility.

Significant contributions of new technology to these three basic objectives are demonstrated here on the basis of A330/A340 (Fig. 5).

Advanced flight control technology, for instance, means the prevention of excursions outside the aircraft design envelopes, such as stalling, overspeed and structural overload.

Extensive use of new materials and processes means lighter aircraft, which is the most direct way of reducing lift dependent drag and engine thrust requirements, which means lower operation cost.

In the case of cabin furnishing materials, for example, Airbus Industrie has developed its own standards in terms of fire resistance, smoke and toxicity, well in advance of national authority action, thus making a significant contribution to increased safety.

Today's high by-pass ratio turbo-fans are inherently quieter than the previous generation of engines. Part of the big improvement in

efficiency has been used to carry the weight of extensive sound absorption treatment in the nacelle ducts.

A330/A340 Key data/general arrangements
The latest members of the Airbus product line are essentially two different versions of a single type. Both are being developed for entry into service in the early 1990s (Figs 6-8).

The A330 twin will be able to carry a typical mixed class load of 328 passengers out to 5000 nm range. Maximum seating is for up to 440 passengers. The A330 will carry 30 LD3 containers or up to nine 96 in x 125 in pallets, using the same fuselage cross-section as the A300 and A310; thus it constitutes a logical extension of our present twin aisle twin product line.

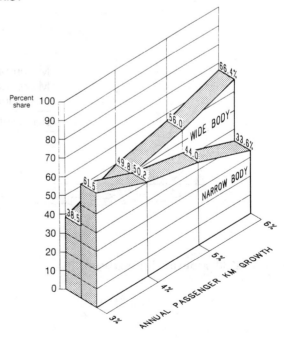

Fig. 4. Aircraft size distribution: year 2006

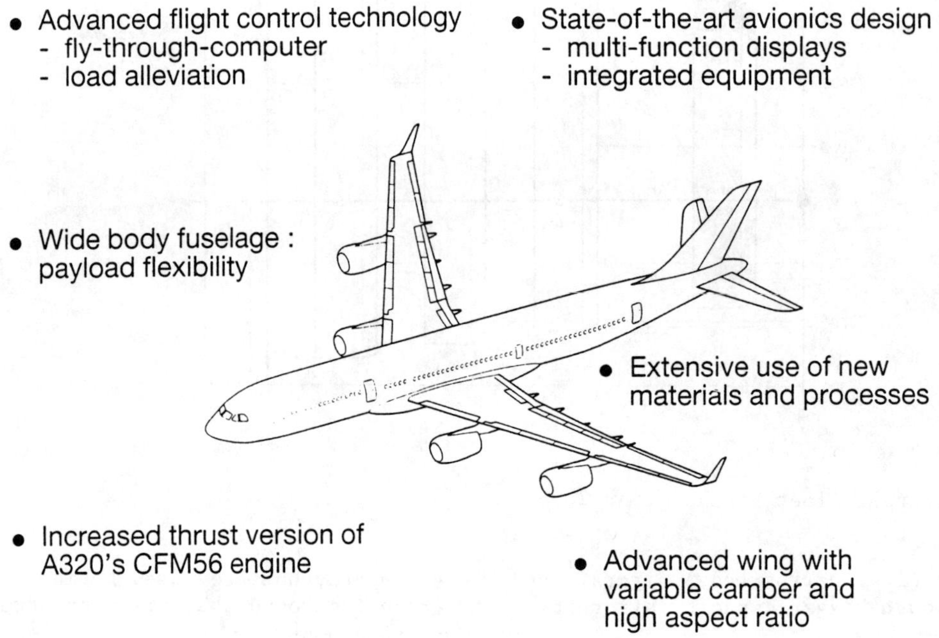

● Advanced flight control technology
  - fly-through-computer
  - load alleviation

● State-of-the-art avionics design
  - multi-function displays
  - integrated equipment

● Wide body fuselage :
  payload flexibility

● Extensive use of new
  materials and processes

● Increased thrust version of
  A320's CFM56 engine

● Advanced wing with
  variable camber and
  high aspect ratio

Fig. 5. Aircraft design evolution: A340 highlights

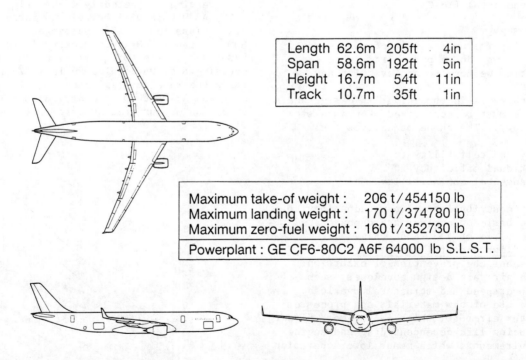

Length	62.6m	205ft	4in
Span	58.6m	192ft	5in
Height	16.7m	54ft	11in
Track	10.7m	35ft	1in

Maximum take-of weight :	206 t / 454150 lb
Maximum landing weight :	170 t / 374780 lb
Maximum zero-fuel weight :	160 t / 352730 lb
Powerplant : GE CF6-80C2 A6F 64000 lb S.L.S.T.	

Fig. 6. A330 general arrangement

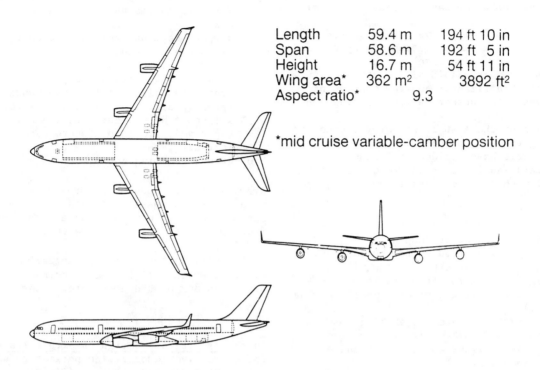

Length	59.4 m	194 ft 10 in
Span	58.6 m	192 ft 5 in
Height	16.7 m	54 ft 11 in
Wing area*	362 m²	3892 ft²
Aspect ratio*	9.3	

*mid cruise variable-camber position

Fig. 7.   A340-200 general arrangement

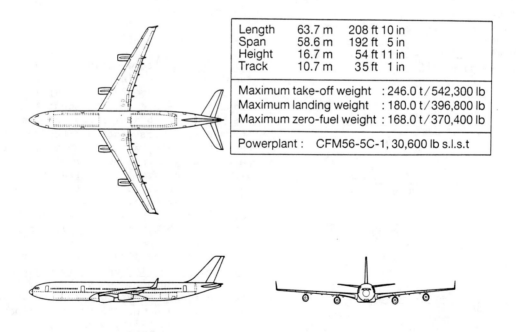

Length	63.7 m	208 ft 10 in
Span	58.6 m	192 ft 5 in
Height	16.7 m	54 ft 11 in
Track	10.7 m	35 ft 1 in

Maximum take-off weight	: 246.0 t / 542,300 lb
Maximum landing weight	: 180.0 t / 396,800 lb
Maximum zero-fuel weight	: 168.0 t / 370,400 lb

| Powerplant : | CFM56-5C-1, 30,600 lb s.l.s.t |

Fig. 8.   A340-300 general arrangement

The four engined A340-200 will carry its standard three-class intercontinental load of 262 passengers on stages out to 7700 nm, while the A340-300 carried 295 passengers 6850 nm. The A340 will provide airlines with an attractive non-stop wide body service in distant city pair markets which cannot sustain economic 747 operations.

The A330 and A340 with a very high degree of commonality cover a wide spectrum of payload and range requirements. The size and range characteristics of the A340 will enable airlines to avoid main traffic hubs and the consequent loss of revenue to another carrier feeding the remote hub.

To ensure that the A340 is properly matched to the existing regional airport infrastructure, Airbus Industrie have decided to fit an auxiliary main landing gear to reduce pavement loading below those of current long range wide bodies.

Wing span against aircraft length
One aspect which will need to be considered very carefully in future airport planning, for taxiways, apron and apron frontage in particular, is the trend towards increasing wing span (Fig. 9).

In the interest of reduced operating cost (reduced drag), aircraft designers have been attracted towards higher aspect ratio and hence higher wing spans.

Advancing aerodynamic knowledge, more refined wind tunnel methods and better wind tunnel facilities allow thicker wings of moderate sweep back, while maintaining high cruise speed capability without the weight penalties normally linked to increased wing span.

How will future aircraft designs cope with existing and future airport infrastructures? The growing need for improved communication between all those participating in the air

transport system has led us to initiate compatibility studies. Under the heading 'Airport enquiry', the following issues were considered

- development of passenger traffic and aircraft movements, future aircraft type mix
- airport terminal and gate layouts, minimum allowable clearances
- landing guidance equipment
- main factors limiting airport capacity: runway capacity, taxiway clearance, apron/gate/ground clearances; aircraft weight, ACN/PCN; curfews, obstacles
- (approved) plans for future capacity increase
- ground handling equipment

Growing airport congestion problems in all areas of aircraft and passenger handling have strongly encouraged us to consider these airport-related factors in our design requirements.

What will be the design parameters for the aircraft which will be needed to meet the market demand in any of the above growth cases?

Inpact of aircraft design on airports/airspace
There are five major design parameters which affect airports and airspace (Fig. 10). These are:

. size
. airframe and systems
. propulsion
. performance
. payload flexibility

Aircraft size is determined by payload and range requirements, and it directly affects airport facilities. Bigger aircraft will certainly reduce runway and airspace congestion, but they must be compatible with the infrastructure. Substantial investment in extending the facilities which exist today will be required, particularly as the numbers of large size aircraft increase. Smaller aircraft are perhaps easier to handle at airports, but they certainly will not prevent airport and airspace saturation, except where they are used to bypass congested hub airports, enabling airlines to develop new routes.

The next three parameters - airframe and systems, propulsion and performance are the traditional domains for technology improvements where aircraft manufacturers improve safety, reliability and operational efficiency.

Payload flexibility means separation between passenger handling and, in particular, cargo handling on pallets or in containers with high interlining efficiency to allow fast turnrounds and hence increased utilisation, or to gain a useful schedule slack to soak up inevitable ATC delays. For instance, the A320 offers interline capability for containerised cargo, which can be loaded on A300s or A310s or any other airplane capable of taking the standard LD3 containers.

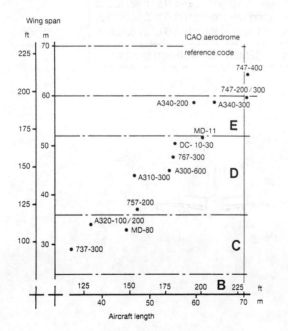

Fig. 9. Trend in wing span and aircraft length

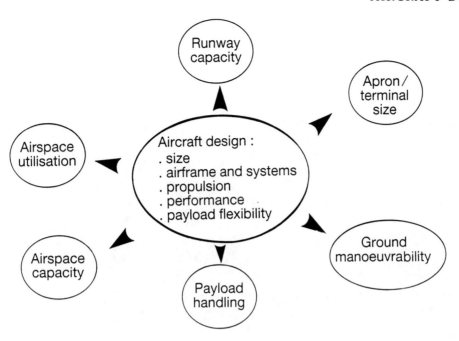

Fig. 10. Impact of aircraft design on airports and airspace

CONCLUSION

The future fleet composition of the world's airlines will show

. around 50% more aircraft within the next 20 years
. a significant shift towards aircraft of larger size and geometry.

History has shown that the civil aircraft manufacturers have done their job in providing economy, reliability and safety. Future developments will more and more be influenced by non-aircraft problems. The operators of our equipment will be increasingly constrained in benefiting commercially from the high technology items incorporated in today's aircraft design. The use of the equipment is limited by the operating infrastructure which often lags behind the appropriate technical and organizational standards which would meet today's transportation needs.

To maintain a functioning air transport system and to avoid 'suffocation' at major airports, airport, ATC and government authorities have to realize the need for improved communication, especially in the area of long-term investment planning and the allocation of funds – as well as the efficient use of investments already made.

Discussion

The search for a second Sydney Airport site
(SSA) has been a long one. In fact, way back in
May 1973, I reported to the First International
Conference on Off-Shore Airport Technology in
Washington, on the results of a feasibility
study for an off-shore airport in the Sydney
region, and advised that, similar to Denver as
outlined in Paper 3, such a proposition was 'not
on' owing to high costs and major technical
problems. It therefore gives me great pleasure
to be able to comment on a study which has
resulted in a decision to purchase a site for a
second major airport in the Sydney region.

Paper 7 reports on the fourth major study in
15 years. The first study began on 1 April
1969, a propitious date when one considers the
ensuing saga of studies. The study reported on
in the Paper was brought to a successful
conclusion and I ask the question why. One
major factor was, I would suggest, that a
consideration of PEOPLE was a primary concern in
the study; and by PEOPLE I am thinking not only
of air passengers, but of those who work on and
around the airport, or who are affected by the
airport in some direct or indirect way.

A new Government was elected in Australia in
February 1983 and a new study was instigated to
find a site for a second airport. The
Government perceived that there was a
requirement to reserve a site for a second major
airport for the following reasons: continued
growth in air travel was more likely than zero
growth; runway capacity of Kingsford Smith had
been reached, as defined by an average 4 minute
delay to all aircraft throughout the day;
possibilities of traffic rationalisation existed
but these were only playing with the margin;
there was a dwindling supply of suitable land in
the Sydney region. Market research was
conducted in December 1983, by way of telephone
surveys, to determine the attitude of people to
a SSA. Results showed that a majority of people
believed a new site was required and should be
selected now, and that the existing airport
could not continue to be developed indefinitely.

We concluded from the survey that the airport
site decision for Government was a people
problem and the SSA Site Selection Study was
therefore designed to proceed according to
environmental impact statement processes, as
required in legislation, with people in mind.

The major concerns, apart from the most
important one of having a site on which it was
technically feasible to construct and operate a
major airport, was to seek a site which would:

(a) conveniently serve people travelling by
air
(b) have the minimum impact on people living
and working around the new airport.

A further concern was a desire to inform
people, by way of a public access programme and
information centre, of what was going on during
the study; we also encouraged their input. This
led to the inclusion of two additional sites in
the long list for initial evaluation. What the
study processes did then was, broadly

- to identify potential sites: ten sites in
all were identified
- to select two or three sites most suitable
for airport development, by the detailed
process described in the Paper
- to devise an airport layout on each site
which had the least effect on people
outside the site
- finally, to prepare a draft Environmental
Impact Statement (EIS) on the effect of an
airport on each of those sites.

Two sites were studied in depth: Wilton and
Badgerys Creek. The first site was Wilton, some
81 km and 102 minutes' travelling time by road
from the CBD. This site would cause ten people
to be displaced and would have 130 people
potentially within the 20 ANEF when the new
airport was operating at its maximum capacity.
It was closer to only 5% of the people in the
Sydney region than Badgerys Creek. The second
site was Badgerys Creek, some 46 km and 69
minutes' travelling time by road from the CBD.
The Badgerys Creek site would cause 750 people
to be displaced, and 1950 people were
potentially within the 20 ANEF. It was closer
to 95% of the people in the Sydney region than
Wilton.

The draft EIS was written from the point of
view of: people directly affected on and around
the site; people who would work at the airport;
people who would use the airport as air
travellers. The Government was left with a
choice between two sites: one at Wilton, which
had virtually no effect on people; and one which
affected a limited number of people but was
closer to 95% of the people in the Sydney
region.

With the effect on all interested parties

identified, the Government was left with a clear choice, whereupon it decided on Badgerys Creek as the site for a future second major airport to serve the Sydney region. The purchase of properties on the site is now proceeding and, so far, some 54 properties have been purchased at a cost of about $10.5M; the programme of purchases is continuing.

I would maintain that the programme was successful in gaining a positive decision by Government because the consideration of people was a major concern in it. After all, airports exist to serve people, and, just as importantly, the decision was taken by politicians who are answerable to the people.

MR G. D. BELL, Gatwick Airport Limited, London
Could the Authors give further details about security and anti-terrorist measures employed at their respective airports? To what extent have these measures influenced aiport design?

MR W. O. TOEPEL (Paper 5)
The design of the new Munich airport strictly observes security and anti-terrorist measures as required by international and national standards. For example, each of the four departure modules contains six security control counters for passenger and hand-baggage check. A strict separation of departing and arriving passengers will be achieved by using a two-level concourse at the apron side of the terminal building. Transfer passengers will be subject to a security control if they have arrived on an 'unclean flight'. Furthermore, a special terminal is planned for handling passengers on security-relevant flights.

BRIG. T. P. DA SILVA (Paper 6)
At São Paulo Airport, the design philosophy applied to the passenger terminals and to the network of roads within the airport complex has sought, by means of strategically placed control points, to prevent the access of unauthorised persons. Electronic equipment for searching individuals and for baggage inspection is currently in use at these locations.

The airport employs a team of trained security personnel, and drills involving all operations staff are periodically carried out to test recommended procedures.

The airport also has facilities for the movement of high profile individuals requiring special security measures. On such occasions, the aircraft can be diverted to a smaller, isolated terminal.

MR I. WOONTON (Paper 7)
No decision has yet been taken on a timetable for development of the Second Sydney Airport. Therefore, to date, no detailed consideration has been given to security and anti-terrorist measures for the new airport, as the terminal areas and terminal buildings will be designed taking account of the circumstances prevailing at that time.

It is worth noting that all international terminals in Australia are designed and constructed in such a way that departing passengers are kept quite separate from arriving passengers, from the security check point for departures to leaving the Customs Hall for arrivals.

MR S. DE LANGE, Schiphol Airport, Amsterdam
How flexible is the terminal design to allow for possible future expansion of the airport?

MR TOEPEL
The first stage of the passenger terminal is designed for a capacity of 12 million passengers per annum, which are expected by the mid 1990s. The second stage of the terminal can be developed to the east of stage one, where sufficient space is available for increasing the capacity to 25-30 million passengers per annum. The design of stage two might be different from that of stage one, taking into account the probably changed requirements of the future.

BRIG. DA SILVA
The master plan of São Paulo Airport has sought to maximise land area utilisation. Phase one of the works entailed the construction of Terminals I and II. Terminal I has been in operation since January 1985 and Terminal II is scheduled for completion in 1990. Construction of Terminals III and IV is not envisaged before the year 2000. (See Fig. 1 for further details of the construction stages.)

Each terminal has the capacity to handle 7.5 million passengers per annum. In the period 1985-86, the airport registered 5 million passengers, and studies estimate that this figure will increase to 7 million passengers per annum in 1990 and 12.5 million passengers per annum by the year 2000.

MR WOONTON
The design of the terminal for the Second Sydney Aiport has not begun because, as yet, there is no timetable for the development of the airport.

However, in determining the preliminary master plan for the development of the airport, a good number of terminal designs were examined. This was done in order to ensure that sufficient

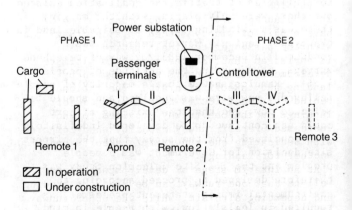

Fig. 1. Construction stages of São Paulo Airport, Brazil

space was provided between the parallel runways to provide the airport developer with the freedom to select whichever terminal design would best meet the criteria at that time. There is enough space between the parallel runways for development of terminals in the course of time to match the capacity of the runway system.

MR G. JONES, Coopers & Lybrand, London
Could the Authors give further details of how the airports will be operated when they become fully operational?

MR TOEPEL
The new Munich airport will handle international as well as domestic air passengers. The module-type terminal allows an excellent separation by modules of different types of passenger. Module A will handle all domestic passengers; Module B will serve international passengers of the national carrier Lufthansa; Terminal C will be reserved for all other international airlines; and terminal D will house non-scheduled carriers. On the apron there will be 20 gate positions - five assigned to each module - plus 30 remote positions served by buses which can be very flexibly used.

BRIG. DA SILVA
The new São Paulo Airport has been in operation since January 1985.
The administration of Brazil's commercial airports is undertaken by Infraero, a state-owned organisation under the general control of the Aeronautical Ministry.
Congonhas Airport, which is now completely enclosed by town development, will continue to operate under curfew conditions between 06.00 and 23.00 hours on account of noise considerations. It will continue to provide a shuttle service, between São Paulo and Rio de Janeiro, currently used by approximately 2 million passengers per annum.

MR WOONTON
It is planned for the Second Sydney Airport to have a pair of widely spaced parallel runways with the passenger terminals between them. It is envisaged that, at the airport's ultimate development, both runways will be used by landing and takeoff aircraft. The rationale behind this decision is that mixing takeoffs and landings on the one runway provides for an increased overall runway capacity when compared with dedicating one runway for takeoffs and another for landings.
At an interim stage of development, it may well be that one runway can be used for landing and departing aircraft, while the other runway is used for general aviation aircraft engaged in training activities and doing touch and goes on that runway.

MR A. W. THOMPSON, Thompson Consultants International, New York
What are the prospects for privatisation in the Authors' respective countries, taking into consideration the privatisation of British Airports, and that of Washington-National and Washington-Dulles?

MR TOEPEL
All international airports in Germany are operated by limited liable companies, and in one case (Frankfurt) by a shareholding company. The owners of these companies are public entities, namely Federal Government, State Governments, municipalities. This form of organisation would readily facilitate privatisation of the airport operators if this were deemed desirable in the future.

BRIG. DA SILVA
It is unlikely that Brazilian airports will be privatised in the near future.
Air passenger traffic in Brazil is still quite small, and of the 62 airports under the administrative control of Infraero, only those in Rio de Janeiro and Sao Paulo handle movements in excess of five million passengers per annum. Six other airports - namely Porto Alegre, Brasilia, Salvador, Recife, Congonhas and Santos Dumont - have movements in excess of two million passengers per annum. The remainder handle fewer than one million passengers per annum.
In terms of the overall economic performance, Infraero, the state-owned administrator, has, in the fifteen years since its inauguration, managed to meet its budget and maintenance costs. However, turnover is not sufficient to fund new investments, and this is likely to present the greatest obstacle in the way of any proposals for privatisation.

MR WOONTON
In 1985, the Federal Parliament created an Act to establish a Federal Airports Corporation: the national government owned statutory authority.
The Act provides for 17 major airports in Australia to be owned and operated by the Federal Airports Corporation, which is charged with the responsibility of developing and operating these airports in a cost-effective manner. The Federal Airports Corporation was due to commence operation on 1 July 1987.
However, in May 1987, the Government announced that it was investigating the possibility of selling the leases of international terminal complexes on each of these major airports to private enterprise, to develop and operate as the leaseholder saw fit: that is, to privatise international terminals.
As a result of this decision, the commencement of operation of the Federal Airports Corporation has been deferred while the Government completes the investigation of this proposal to privatise international terminal complexes at government airports.
It is expected that the Government will take a decision on this matter by the end of 1987.

5 The development of Gatwick Airport

8 The development of Gatwick Airport

G.D. BELL, Chairman and Managing Director, Gatwick Airport Limited, UK

The air transport industry is all about change: it thrives on it. And the physical development of
of Gatwick Airport in recent times - undertaken in a climate of a Government White Paper on
Airports Policy and the Airports Act 1986, the privatisation of the British Airports Authority and
a continuing debate on future runway and passenger terminal capacity in the South East - is a
first-rate example of this. Gatwick Airport in general, and the North Terminal development in
particular, has evolved the way it has because its operator, Gatwick Airport Limited, has listened
to its customers and its colleagues in the industry and has been willing to accept change and
indeed be motivated by it.

INTRODUCTION

1. The success story of Gatwick Airport's
development from its re-opening in 1958 to its
emergence in 1986 as the third largest international airport in the world is one which I
never tire of repeating. However, the topic I
would like to address here is not the history
of a major international airport. It is instead the challenges and the changes which arise
at an airport which has already emerged internationally and is looking forward to its
maturity.

2. And what I hope to describe to you - what
you will also largely see for yourselves during
the tour to the North Terminal Site - is how
Gatwick Airport Limited (GAL) has responded in
the recent past to the challenge of planning
and operating Gatwick Airport. I shall also be
describing how it sees this task in the future
as Gatwick grows from its present throughput of
16 million passengers per annum (mppa) to some
25 mppa in, we expect, the mid 1990s.

3. It is a story about change and the reaction to change. And its message, as such,
reflects the 'Airports for People' theme of
this Conference: that if you want to manage
change and manage it well, you have to listen
to people.

THE PRIVATISATION OF THE BRITISH AIRPORTS AUTHORITY

4. I am the first Chairman and Managing
Director of Gatwick Airport Limited, a sub-
sidiary company of BAA plc formerly the British
Airports Authority. On 1 August 1986 the
property, rights and liabilities of the British
Airports Authority were transferred to BAA plc.

The shares in BAA plc are held at present by
the Secretary of State for Transport on behalf
of the Government and it is expected that the
whole of the share capital of the company will
be sold to the general public during the
Summer of 1987.

5.Under the new BAA plc company structure
shown in Fig. 1 Gatwick Airport Limited is
currently one of seven airport subsidiaries.
All I wish to say on this topic at the moment
- apart from introducing it to you as the
change within which all other changes are
taking place - is that BAA plc is the world's
leading international airport group. The subsidiary companies of BAA plc handled 75% of UK
air passenger traffic and 85% of air cargo
tonnage in 1985/6 and when it is in the private
sector it will be the first and only significant airport system to be privately owned and
quoted on the Stock Exchange. It is a
challenge which all of us at Gatwick and the
other companies in the plc look forward to with
relish.

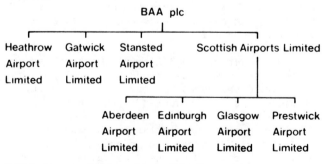

British Airports Services, Commercial Services and Safety and
Security are divisions of BAA plc.

Fig. 1 - BAA plc Company Structure

Airports for people. Thomas Telford Limited, London, 1988

65

THE NORTH TERMINAL DEVELOPMENT

6. For the purposes of this paper, Gatwick embarked on its journey as a mature airport on 9 November 1982. That may seem somewhat precise and - to those who are familiar with Gatwick passenger traffic statistics (Fig. 2) and who know that in 1982 the airport was already handling some 11 mppa - a somewhat grudging tribute. Not at all. My sole reason for choosing that date is that on 9 November 1982 the Secretaries of State for Environment and for Trade granted planning permission for the North Terminal and, with it, the opportunity for the airport to fulfil the role which the then BAA had long planned for it.

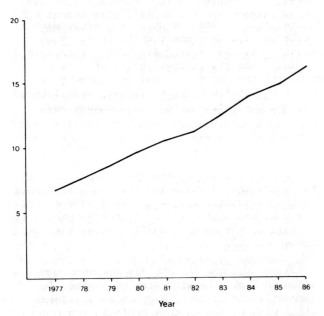

Fig. 2 Gatwick Passenger Figures (Millions)
1977 - 1986

7. The grant of planning permission did not come to us, of course, like a bolt from the blue. It was not as if we had been given something we did not want. Plans for a second terminal at Gatwick were first published in 1970 in a Draft Land Use Plan which also safeguarded for, among other things, a second parallel runway. As a consequence of the Government's decision to build Maplin, the BAA abandoned the safeguarding of the line of this runway in 1971. The area to the north-west of the existing terminal thus became available for a second terminal.

8. Thereafter, the BAA's 1974 Master Plan Report for Gatwick described the developments that would be needed to provide the capacity of 16 mppa. It also referred to the continuing need to provide terminal capacity commensurate with the growing use of larger aircraft even after Gatwick had reached 16 mppa. The same area was indicated as the most favoured site for a second terminal.

9. The plans for the North Terminal, prepared over a period of some fifteen years, and finally subjected to the most rigorous examination of a Public Inquiry lasting 75 days, were at the foundation of how Gatwick would provide capacity during growth of demand from passengers and air transport movements.

THE SOUTH EAST AIRPORTS SYSTEM

10. But of course, Gatwick Airport does not exist in a void. The context for its development is that the South-East Airports of Heathrow, Gatwick, Stansted and Luton (Fig. 3) are viewed by both the Government and BAA plc as a system. The increases in capacity that will occur as the system develops will mean that the role of the four airports will change over time. This changing share that each airport has of the total passenger traffic within the South-East region requires a strategy to ensure that the system develops in the most economic and efficient manner.

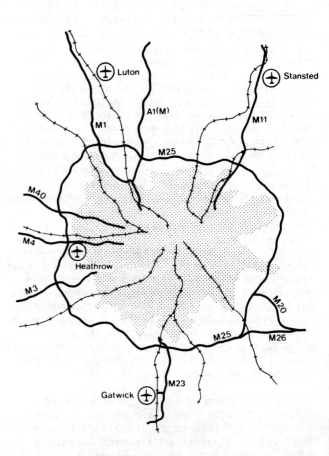

Fig. 3 The South East Airports

11. The Government White Paper on Airports Policy (Cmnd 9542), presented to Parliament in June 1985, sought to protect the UK's leading position in world aviation through a series of proposals for legislation which were contained in the Airports Act 1986.

In respect of traffic distribution between the four South East Airports the Government indicated it would be guided by four principles:

- our international obligations;
- the authority of the Airport Scheduling Committees;
- the additional authority, where necessary, of specific formal guidance or rules; and
- a larger role for the market;

And in its responses to CAP510 and CAP517, the Civil Aviation Authority's consultation documents on the topic of traffic distribution, BAA plc and GAL supported a policy which relied on the market and the Airport Scheduling Committees to work the system. It will be interesting to see how these two instruments are able to control the supply and demand equation of air transport over the next few years as the debate on additional runway and passenger terminal capacity in the South East gathers momentum.

THE DEVELOPMENT OF GATWICK AIRPORT

North Terminal

12. But let us get back to the present, and the changes that are already with us. The scheme for the North Terminal permitted by the Secretaries of State (Fig. 4) showed a wholly international terminal with 19 aircraft stands, 12 of which ultimately would be pier-served. Of those 19 stands 17 would cater for the 747-200 series, the one currently in service, and the remaining 2 for wide-bodied aircraft of DC10 or Airbus size. The terminal was designed in a way which permitted the mixing of arriving and departing passengers in the piers, and also made no allowance for any changes to the status of passengers which might be contemplated by our friends in the European Community. It was provided with roads, a staff car park, multi-storey car parks, a long term car park, an inter-terminal tracked transit system and other items of infrastructure. And the provision of these items - like the provision of the terminal's check-in desks, baggage handling systems, Immigration combs, security system - were planned to match, in phases, the expected passenger growth, by number and by type, in the terminal.

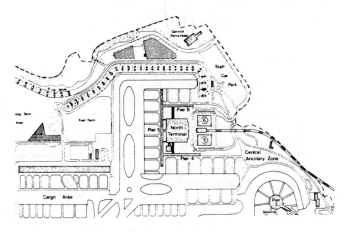

Fig. 4 Layout of the North Terminal

13. Now, if on the morning of 9 November 1982 you would have asked Pat Bailey, then the Airport Director: 'Have you got this terminal right?', his answer: 'Yes, so far' would have been a shrewd one. Our business is changing constantly and it would have been a reckless man who would have said the original scheme as envisaged by the BAA would be the one adopted by the airlines on opening day. In retrospect, and this is another reason why I have chosen 9 November 1982 as the date from which Gatwick began its adult life, the planning of the terminal in many ways gathered pace from then.

14. On the planning programme alone, nine separate submissions were made to Crawley Borough Council, the local planning authority, seeking approval for matters reserved by the permission granted by the Secretaries of State. These ranged from the overall site layout and phasing and the diversion of the River Mole which ran across the site, to the terminal building itself, its west pier and the inter-terminal tracked transit system.

15. And of course all the time this complex and demanding project was being managed the BAA, as a nationalised industry, had the task of seeking Government approval to the release of funds to pay for the work.

16. But throughout the development - with all the limitations of time, space and money - Gatwick listened to people. It listened to its customers in the industry, the airlines and the plane-makers, who were telling it to keep aircraft stands flexible and to safeguard for the next-but-one generation of jets. It listened to the passengers passing through the existing terminal who were telling it what standards of service they wanted on the departures concourse and in the catering outlets. It listened to its bosses, the Government departments and their Ministers. And it listened to its Consultative Committees and local authorities who wanted more trees planted, fewer lorries on the road, less airport ground noise and more details of the airport's future development plans.

17. And not only did Gatwick listen, it responded. Not every time, I might add. But the net result has been many many changes to the concept of the North Terminal. Not just from how it was envisaged to operate during its fifteen years on the drawing board, but even from how it was planned to work as recently as 9 November 1982. Most significantly, these changes have taken place on the aircraft aprons, in the terminal itself and in the piers - and have been improvements to the core of our business: the safe, swift and convenient passage through our airports of passengers and planes. Let me give you some examples.

18. On the apron, GAL has taken the initiative to introduce the MARS concept - Multi Aircraft Ramp System - to the North Terminal stands.

In the first phase of the development 4 of the 7 Pier 5 stands, which are now capable of accommodating 747-400 will each be able to handle two aircraft up to the size of 737-300 independently of each other. A further 3 Pier 4 stands will now be available for similar use in the later phases of the project. By this method GAL has increased its North Terminal stand capacity from 19 to 26 and introduced a more flexible use of the concrete available to it. For the future, GAL is looking at how the next-but-one generation of super jumbo aircraft, the 747-500 series, might need to be accommodated at Gatwick's North/South Terminals and what implications its size might have for the design of the later phases of the North Terminal site.

19. There have also been changes imposed upon us by circumstances outside our control. The most serious example being that brought about by the threat of terrorism. An airport operator must needs react in many different ways to such a threat. Some of you will remember the Herculean efforts made by the Management and staff of Terminal 1 at Heathrow when, over a single weekend in January 1986, El Al was provided with check-in facilities, a ramp office and a sales and reservation desk in that terminal. Our task at the North Terminal was different. The western pier, Pier 4, was originally designed on a large open gateroom concept in which arriving and departing passengers could mix. We were required by the Department of Transport to segregate those passengers. In order to formulate the most effective proposals, given the priorities of departing passengers, GAL held detailed discussions with the Airport Consultative Committee and a design is now in preparation which provides a corridor for arriving passengers on the east side of the pier with manned security points at the exits from the departure lounge.

20. And as GAL looks forward to the next decade, potentially even more significant are the changes to both Terminals which could be necessary as a result of the European Community's intention to complete the internal market. Although it appears to be the Community's long term wish for all intra-EC air travel to become domestic, thus dispensing with Customs or Immigration formalities, the reality in the initial stages at least is likely to fall short of this and perhaps require the retention of one of the control authorities. Full harmonization - where the current two-channel system within passenger terminals would continue except that EC traffic would become domestic - would be difficult. An intermediate stage requiring three channels - one each for domestic, EC and other International - would be even more challenging.

21. These are just some of the changes to a £200m investment which had taken some fifteen years to plan. The first phase of the terminal is due to be completed in November 1987 and open for business in February 1988. No doubt further changes will be made to its proposed operation between now and then. Its later phases, which include one-third of the building area, 28 check-in desks and 12 aircraft stands, will almost certainly alter in both shape and function before they are brought into operation.

22. On 21 January this year I was able to announce that GAL and British Airways had agreed in principle that the airline would transfer all its operations at Gatwick Airport to the North Terminal, subject to the successful conclusion of detailed discussions. This would include the 19 British Airways Gatwick-based scheduled services, the British Airways charter services and all the airlines handled by British Airways at Gatwick at the time of the transfer. Now when British Airways makes the journey across the airfield from the South to the North Terminal - and I'm sure when it happens it will be just as impressive as the one it made across the airfield at Heathrow to Terminal 4 in April 1986 - we do not know now what other carriers it will take with it. The view of GAL on the opportunity - I am tempted to call it the North Terminal Share Opportunity - to occupy a brand new terminal is of course a strongly optimistic one. It is an excellent terminal; it will work; and GAL wants to maximise its investment. I am determined that the new terminal will pay its way and that the system of a two terminal airport will in time maximise the use of both buildings. This will be one of the crucial elements in the development of the business of managing Gatwick and now the airport has the commitment of a major operator for its new facility that work can begin in earnest.

South Terminal

23. But development at Gatwick is not restricted to the new terminal. The existing building, the South Terminal, has since its original construction been altered more times than I can count. It has been gutted and refurbished, extended on every face at almost every level, replanned and replenished. It was equipped, in 1983, with a £24m satellite terminal connected to it by a rapid transit system similar to that now being installed between the South and North Terminals. Other significant improvements to the attractiveness of the terminal include the Gatwick Hilton, which opened in 1982 offering 330 bedrooms and which by April 1987 will offer some 570 in total, and the rebuilding of British Rail's Gatwick Station which was completed in 1980. And we are just about to commence one of its most radical changes as we completely replace the existing outbound baggage system and at the same time provide for another extension to the building, this time on the western, airside face.

24. The existing baggage handling system which was installed progressively between 1976 and 1983 will shortly be coming to the end of its assessed life. The window of marginally lower passenger throughput figures which the opening of the North Terminal provides will be used to replace the existing system, and this will take place, following full consultation with the handling agents at Gatwick, between 1988 and 1990. Of course, during the time the baggage system is being replaced the South Terminal will be operating at something like 12 mppa - equivalent to its annual throughput in 1983 - so it will not be an easy task. There also remains the question of the character of the relief which the South Terminal will enjoy. Will it be charter or scheduled? long haul or short haul? Will it have a high or low inter-line content? These are crucial questions when assessing the capacities of what remains available for use.

25. So it remains all change at Gatwick. Changing and improving a passenger terminal as it takes shape and changing too one which has already changed so much since 1958 that it is unrecognisable.

The Development of the Business

26. Change is also a strong feature of the way we are looking at the rest of our business beyond the airfield and the passenger terminals. It is a change coincident with the privatis-ation of what was once the British Airports Authority and which is now called BAA plc. Part of my responsibilities as Chairman and Managing Director of Gatwick Airport Limited has been to set up a business development section within the management structure of the airport. Now, to date, BAA in general and Gatwick particularly of late have been very successful businesses. The BAA has been con-sistently profitable (Fig. 5) since its for-mation in 1965 and has in that time funded with minimum Government borrowings some of the largest development projects in the country. Gatwick has been profitable (Fig. 6) every year since 1981/2. So success is not new to us. Why, then, appoint a Business Development Manager?

27. Under the umbrella of my Business Development Manager will fall the property and estate management of the airport, airport plan-ning, the management of our public and staff car parks and the information services. And over those areas it is the responsibility of the Business Development Manager to do just that - develop the business: generate fresh ideas, introduce new angles on established practices and generally enlarge the business potential of the airport to the benefit of Gatwick Airport Limited. It will be all about the management of change. I am not saying that the face of Gatwick will change overnight, but changes there will be.

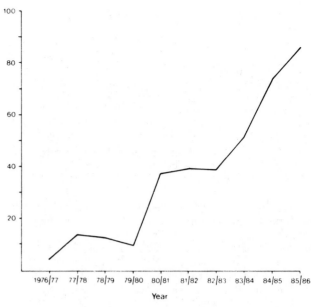

Fig. 5 BAA Trading Profit: 1976/7 - 1985/6 (£ millions)

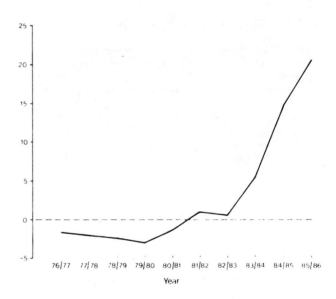

Fig. 6 Gatwick Trading Profit/Loss: 1976/7 - 1985/6 (£ millions)

Changes there must be if Gatwick Airport Limited is to prosper and continue to respond to changes in the aircraft industry and changes in its competitive position with other landowners and businesses in the area.

28. The last future Land Use Plan published by the BAA was an illustrative one which appeared in the back pocket of the Gatwick Airport Master Plan Report 1983. That Plan identified three zones within which the airport would wish to see developments take place as

Gatwick grew to its planned capacity of 25 mppa: those zones were located south of the runway, east of the London-Brighton railway line and to the north-west of the airport's landholding. While those three areas will continue to provide much scope for developments associated with warehousing, aircraft catering, car parking, cargo facilities and aircraft maintenance - together with road and service infrastructure and landscaping - there will now take place I believe changes of use on airport land already developed for airport-related activities. These changes may involve the intensification of the current use or a change of use altogether.

29. But here again, we must listen to others. We cannot act in isolation. In all of those activities I have just mentioned Gatwick Airport Limited is very much in competition with or constrained by forces outside the airport and we must tailor our business to take account of that. I am certain we are better equipped to do that now than any time in the past. But it must always be remembered that Gatwick Airport Limited is in the business of running an airport: Gatwick Airport. That is where its prime expertise lies and it is that expertise which I want to motivate.

FUTURE CHANGES AT GATWICK AIRPORT

30. That, then, briefly, covers the recent development of Gatwick into a two terminal airport with a capacity to handle some 25 mppa. That potential will start to be realised in February 1988. It is an airport which, within careful long term planning strategies, is always changing: as the industry changes, as technology changes, as the expectation of the public changes.

31. And what of the future? How will Gatwick's role in the South East Airports system change as the other components - Heathrow, Stansted and Luton - themselves change? There has already been some speculation over how Stansted might start to build up its passenger numbers and of course the way in which it does will affect the development of both Gatwick and Heathrow. Where in the south east growth of the charter and scheduled markets takes place is a matter which will engage the minds of the UK air transport industry over the next few years, rather than months. But as that debate goes on Gatwick will look to the continued health of its charter market, the establishment of its recent US and European scheduled services, and growth from Europe, North America and the East.

32. How the airport processes the passengers these new services will bring will be a major challenge to GAL and to the handling agents. But GAL will continue to listen to its customers and its colleagues before it makes the decisions which it believes to be the right ones for Gatwick. Managing a mature airport, as my colleagues down the road at another place will tell anyone who cares to listen, is a mixed blessing.

33. As the conference theme asserts: airports are for people. I hope I have explained how this rapidly changing industry in which we work is affected by the very people who rely upon it. The one feature which I have tried to stress as representative of the business we are in is change, and that a willingness to accept it and be motivated by it is vital if the right sort of changes are to be made.

9 Airport — City centre — rapid transit

Dr J.D.C.A. PRIDEAUX, Director of Intercity, British Railways Board, London

This paper discusses the benefits of providing a rapid rail link between an airport and city centre. It explores the advantages to travellers and indeed the benefits to the airport itself and the railway company. The essentially symbiotic relationship between the airport and the railway company is revealed.

INTRODUCTION

1. The provision of a rapid rail link between an airport and a city centre brings important benefits to the traveller, the airport and the railway company offering the service. The relationship between these three is fundamental.

2. The primary example taken in this paper to explore these relationships is British Rail's InterCity link between Gatwick Airport and London Victoria Station - the "Gatwick Express". The development of this service and the success which it represents in providing a rapid rail link are looked at in some detail as an example rather than as a model. The essential elements that are criteria for its success are looked at in order to draw more general conclusions and reference is made to the development of the rail link to Stansted Airport where many of the lessons learned have been applied.

DEVELOPMENT AND HISTORY OF GATWICK EXPRESS

3. When the new airport was built at Gatwick in 1958 a conscious decision was taken to move the main building to lie adjacent to the existing railway line - the main London-Brighton line. British Rail at the same time built a new railway station to serve the Airport directly. During the 1960's, the airport grew from 475,000 passengers a year to 3 million by 1969 but could not attract many scheduled airlines. Not until the 1970's did major growth occur and by 1980 the airport was dealing with some 9million passengers a year. By the Mid 1970's British Rail were investigating the possibilities of changes to the station and changes to the train pattern. A new railway station was built in 1980 with better passenger facilities and a revised structure to improve interchange.

4. During the whole of this period there was no specific, dedicated train service for the airport but rather a variety of trains which called at the airport. The general pattern was for 3 or 4 services an hour stopping at Gatwick Airport. These train services also stopped at Redhill, East Croydon and Clapham Junction before reaching London Victoria. The services were well used but were not designed specifically for the airport. With the opening of the new station in 1980 and the continued growth of the airport, it became clear that there were opportunities to dedicate the service and create a rail link which ran independently from the commuter services. For reasons that will be discussed later, the airport and the airlines using it were enthusiastic that such a development should take place. It was also clear that the dedicated rail link would be an important business opportunity for British Rail.

5. In 1984 the Gatwick Express was launched to provide a dedicated rail link between airport and city centre. The new service, (fundamentally as the service currently operates) comprised specially modified rolling stock and offered a non-stop service of 30 minutes duration, dedicated platforms at Victoria and a fixed 15 minute interval to services during the day.

6. There are several important elements in this service which represent the prime ingredients in ensuring success and these will be dealt with in some detail later. It is worth, however, reflecting on the legacy of history and to consider what advantages and disadvantages have accrued.

7. Firstly, the fact that the building of airport and station was coincidental should have given significant benefits. However, the developments were undertaken by different organisations and, although discussions took place between them, the interchange facilities between the two reflect the existence of two principals. Additionally, as development funding was separate, increased throughput at the airport led to separate funding by British Rail of improved facilities at a later date. Had the British Airports Authority seen the importance the rail link was to acquire, there might have been a greater willingness to see the station as an integral part of their airport infrastructure. Such close co-operation has subsequently been the case over the design of the new air terminal and railway station at Stansted Airport.

8. Secondly, that the Gatwick Express has been developed out of existing train services using an existing network has both advantages and

disadvantages.   The fact that the railway lines are shared with other services gives advantages in the ability to share railway infrastructure costs.   The use of existing tracks and to existing stations has given cost savings compared with building a separate, new railway line and has allowed investment to proceed incrementally in line with growth.   The alternative - a separate line - either implies a willingness to fund very heavily from the outset,when it is unlikely that such an investment will pay back for many years, or creating a new line into an established airport where traffic patterns have developed round other means of transport.   The latter not only requires large investment into a market where the competition is already established but creates disruption to both railway and airport infrastructure.   For Stansted Airport, British Rail is creating a new spur from existing lines to a new station fully integrated with the airport complex.   In these circumstances, the benefits of existing infrastructure and the construction of new track are combined to coincide with the planned growth at the airport.

9. By using existing track, the links with the rest of the rail network allow a diversity of rail services from the airport to other points in the country rather than just Central London. For example, during 1986 InterCity introduced Cross-London services which run direct from the North West through London to Gatwick and beyond. The new services northbound provide passengers arriving at the airport with direct train services to Birmingham, Liverpool, Manchester as well as the links to London, Brighton, Portsmouth, Reading that existing services provided.

10. However, the competing demands of other services on the railway create less than perfect operating conditions.   Any delays and operational problems to other services inevitably have a knock-on effect upon the Gatwick Express.

ADVANTAGES OF A RAPID RAIL LINK - DEALING WITH THE TRAVELLERS' NEEDS

11. The traveller has the choice of several modes of transport.   In seeking ways to forecast the potential use of rail links to airports,British Rail has developed a model based on extensive research which quantitatively assesses the likelihood of airport passengers choosing from a range of available modes of transport.   Whilst the business and leisure travellers' decision processes differ and the options open to overseas visitors are usually different from travellers originating in the UK, the decision tree for access mode can be generalised thus:-

<u>Airport Users</u>

Private Car   Public Transport

Park & Ride Kiss & Ride   Taxi   Mass Transport

Rail   Bus/Coach

The primary variables influencing travel decisions at each stage are cost and time, but frequency and interchange variables are also included for mass transport.   Travellers' perceptions of comfort and reliability are taken into account within the model by a constant term for each mode.   The forecasting model itself is complex and incorporates a number of recent developments in transport economics, this outline serves only to illustrate its essential structure.

12. Reviewing the model, it can be seen that the principal decision is between use of private car and public transport.   The private car provides the traveller with the greatest flexibility in terms of door-to-door transport and is clearly the greatest competition to any rail link.   1986 Gatwick Express survey information shows that around 50% of all passengers using the Gatwick Express had a car available to use as an alternative but chose not to.   Indeed only just over 30% passengers had even considered using an alternative mode. Whilst it has great flexibility, the car does suffer from inherent disadvantages.

13. Firstly, journey times, particularly in and around big cities, are not necessarily reliable as traffic and weather conditions affect journey speeds, congestion and routes available.   There is no doubt that even given the current motorway system a car journey from Central London to Gatwick Airport or vice versa cannot compete in journey time with the train - regardless of type of car.   As an example, the South London assessment study of November 1986 by Mott, Hay and Anderson for the Department of Transport identified traffic congestion in the A23 corridor south towards Gatwick as the single most serious problem affecting traffic in the area.

14. Whilst these are specific features relating to Gatwick Airport, the problems of traffic congestion are not unique to London, similar problems are likely to exist in every major city.

15. Secondly, for park-and-ride drivers, car parking at the airport brings its own interchange problems of moving travellers and luggage from the car park to the airport terminal.

16. The problems of unreliable journey time and traffic congestion equally apply to taxis, buses and coaches which form the competing public transport options in the British Rail forecasting model.

17. The relative strengths of a rail link are confirmed by survey information of Gatwick Express passengers.   When asked to rate the importance of key service quality features, the length of journey, frequency of service and reliability of arrival time consistently score highly.

TABLE 1
GATWICK EXPRESS QUALITY OF SERVICE FEATURES
RANKED IN ORDER OF IMPORTANCE TO TRAVELLERS

1. FREQUENCY OF SERVICE.
2. SPEED OF JOURNEY.
3. RELIABILITY OF ARRIVAL.
4. PRICE OF JOURNEY.
5. ABILITY TO GET SEAT.
6. SPACE FOR LUGGAGE.
7. SEATING COMFORT.
8. EASE OF OBTAINING TICKET.
9. AVOIDANCE OF CHANGES EN ROUTE.

18. Of primary importance to the customer is the frequency of the service. A half-hour journey time would be meaningless if it was provided only every 2 hours. Given the concern about "catching the plane" for the traveller and checking-in on time, anything more than 30 minute intervals of service is insufficient to provide the peace of mind desired.
19. The duration of the journey itself for the traveller between airport and city centre is more important in terms of comparison with other modes than the actual journey time which is clearly a function of distance. Clearly a journey time that is too great in traveller perception will be to the detriment of the airport development whatever the mode. The 30 minute journey time of the Gatwick Express effectively brings Gatwick "nearer" to Central London than any other transport mode.
20. The non-stop nature is an important psychological factor, particularly for travellers to the airport. Whilst an intermediate stop may only add 2 minutes to the overall journey time, the perception of reliability and urgency that a non-stop service provides is important in the passenger viewpoint - the traveller's main anxiety is to check-in on time.
21. The fact that price of journey has a lower rating than these factors not only reflects that airport passengers are more concerned with journey time and frequency benefits, but also reflects the type of traveller carried. The Gatwick Express carries a very large proportion of International holidaymakers (whose airport access mode represents a very small proportion of their overall journey cost) and also a higher proportion of employed and self-employed than for other services.

TABLE 2
GATWICK EXPRESS PASSENGERS - JOURNEY PURPOSE
(CUMULATIVE SURVEYS 1985-86)

HOLIDAY	37%
TO/FROM WORK	17%
EMPLOYERS BUSINESS	14%
VISITING FRIENDS/RELATIONS	11%
PERSONAL BUSINESS	6%
DAY OUT	5%
SPORT OR ENTERTAINMENT	3%
SHOPPING	3%
OTHER/NOT STATED	4%

TABLE 3
GATWICK EXPRESS PASSENGERS - OCCUPATION OF
TRAVELLER (CUMULATIVE SURVEYS 1985/86)

	GATWICK EXPRESS
STUDENT	9%
RETIRED	2%
UNEMPLOYED/NOT WORKING	2%
HOUSEWIFE	3%
EMPLOYED	67%
SELF-EMPLOYED	12%
NOT STATED	5%

It is clear, however, that whatever the journey purpose is or the type of traveller the key requirements relate to the journey time, frequency, reliability and quality of journey.
22. It should be remembered, however, that it is not just airline travellers that use the "Gatwick Express". It is inevitable that when an up-market service is created, regular travellers will change their travel patterns to take advantage. Consequently, at certain times of day, there are large numbers of commuters using the service although they do not form part of the primary market that the rail link was created for.
23. It can be seen that two types of market analysis are required to plan a successful airport rail link. Firstly, the British Rail model for airport travellers helps to forecast the rail share. This share, combined with the airport throughput forecasts, assists British Rail to plan a level of service to satisfy passenger requirements given the constraints of airport location and throughput. Secondly, passenger surveys permit effective identification of the travellers' requirements, type of passenger and journey purpose. These are important in order to ensure that the type of service provided is appropriate.
24. Similarly, regular checks of customer perception of the quality of the product form the most important base for decision-making in adjusting the service.
25. The key elements of journey time, the frequency of service and reliability of transit are in themselves primary requirements and are consequently highly marketable properties to the potential rail customer. However, the quality of the rolling stock, and the overall quality of the journey itself are also extremely important to the traveller and are likely to make the difference between a successful and an adequate rail link.
26. It was for this reason that one of the primary changes made when the "Gatwick Express" was instigated in 1984 was the provision of dedicated, specialised rolling stock. The current rolling stock comprises of air-conditioned, InterCity coaches with additional luggage space and is quite separate and distinct from the vehicles used for local services. Back-up stock is also provided at a level which reduces risk of alternative (non-Gatwick) stock being used. It is imperative that wherever possible only this dedicated stock is used. There are inevitable occasions when failures in service

mean that alternative stock is pressed into service but this iskept to a minimum.

27. The maintenance of this stock in good condition and in a clean state is a primary requirement.   The shuttle nature of the service means that the trains each complete 10 circuits a day i.e. 10 trips to the Airport and 10 trips to Victoria.   The amount of litter generated by each train carrying up to 4,000 passengers in the course of a busy day is considerable and every vehicle receives a clean at the end of each trip, a further clean at the end of each day and a heavy clean every fortnight.   There is nothing worse from a passenger viewpoint than travelling in a dirty train, travelling in a train with nowhere to put their luggage or finding toilets out of order.

28. The quality of journey has been further improved by the installation of telephones and the provision of trolley food services, but for the traveller the critical part of journey quality associated with the service is interchange at the Airport and access to the Rail system at Victoria.

29. When the Gatwick Express was launched a complete package was formulated which went beyond the rail link itself in order to make the overall journey as easy as possible for the passenger.   A major new station development at Victoria station will be completed in 1987 with a dedicated Gatwick Express terminal built on a "raft" above the platforms.   The new terminal will provide escalators and lifts between the dedicated platforms that allow the transfer of luggage trolleys, immediate access to taxi ranks and private vehicles and a full range of shopping facilities complementing the terminal.

30. Travellers using the "Gatwick Express" at Victoria have benefitted from the start of the service from the Central London Check-In facilities operated by British Caledonian Airways as one of the three Handling Agents for Gatwick Airport.   Check-In for Airline travellers can therefore be at the railway station in London, thus allowing passengers to travel to the Airport without carrying their luggage.   It is security checked in the normal way and travels, sealed, on the Gatwick Express to the Airport where it is transferred to the aircraft.   For these passengers the Railway station is simply an extension of the Airport. The further development of Victoria station includes rebuilding of check-in facilities on the "Raft" and the interchange facilities are improved even further.

31. The facilities at Victoria are being restructured with the passenger movements and Gatwick Express interchange specifically in mind.   At Gatwick, however, as has already been noted the situation is the product of separate development by British Rail and British Airport Authority.   Whilst the layout at Gatwick is exceptionally good, in terms of minimising distances between train and plane, the facilities for transfer of people and luggage are not perfect and need constant review.   The platforms at the railway station at Gatwick are unfortunately too narrow safely to allow the direct transfer of trolleys between airport concourse and the platforms.   This throws even

greater emphasis upon the provision of lifts, and a further set was opened in 1986. Additionally, further escalators are being built in early 1987 to cater for increased passenger flows created by the opening of the second terminal at the Airport.

32. Interchange facilities are critical to the overall journey experience and the ability to deal effectively with passengers <u>and</u> their luggage is essential.   Any airport/rail interchange needs to give this aspect particular attention because from the travellers' viewpoint this represents one of the greatest areas of potential inconvenience.

33. At Stansted it has been recognised that the railways would prove an important asset to the expanded airport.   However, early designs put the railway station parallel to the new air terminal and about 100 metres from it, requiring some passengers to walk as much as 200 metres in total from train to departure concourse.   This was clearly unsatisfactory for a public transport mode designed specifically to capture a high proportion of travellers to and from the airport.

34. A series of revisions was made, in collaboration with BAA's designers, to bring the station much closer to the airport, culminating in the configuration now adopted. This places the station immediately under the front face of the air terminal building, requiring only vertical movements under cover, via escalators or ramps, to move between the two facilities.

35. The airport terminal has been so designed that departing passengers enter in the westernmost half of the concourse whilst arrivals use the eastern half.   This arrangement has the merit of simplicity, with maximum effectiveness in avoiding conflicting passenger movements.   British Rail has designed the railway station so that this approach can be continued in the vertical interchange arrangements to platform level. When a train arrives the passengers will have the choice of using either escalators or a fixed ramp to move up to the airport concourse without the need to pass through a ticket barrier and without conflicting with passengers moving down to the station. Passengers moving down to the station will leave the escalators or the fixed ramp within the station Travel Centre and will normally pass the ticket sales point and travel information facilities, in progressing towards the waiting trains.   There will be no ticket barrier.   Lifts will be provided in either direction, for use by the disabled.

36. To summarise, a rapid rail link can satisfy a large number of travellers requirements.   In reality these requirements are only likely to be met if due attention is given in the first instance to planning with the traveller in mind and if the service quality provided is sufficiently high in standard.   There are additional advantages that accrue to passengers in ease of interchange and flexible check-in facilities to make luggage carrying less of a problem.

ADVANTAGES OF A RAPID RAIL LINK - THE RAILWAY
VIEWPOINT

37. From a British Rail point of view the
provision of a dedicated service provides
significant opportunities to cater for an
airport market that on every projection is
planned to increase. It is essentially a
business decision. The decision between
offering a dedicated non-stop service and
simply providing services which call at both
Airport and City Centre terminus is, however,
more complex. The fact that a non-stop
service improves customer perception is
countered by the fact that intermediate points
cease to become catchment areas for the service.
The "Gatwick Express" for example passes
through some of the most densely populated areas
of the UK. These potential airport passengers
are served instead by commuter services and not
by the dedicated service as the primary market
that British Rail is aiming for is the Airline
traveller.

38. Non-stop services may not, however, prove
the right solution in other locations.
Existing plans for the rail link to Stansted
include an interchange stop in North London to
link with the Underground system, to increase
the catchment area of the service and to
provide an effective link with the west end of
London.

39. Therefore, the size of the market area to
be served is central in any railway decision to
instigate a non-stop service; if the City and
its market is not large enough the loss of
potential customers by running non-stop would
force a stopping service to be provided on
economic grounds.

40. The size and scale of the airport is
equally critical. A major international
airport by definition has more passengers, more
visitors, more staff and, therefore, more
potential customers for the rail link.

41. Clearly, these are essential marketing
issues that assume a railway system whose
decisions are fundamentally commercial in nature
and independent in planning from either the
airport or city authorities. The decision on
frequency, stopping pattern and size of train
will inevitably be made in such a way as to
optimise the Railway Company's finances.
Assessing traveller performance is fundamental.

42. For the Railway Company there are
advantages in providing a high quality link that
extends beyond the direct financial benefits.
Overseas visitors can be introduced to the
Railway system at the earliest stage of their
visit. If the impression is good then the
likelihood of travel elsewhere by train is
improved. Surveys of Gatwick Express
passengers show that 9 out of 10 respondents
felt that they were more likely to travel on
InterCity services in future than before the
current journey. The potential revenue
generation to British Rail as a whole is,
therefore, considerable.

ADVANTAGES OF A RAPID RAIL LINK - THE AIRPORT
INFRASTRUCTURE

43. The airport's primary source of
passengers is, of course, from the air, but the
accessibility of the airport to its primary
market, the city centre, is the key to its
success. To attract scheduled airlines and
the business market, the links are even more
critical than for the charter leisure market
where time dependency is not so marked. To
achieve full international airport status,
therefore, the accessibility is of primary
importance. In a real sense, therefore, the
viability of an airport is closely related to
the provision of its transport infrastructure.

44. Government planning authorities also
recognise this and the Departments of
Environment and Transport made the "provision
for public transport facilities including a
British Rail link, railway station and bus
station" a condition in granting Planning
Permission for extension of Stansted Airport in
1985.

45. If the travellers' perception of access to
an airport is a function of location, the
available modes and the confidence he or she has
in their reliability, then an Airport such as
Gatwick which is a greater distance from
Central London than Heathrow, becomes heavily
dependent upon ease of access in order to
compete. The "Gatwick Express" effectively
brings Gatwick nearer to Central London than
Heathrow in journey time. The travellers'
perception, therefore, in terms of time
isographs is that Gatwick is "closer" than
Heathrow to Central London and allows Gatwick
to compete effectively as an international
airport. The role a rail link plays is,
therefore, crucial in providing the necessary
accessibility but also gives several other
specific advantages to an Airport.

46. Firstly, land values tend - in general - to
be cheaper further away from the city centre.
If journey times can be kept short, but at the
same time distance from the city centre can be
increased, there is a consequential financial
benefit when expansion of space and ancillary
service industries around the airport are
required.

47. Secondly, a successful rail link requires
less land to be dedicated to transport
facilities than if all the travellers arrived
by road. The Airport is consequently able to
devote more of its land and resources to other
activities than simply vast areas of car
parking. Land is released for other attractive
airport related developments and potential
constraints on Airport expansion may be relaxed.

48. Thirdly, the provision of a dedicated
rail link exclusively for an airport becomes a
major marketing tool for the airport by
providing the tangible evidence of reliable
access that is critical. Additionally, the
rail link allows access into the rest of the
railway network allowing a national catchment
area for the airport.

49. Fourthly, a railway link allows improved
airport terminal design due to the greater
concentration of passengers at one point and
makes passenger interchange easier.

50. This critical relationship between
reliable access and Airport success implies a
strong interdependence between the Railway and
the Airport Authority. It is the joint

intention of British Rail and Stansted Airport Limited that, not only is the infrastructure integrated but also that there will be compatibility of design. This will include such items as signing, passenger information displays, retail outlets and even floor finishes and colour schemes.

51. There is clearly a symbiotic relationship in that the well-being of both is dependent upon the other. It is, however, a matter of survival for the Airport whereas it is a business opportunity for the Railway. The consequences for an airport such as Gatwick of not having the "Gatwick Express" are difficult to assess but the growth in scheduled airlines and the business market would be jeopardised and passenger throughput at the Airport would be seriously at risk.

52. In common with all airports in UK, the fact that the "Gatwick Express" is operated independently of the Airport Authority means that the rail service is essentially a "free good" to the Airport. It is not surprising that the Airport was enthusiastic about the inception of the service and that some of the airlines include mention of the "Gatwick Express" in advertising material. Both the airlines and the airport have recognised the importance of the service to the continuing success of their own business and are consequently the most vociferous critics of variations in quality.

MEASURES OF SUCCESS

53. The single greatest measure of the success of any transport link is the number of passengers it carries. The impact that the Gatwick Express service has had on passenger volume is demonstrated by annual London-Gatwick volumes. In 1984 2.8 million passengers were carried between London and Gatwick, and in 1987 4.1 million passengers are anticipated. These figures represent purely the London-Gatwick ticket sales and do not include other rail travellers.

54. However, rail volume figures on their own do not indicate the relative success of the Gatwick Express in comparison with other modes. The 1984 CAA Airports Survey showed that for Gatwick and modal split used for access was as follows:-

Car	48%
Rail	32%
Bus/Coach	13%
Taxi	5%
Other	2%

Clearly the rail links to Gatwick play an important role, but are second to the car in total market share. Significantly, however, the same survey showed that the access mode used by passengers between Central London and Gatwick was:-

Rail	57%
Car	19%
Bus/Coach	17%
Taxi	6%
Other	1%

and even for Greater London as a whole Rail was

the major mode of access.

56. London itself is the main target market for the rail link to the Airport. It cannot and does not seek to serve all the surrounding area as the primary passenger flow is to and from the city centre itself. Since this survey the impact of the Gatwick Express will have strengthened further this position.

57. In addition to the number of travellers using the service the ways in which the service is viewed by the customer is critical, the feedback surveys give is necessary to ensure the service is providing what the traveller requires. Taking the principal features that were regarded as important in Table1 the latest Gatwick Express Survey in 1986 showed these features scoring as follows:-

Feature	UK Resident	Non-UK Resident
	(100 = V.Good, 0 = V.Poor)	
Frequency of service	90	86
No changes on route	87	83
Speed of journey	81	79
Ability to get seat	78	79
Reliability	75	78
Ease of obtaining ticket	72	75
Seating comfort	70	73
Baggage space	64	61
Price of journey	52	56

58. With one or two exceptions the rating of these features is broadly similar to the ranking in importance that was made. The most notable difference is in price of journey, the provision of the service and the level of quality that is necessary does not come cheaply!

CONCLUSIONS

59. The Gatwick Express has been used as an example of how a Railway Company has developed a rapid city link of high quality to satisfy passenger requirements. Many of the lessons learned have subsequently been applied to a rail link for Stansted Airport.

60. For the traveller a rail link provides some specific advantages over other modes of transport:-

(i) Frequent services.
(ii) Rapid journeys.
(iii) Reliability of journey time.
(iv) Short distances and ease of interchange at the airport.
(v) Ancillary benefits such as check-in city centre.

61. Differing locations, airport size and city size will influence the economic equations determining the frequency, scale and stopping patterns of the rail link provided. Whatever the service provided a rail link provides an important business opportunity to be exploited for a railway company. The creation of such services out of existing railway networks is cheaper and more flexible than building new links.

62. Whilst in the UK, the choice of location of an airport is outside the railway decision-making power, decisions on airport expansion have tended increasingly to take railway infrastructure into account.

63. In a very real sense the Airport Authority gains most from the provision of a rapid rail link. Not only does such a link provide for a

more economic use of land and terminal design, but it also has many of the infrastructure benefits that are associated with the railway provided as a "free good". Whilst many airports may wish to have a service at the same level and standard as the "Gatwick Express" the railways can only provide what is economically viable under the specific circumstances.

64. It is a symbiotic relationship whereby the airport gains the ability todemonstrate its accessibility in tangible form and thereby enhances its potential to grow by serving its target market effectively. The need to jointly assess infrastructure requirements to provide the easiest possible interchange for passengers should be clearly understood.

65. The railway gains, in return, access to a potentially expanding market where the precise cost of journey is not necessarily the dominant decision in choice of mode. It would be unfortunate indeed if the separate funding and separate decision-making of independent authorities in future led to a failure to create adequate facilities because each pursued its own financial ends independently.

Discussion

MR S. DE LANGE, Schiphol Airport, Amsterdam
What options were available in the development of Gatwick Airport - that is, new terminal and runway, new runway or just a new terminal? What criteria influenced the final decision?

The present percentage volume of passengers using the Gatwick Express is 57%; what was it before the introduction of the high-speed train?

MR G. D. BELL (Paper 8)
In July 1974, the UK Government cancelled the Maplin project, a scheme to construct a two-terminal, two-runway airport on Maplin Sands at the eastern end of the Southend peninsula in the Thames estuary. It did so for four reasons:

(a) the rapid introduction of large aircraft which suggested that the major constraints at airports in the London area would be the capacity of passenger terminals rather than runways
(b) these larger aircraft were quieter, and noise disturbance from them was expected to reduce over the coming years
(c) the recent rises in the cost of fuel which resulted in traffic forecasts significantly below those previously used
(d) the economic recession in the UK at the time.

In the light of this, the Government White Paper on Airports Policy of February 1978 concluded, among other things, that proposals should be brought forward by the BAA for a second terminal at Gatwick to raise the capacity to 25 million passengers a year and that proposals for a second runway at Gatwick should not be revived. The site for a second terminal at Gatwick, which had been identified in the Government's review of the Maplin project, lay within the area which had been safeguarded for a second runway, parallel to the existing one. The Government's decision at the time was based on the assumption that there was no justification for further capacity up to 1990. Since then, consent has been given to expanding Stansted to provide further capacity for the 1990s.

The 1984 CAA Airport Survey showed that rail was used as the access mode by 57% of passengers from Central London and 32% of passengers overall. Directly comparable figures regarding origination of passengers before and after the introduction of the Gatwick Express service in May 1984 are not readily available. However,

British Rail figures show that 2.9 million passengers travelled to and from Gatwick by train in 1983 and 5 million passengers in 1985. During this period the airport throughput rose by around 2.5 million to 15.5 million. In crude terms, therefore, the rail share rose from around 22% in 1983 to the 32% reflected in the CAA Survey in 1984 after the introduction of the Gatwick Express service.

MR A. W. THOMPSON, Thompson Consultants International, New York
With regard to the prospective privatisation of the British Airports Authority, will the individual airports in the system (e.g. Heathrow, Gatwick, Glasgow) be competing with each other? If so, what plans are there for a non-stop Intercity service to Heathrow to keep the latter competitive? Will the international airlines have a choice of airports (that is, a choice of quality of airport service)?

MR BELL
Privatisation of the BAA will not change the ability of individual airports owned by the BAA to compete with each other. However, the ability of airlines to obtain route licences is dependent on traffic distribution policies within he UK and on bilateral agreements. One of the four traffic distribution rules for Heathrow prohibits any airline which has not previously operated at Heathrow from being granted a licence to operate an international scheduled passenger service at that Airport. In answer to the second question, there are no plans for developing a non-stop Intercity service to Heathrow, although the whole question of surface access into Heathrow is being reviewed.

MR G. F. DOUGHTY, Stapleton International Airport, Denver
What was the cost of the people moving system, i.e. the rapid transit system, at the new North Terminal at Gatwick Airport? Were any other systems considered?

MR BELL
The total cost of the people mover system, including the supporting structure and the stations, was in the order of £20M. The

contract for providing the system itself was awarded to the Westinghouse Corporation following an analysis of a wide range of proposals submitted by other companies worldwide. A traditional road based bus service was also considered but rejected because of the inherent poor quality of service.

MR G. A. KAMDEM, Direction de l'Aviation Civile, Ministere des Transports, Yaounde, Cameroon
If the runway capacity at Gatwick is not increased but remains as a single runway, what can be gained by the construction of a new terminal building apart from contributing towards the comfort of the passengers, especially if the volume of passengers increases at the present rate?

MR BELL
There is no proposal to provide a second operational runway at Gatwick. Gatwick currently has one operational runway and an emergency runway. The two cannot be used simultaneously. The North Terminal will provide additional capacity of 9 million passengers per annum in addition to the capacity of the South Terminal of 16 million passengers per annum. The Airport's total capacity of 25 million passengers per annum is expected to be realised in the mid to late 1990s. Achievement of this level is dependent on the average aircraft load increasing to about 140 to 150 passengers per aircraft.

MR H. HEIJERMAN, Schiphol Airport, Amsterdam
When the new terminal at Gatwick Airport is completed, which new carriers will be recruited? How will passengers be given information on which carriers they will be flying with and from which terminal they will be departing?

MR BELL
British Airways has decided to transfer the whole of its Gatwick terminal operation to North Terminal. British Airways is one of the three handling agents at Gatwick and currently handles about 20 other airlines. Airlines are not being allocated or directed to any specific terminal. Airlines will be free to choose, subject to capacity constraints, at which terminal they wish to operate. Through intensive publicity provided by both the Press and travel agents, it is planned that passengers will be made aware, even before they leave for the airport, from which terminal their flight will be departing. Arrangements are being made to cope with those passengers who arrive at the airport without knowing to which terminal they should have gone.

MR K. DEHN, Flughafen Frankfurt am Main
My question concerns airport employment and the use made of public transport by airport employees. What is the modal split in transport used by employees at Gatwick to get to and from the airport?

What are the airport and transport authorities doing to encourage the use of public transport - subsidised transport, concessionary fares, special arrangements, interest free season ticket loans, etc?

MR BELL
Research carried out on behalf of the BAA plc in June and July 1986 indicated that the main means of transport to Gatwick by airport staff were as follows:

Private car	80%
British Rail	9%
Public Road Transport	3%
Works bus	3%
Other	5%

The issue of Gatwick's transport infrastructure and the problems of staff travelling to and from the airport will be the subject of a special study, led by Gatwick Airport Ltd, which is due to start in November 1987. Some companies already operate schemes on a small scale. In order to meet shift demands, some catering and cleaning companies prefer to operate works buses on a limited basis rather than to rely on public transport.

MR R. C. LAMBERT, Birmingham International Airport
In view of the runway restraints, particularly at peak times, and of the reliance being placed on the increasing use of larger aircraft to meet capacity, what would be the impact of the setting up of a hub and spoke - between say a US and European airline - with resultant demands by surges of connecting flights?

MR BELL
A hub and spoke operation already exists at Gatwick. A great deal of British Caledonia's traffic arises from this type of operation. The question, however, anticipates the possibility of scheduled operations developing to a large extent. Clearly, the proliferation of a large number of high frequency, low load services at peak time could reduce the capacity of the Airport by denying slots to large aircraft.

DR D. COUSSIOS, Commission of the European Communities, Brussels
I would like to come back to the answer that Mr Bell gave to Mr Kamdem. From the design point of view, it is already known that the following five factors are the main determinants with regard to airport capacity: runway complex capacity; airways configuration; passenger terminal buildings; airport access aspects (i.e. road system, public transport facilities, etc.); and airport parking facilities.
It is clear from what has been said that at Gatwick all the above factors can be developed, with the exception of the first one. This means that Gatwick's one runway will remain the dominating factor as far as airport capacity is concerned.

Could Mr Bell indicate, therefore, the highest actual number of runway movements per hour (or per annum) achieved at Gatwick Airport – given that one runway at Heathrow achieved a total number of 53 movements per hour?

MR BELL
Gatwick has achieved an all-time high of 53 movements in one hour on the single runway on two occasions. The first was on 3 June 1987 (the total included two helicopter movements) and again on 15 June 1987 when the total consisted only of aircraft. Fifty-one movements were recorded on 29 May 1986. However, for scheduling purposes a movement rate of 40 per hour is adopted; to adopt a rate significantly higher than this would result in average delays for both arriving and departing flights being at an unacceptable level.

MRS M. PAPATHANASSIOU, Commission of the European Communities, Brussels
Is Luton Airport considered to be part of the London airports system?

Does a direct Intercity link exist between Luton and London? If so, could details be given?

MR BELL
The answer is yes. When considering the capacity of the London airports system, the Government, the Civil Aviation Authority and the BAA plc take into account capacity which exists at Luton Airport. Its role in the London airports system is explained in the 1985 White Paper on Airports Policy (Cmnd 9542).

There is no rail link between London and Luton Airport. The town of Luton lies on an Intercity route (London – Bedford) and services currently operate on a half-hourly frequency during the day and at hourly intervals during the night every day of the week. There is a connecting coach service to the airport. Express coach services operate between London and Luton Airport on a regular basis, either direct or via Victoria Coach Station.

10 Stol: airport access made easy

J.F.B. SHAW, Director, Special Projects, Sales, A.F. TOPLIS, Manager, Market Analysis and Research, and R.K. WILLIAMSON, Supervisor, Special Projects, The de Havilland Aircraft Company of Canada, Ontario, Canada

The history of STOL from a viewpoint of a closely-involved manufacturer leads from an over-powered, noisy, single-engined bushplane to a very quiet, four-engined airliner operating into the centre of a metropolitan area. The design requirements for such an aircraft and the future applications of the concept are discussed.

The History of STOL

On August 16th, 1947 a stubby, high wing bushplane took-off for the first time at Downsview, Ontario. The DHC-2 Beaver, Fig. 1, was designed as a tough passenger and freight carrier. Thanks to a last-minute change in the choice of engine from Gypsy Queen to Wasp Junior, it was a somewhat overpowered aircraft, which made it ideal for its intended operation on floats or skis from small Canadian lakes. One very noticeable feature of the Beaver was its noise at take-off, the ungeared Wasp giving the propeller a tip Mach No. of 0.9. The Beaver was the first of a line of de Havilland aircraft which, through a combination of power and high lift aerodynamics – the Beaver was a very early employer of ailerons which drooped with flap deflection – have had Short Take-Off Landing, STOL, characteristics. On the other hand, all subsequent de Havilland propeller STOL aircraft have been markedly quieter than the Beaver.

The concept of using these aircrafts' qualities in a specialized airline service did not arise until the mid 1960's when the FAA mounted an emergency evacuation exercise in central New York called Metro '66. The Twin Otter and DHC-5 Buffalo were among many aircraft and helicopters which landed and took off at various simulated emergency strips in the city. The Twin Otter used Pier 26 in Manhattan and the Buffalo landed on a baseball ground in East River Park with 44 passengers on board.

The technical feasibility of operating fixed-wing aircraft into confined spaces in the downtown area of a major city was proven by the demonstration, although of course without any of the normal allowances for obstacle clearance and engine failure.

De Havilland reasoned that an aircraft with STOL capabilities could provide a convenient downtown-to-downtown air service. Airports were congested at that time too and a premium service which would save the short-haul business traveller the inconveniences suffered at a major airport, was seen as a potential market for STOL aircraft (ref. 1).

The Northeast Corridor Investigation

In 1968, the U.S. Civil Aeronautics Board instituted the Northeast Corridor VTOL Investigation, whose purpose was to establish the technical feasibility and economic viability of helicopter service between city centres in the Boston-Washington megalopolis. De Havilland saw this as an opportunity to promote the concept of fixed-wing STOL aircraft and submitted an extensive market forecast, modal split, and economic analysis of a STOL system in the corridor (Ref. 2). It discussed the sites required, the aircraft types involved from the Twin Otter to a future Augmentor Wing Aircraft, forecast the traffic on each route over time, and showed that the system would be profitable. One hundred and one Dash 7s would be required by 1978, the de Havilland brief stated and 174 by 1982.

Fig. 1. DHC-2 Beaver floatplane take-off

Phase 1 of the Investigation concluded on an upbeat note. The CAB Examiner stated:

'A new additional air service between major cities in the Northeast Corridor, to be provided by STOL, VTOL and VSTOL aircraft using central city landing sites and sites in densely populated suburban areas is technically and economically feasible and it will fill a pressing need to reduce congestion and delay, and enhance the quality of air transportation in the markets.' (Ref. 3)

In Phase 2, the cities involved in the inquiry were scheduled to recommend potential sites for STOLports. Eastern and American Airlines conducted trials with the Breguet 941, or MD-188, as it was known in the U.S.A. under McDonnell-Douglas sponsorship. This was a military, four-engined STOL turboprop aircraft with almost the entire wing enveloped in the propeller slipstream. As a safety feature, like the present-day V-22 Osprey, the engines were interconnected by a shaft. The trial showed that non-interfering flights into unused runways at major airports were feasible and could considerably increase airport capacity.

In May 1970, de Havilland received a Request for Proposal from American Airlines for six DHC-5 Buffalo aircraft equipped to airline standards and certificated to operate from 2,000ft. STOLports. These aircraft were to carry 36 passengers each. The Buffalo had been in production for some five years for the military but would have required considerable modification and offloading to meet the 2,000 ft. field length requirement under civilian rules. American intended the six Buffalo for a demonstration service between Washington D.C. and Manhattan. They felt that the New York area was the key and that a demonstration elsewhere would have little impact. It was decided to use Chelsea, on the Hudson River, as the 'for-instance' site of a New York STOLport (ref. 4).

Public Opposition to STOL

In June 1970, the FAA accepted an unsolicited

proposal from American Airlines to study the concept of a temporary STOLport in the Manhattan area. The idea proposed was FIMS, a Floating Interim Manhattan STOLport. FIMS was to consist of a deck mounted on top of a number of scrap ships (Fig. 2) It had the advantage of being relatively cheap, 14.5 million dollars, and could be towed to other locations as necessary. The citizens of Chelsea only became aware of the American Airlines' study when a press release was made, announcing the contract award and the possible location of the STOLport. A citizen's group, 'Chelsea-against-the STOLport', which was in existence already as a result of the CAB's hearings, actively demonstrated outside American's office, held meetings, and lobbied energetically until the FAA Transportation Secretary cancelled any further consideration of the FIMS in March 1971 (ref. 5).

The Dash 7 Specification

The Dash 7's initial design stems back to January 1968 when a 'Planning Brief in Respect to a new DHC Airplane, DHP-35' (ref. 6), laid out the concept in the following terms:

'There is now developing a high priority requirement to accelerate the introduction of economic STOL aircraft operating from special STOLports close to city centres and using separate navigation and approach devices at major airports'.

It went on to note that a 'new medium STOL' passenger/cargo aircraft should be ready to enter service in 1971...'

Table 1

Dash 7 Development

	Proposed Aircraft		Current Aircraft
	DHP -35	DHC -7	Dash 7 S.100
			In
	Jan.	Dec.	Service
Date	1968	1968	1977
Passenger Capacity-Seats	35	40	50
Engines CP and W PT6A	-27	-50	-50
T.O. SHP	620	840	1,120
Max. Takeoff Weight-lb	26,500	30,640	44,000
Max. Landing Weight-lb	26,000	30,000	42,000
Operational Wt.Empty-lb	16,500	19,740	27,690
T.O. Field Length, ISA, SL at Max. T.O.W.-ft.	1,600	1,900	2,260
Land. Field Length, ISA, SL at Max .Landing Wt.-ft.	1,600	1,900	1,950
Max. Cruise Speed-KTAS	200	235	231

Source: Refs. 6, 7 and 8

Fig. 2. Floating interim Manhattan STOLport

Investigation of the performance requirements showed that a four-engined aircraft would be needed, and the main characteristics of the aircraft were as shown in Table 1. By December 1968 it had grown from an initial concept of literally a double Twin Otter with 30/38 passengers and four 620 SHP PT6A-27 engines to a 40-passenger, four 840 SHP PT6A-50-engined aircraft. The specification noted that the noise levels would have to be low, and the target was set at 95 PNdB at 500 feet at takeoff. The empty weight was to be 19,740 lb. and the takeoff weight, for a 200 n.m. stage with full passengers and reserves for a 1,900 ft., Part 25 takeoff, was 39,640 lb.

Surveys of potential customers indicated a need for a larger aircraft, and the final aircraft with help from a co-operative engine manufacturer, came close to the expected field length and cruise speed, although carrying some ten more passengers. The design effort required to meet the demanding specification for downtown STOL service and yet maintain the desired noise target was nevertheless significant.

The aircraft first flew in March 1975, receiving certification in the spring of 1977 (Fig. 3).

Profitability of Operation

The targets for the Dash 7 design were that it should:

- be capable of consistent, scheduled operation from 2,000 ft. STOLport.

- offer a comfort level acceptable to regular travellers on trunk air lines.

- operate unobtrusively with very low noise and no visible smoke.

- be capable of profitable operation over stage lengths from 50 to over 300 miles.

The question of the 2,000 ft. field length, whether it should be 1,500 ft. or 3,000 ft. or some other value, has always been a moot point. Ref. 9 stated ... '2,000 ft. was considered (by de Havilland) to be

- about the upper limit for a downtown STOL-port, because of land building costs. Two thousand feet is by no means an extraordinary building length. The buildings of a large shopping plaza are about the same length as a STOLport.

- Feasible for addition to existing hub airports.

- A field length of the same order as our Twin Otter customers were used to - although, of course, to different operating rules.'

The comfort level for any aircraft with the Dash 7's wing loading, 51 psf, cannot match that of a typical jet, but the Dash 7 has proven to be quite acceptable to passengers in places as widely separated as England, New England, Guinea and New Guinea.

The Dash 7 has established a standard of quietness and environmental acceptability which has been accepted worldwide.

When the Dash 7 operator takes advantage of the aircraft's STOL and other unique characteristics, there can be a very positive reflection on the profitability of operation.

MacGregor (Ref. 10) has shown that the Dash 7's ability to make use of separate access landing system (SALS) runways can provide a competitive advantage for its operator. Figs. 4 and 5 compare the Dash 7 Series 200, a proposed development of the Dash 7, with the Dash 8 Series 300 and indicate that there is a saving in trip direct operating costs through using SALS. Another comparison, operation from 800 metre runways at ISA+15 deg.C, is given in Figs. 6 and 7. The Dash 7's savings in this case are rather more dramatic.

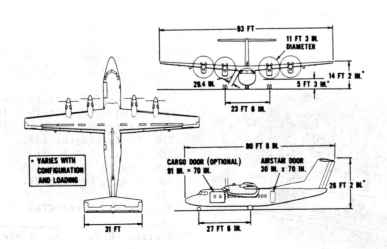

Fig. 3. Dash 7 general arrangement

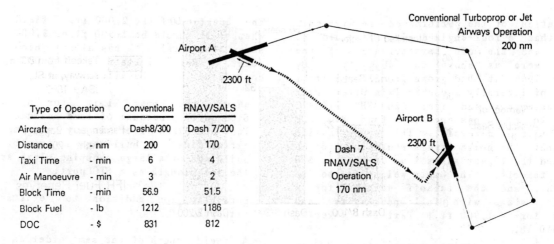

Type of Operation		Conventional	RNAV/SALS
Aircraft		Dash8/300	Dash 7/200
Distance	- nm	200	170
Taxi Time	- min	6	4
Air Manoeuvre	- min	3	2
Block Time	- min	56.9	51.5
Block Fuel	- lb	1212	1186
DOC	- $	831	812

Fig. 4. RNAV/SALS alternative

WORLDWIDE APPLICATIONS

The design characteristics of the Dash 7 lend themselves to a wide variety of applications around the world. STOL performance characteristics provide a means of developing suitable approach and departure routings in a number of difficult airport and airspace situations.

London City Airport

At London City Airport, both the environmental and physical constraints of the site have made it necessary to utilize STOL technology in the overall airport plan. The installation of an airport in the midst of a redevelopment project such as the London Docklands area is possible because of the small amount of real estate required to accommodate a STOL aircraft. The Dash 7's high angle glide path and steep departure path provide a safe and logical method of approaching over other structures in the area. The aircraft's low noise footprint drastically reduces the environmental impact London City Airport will have on the surrounding community.

The Dash 7 will use a 7.5 deg. glideslope to approach the runway at the London City Airport from either east or west. Guidance will be provided by a special high glideslope angle Instrument Landing System. All weather operations will be accommodated down to limits of at least 300 foot ceiling and one mile visibility. As is usual, when experience is gained, these approach limits may be lowered.

Although radar will be available for all London City Airport arrivals, some operators will use onboard Area Navigation (RNAV) in order to enhance the transition onto the approach through the London TMA. Other air traffic at Heathrow, Stansted and Gatwick will be taken into consideration during the initial approach procedure to London City Airport. RNAV can be used to navigate the aircraft automatically on a predetermined flight path through the TMA and onto the final approach to the runway. In this way, the aircraft will be able to approach on a dedicated flight path to the airport in accordance with required spacing from other traffic in the area and free of other control zones in proximity of the approach. The RNAV equipment will provide the

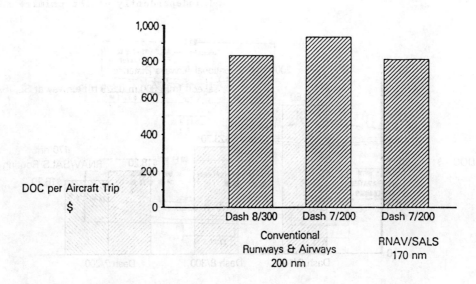

Fig. 5. DOC reduction using RNAV/SALS

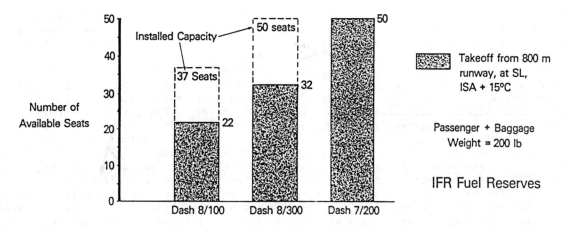

Fig. 6. Payload capability on 200 nm sector

vectored guidance and the controller will only monitor the approach with considerably reduced workload.

Accessibility to the airport is just as important in the air as it is on the ground. If flights coming into and out of London City Airport are delayed by other air traffic in the area, the advantage of using this STOLport is lost. Utilization of special avionics, coupled with the STOL performance capabilities of the Dash 7 can provide separate and discrete access to the STOLport, bypassing the normal traffic delays associated with a busy terminal hub area.

Ground accessibility to the airport is also convenient and time efficient. The London City Airport is located just 6.5 miles from the City of London, or a mere 20 minute taxi ride from St. Paul's. Also light rail transit, a part of the overall Docklands redevelopment scheme will no doubt, eventually be constructed to the STOLport site.

Washington National Airport Separate Access

Some elements of the London City Airport approach procedures are being used to enhance airport accessibility in other locations. Washington National Airport is one of America's busiest hub airports located on a relatively small acreage close to the center of the U.S. capital. During the late 70's, Ransome Airlines, one of the more prominent commuter airlines serving the North-East Corridor was experiencing difficulty in accessing Washington National Airport. The higher operating costs of flight delays due to air traffic congestion and diversion were reducing the airline's profitability. By using an on-board 3-dimensional Area Navigation System and the STOL capabilities of the Dash 7, Ransome Airlines developed a concept called the Separate Access Landing System (SALS).

The SALS concept uses RNAV to lead the aircraft through a busy terminal area, usually by a discrete route, and onto an intersecting stub runway or secondary reliever runway where the aircraft stops short of the major runway in use. The operation takes place simultaneously and independently of the primary runway in use.

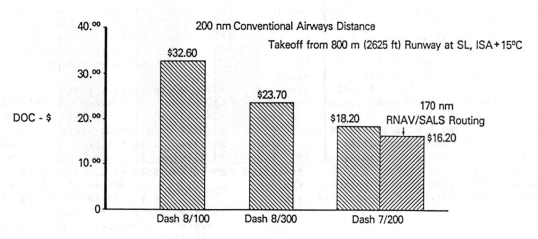

Fig. 7. Direct operating cost per seat trip

At Washington National, Runway 33 is used as the stub when Runway 36 is the primary runway in use. From the threshold of Runway 33 to the intersection of 33/36 there is 2,380 feet of available landing distance for the aircraft. This landing distance is well within the Dash 7's capabilities. If a balked landing is necessary the aircraft is even able to touchdown at the threshold, suffer an engine failure, take-off again and turn in plenty of time to avoid any portion of the intersecting runway. Ransome has been using the Washington National SALS approach procedure for the past five years. Recently, the airline has been purchased by Pan American Airlines as its commuter arm. Ransome/Pan Am Express is now using the same SALS concept to more efficiently access JFK Airport, Pan Am's largest hub.

Mountain Stolports

STOL performance capabilities can also provide accessibility to airports surrounded by high terrain. Often, more than enough landing space can be provided on the bottom of a valley floor, but the surrounding terrain can inhibit the development of an all weather instrument procedure suitable to accommodate the shallow 3 deg. glideslope angles common to most conventional aircraft. The Dash 7 is capable of a 7.5 deg. glideslope in IFR conditions. Its engine-out climb performance is higher than normal because of its 4-engine configuration. If one engine fails, only 25% of power is lost as compared to the 50% lost by a twin-engined aircraft.

Protected airspace requirements surrounding approach routings are tailored so as to fit the steeper arrival and departure routes. New precision approach aids, such as the Microwave Landing System (MLS) provide reliable and accurate signal propagation in areas with high surrounding terrain. MLS can also generate high angle glidepaths of up to 10 deg. and therefore provide an excellent navigational aid for high terrain STOL approaches.

In Norway, Wideroe's has been an operator, first of the DHC-6 Twin Otter and currently of Dash 7's, on a chain of STOLports stretching along the rugged coastline. Some STOLports are only 800 metres in length but service continues throughout the year in some very difficult meteorological conditions.

In the U.S.A., Valdez Alaska is an excellent example of how STOL can provide a decisive advantage over conventional approach methodologies. The conventional approach procedure into Valdez is a localizer/DME (no glideslope) approach with limits of 3,000 ft. ceiling and five miles visibility. The STOL MLS approach operates to limits of 500 ft. and 3/4 mile visibility. All Weather operations are thus greatly enhanced through the use of STOL performance characteristics.

Pemberton, sited in the Rockies in British Columbia, is the site of a current investigation and flight test program. Pemberton is about 19 miles from one of North America's largest ski resort areas. The airport is located on the bottom of a meandering valley floor, some 677 feet above sea level. The coastal mountain chain which lines each side of the valley reaches altitudes of 7,000 to 8,000 feet ASL. A 7.7 deg. MLS glideslope guides the Dash 7 down into the mountain valley and ultimately to the Pemberton Airport. However, if the flight crew fails to gain visual contact with the runway, a second MLS azimuth and two Non-Directional Beacons provide precision track guidance from the Missed Approach Point out through the valley and back to a safe altitude.

The missed approach procedure incorporates three turns which follow the valley floor in order to provide the required clearance for the aircraft. Pemberton will be a challenging procedure, and when certificated will allow airline operations in yet another difficult airport environment.

Other Applications

STOL technology can provide reliable all weather accessibility to a number of airport locations at which operations under conventional methods may be very restricted. Proposals are being considered for sites, such as in the Amsterdam harbour area and also at Sheffield to provide a link with London's City Airport. In Hong Kong, STOL technology may provide an answer to increased congestion at Kai Tak International through the addition of a second runway suitable for special STOL procedures.

In Hawaii, the West Maui Airport opened on March 1st as the state's first Stolport. Hawaiian Airlines' Dash 7 fleet will use the new facility in order to provide a quiet and efficient access to one of Hawaii's foremost tourist destinations.

Future Concepts

At some point in the future, the price of fuel will rise once more and exploration and drilling for oil far out in the ocean will start once again in volume. When that happens, an innovative concept for the use of STOL, which has been around for several years, will be revived. Fig. 8 shows the Seaforth STOLport, a concept of Seaforth Maritime of Aberdeen. It consists of a 1900 ft. deck mounted on below-surface pontoons, with hangars, recreation, crew and propulsion facilities at lower levels. One such vessel could be anchored at the centre of a developing oil field and act as the major airport for oil workers of the field. Its justification lies in the large difference in operating costs between helicopters and fixed wing STOL aircraft and in the limited range and

Fig. 8. Dash 7 - Seaforth STOLport for offshore transportation

relatively slow speed of existing helicopters. Because of the provision of recreation facilities, it would also be possible to extend the time of service of the crews on the rigs, thereby achieving further savings.

Looking even further into the future, Fig. 9 illustrates a possible civil development of the Boeing-Bell V-22 Osprey operating out of a downtown heliport. With cruise speeds of some 300 Kt this vehicle would outstrip present day, fixed wing STOL aircraft and, with much of the development costs paid for by its military progenitor, could bring its cost of operation into the range of viability for airline applications.

Conclusions

Downtown STOL has had a very long gestation but is now about to begin its most important world application here in London. Once the convenience of the system has become appreciated by the travelling public and once the surrounding neighbourhoods come to realise the minimal nature of its environmental impact, the spread of these handy STOLports to other cities in Europe becomes inevitable.

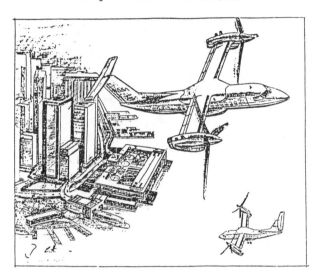

Fig. 9. Potential future downtown tilt - rotor operations

References

1. TOPLIS, A.F. 'Downtown-to-Downtown STOL Air Service' Royal Aeronautical Society Symposium Urban STOL operations, 28 March 1984.

2. DE HAVILLAND AIRCRAFT OF CANADA 'An Intercity STOL Transportation System' NECI CAB Docket 19078, Direct Exhibits, May, 1969.

3. CIVIL AERONAUTICS BOARD 'Northeast Corridor VTOL Investigation' Docket 19078, Initial decision by Examiner E. Robert Seaver, February 2,1970, CAB, Washington, D.C.

4. RANSONE, R.K. 'Chelsea STOLport--The Airline View' SAE Paper 760523, May 18-20, 1976, SAE Inc., Warrendale, Pa.

5. SCHWARTZMAN, Jacqueline 'STOL and the Residential Community' SAE Paper 760524, May 18-20, 1976, SAE Inc., Warrendale, Pa.

6. DE HAVILLAND AIRCRAFT OF CANADA 'Planning Brief in Respect to a New DHC Airplane'. Project Designation DHP-35, DHC Corporate Planning Market Research, January 12, 1968.

7. DE HAVILLAND AIRCRAFT OF CANADA 'DHC-7 Preliminary Design Specification' 7/PM/5, Appendix 1, December 1968.

8. DE HAVILLAND AIRCRAFT OF CANADA 'Dash 7 Performance Data' Aeroc 7.2.AC.20, Issue 6, February 1979.

9. BULLER F.H. and TOPLIS A.F. 'The DHC-7, First Generation Transport Category STOL - Particular Design Challenges'. AIAA Paper 72-809 Los Angeles Aug. 7-9, 1972.

10. MACGREGOR R.I. 'Direct Operating Costs and Related Considerations in the Selection of Regional Airliners'. Regional/Commuter Operations Symposium. Tokyo, 23 October, 1985.

11 London City Airport — a new approach to city centre travel

R.N. SAINSBURY, Director, John Mowlem and Company plc, Brentford, UK

The London Docks will soon become the base for a new form of international traffic when Britain's first inner city airport opens for business this autumn. The airport facilities are described and the progress of gaining planning consent and committing the development is recounted. The investment perspective is explained. The business passenger has been identified as the target market; the manner in which the airport and its management are aimed to serve this market is described. Means of access to and from London City Airport and its place in the overall renaissance of Docklands are also considered. The final subject area addressed is that of airline attitudes and public response.

INTRODUCTION

1. This paper does not aim to describe the design and construction of London City Airport as an engineering project, though perhaps one day such a paper may be written. Instead it sets out to record the project in human terms, by reference to the passengers it will serve and the facilities it will offer them, the planning and environmental issues and the political dimension of the project, the response of airlines and public to its creation, and the investment perceptions which have been the guiding force behind the development.

2. Before embarking on a detailed case history it may be well to give an outline description of the project as currently being built.

3. The site lies between the King George V and Royal Albert docks in the London Borough of Newham (see Fig. 1). It is within the Royal Docks development area, a part of the overall 2000 hectares of obsolete docklands being redeveloped under the auspices of the London Docklands Development Corporation (LDDC). It is within 10 km of the financial centre of London - the City.

4. Fig. 2 shows in simple outline the facility being provided. The overall runway length is 1080m but is misleading, for the declared runway length is 762m; the explanation is that there are two overlapping runways, this displaced threshold solution being required to meet planning constraints in relation to existing or possible future structures. The principal candidate aircraft with the STOL (short take-off and landing) characteristics

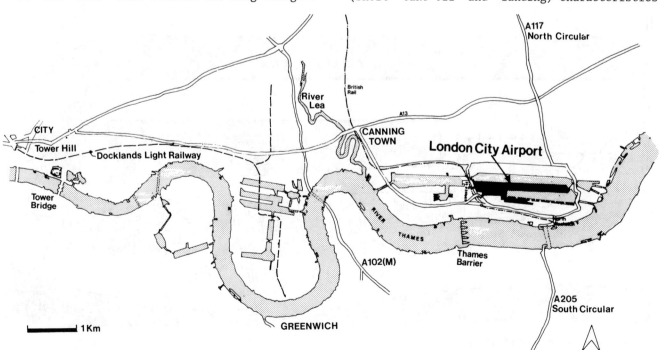

Fig. 1. Location of London City Airport

Airports for people. Thomas Telford Limited, London, 1988

required for the airport is the de Havilland Dash 7, a 50-seat fully pressurised turboprop aircraft with exceptionally good noise characteristics.

5. The passenger terminal is situated at the western end of the King George V dock, the departure pier extending westwards and offering ten aircraft stands. The fire, rescue and maintenance (FRM) building, fuel store and maintenance hangar are all sited at the west end of the airport. Car parking, at ground level, will be close to the terminal, on the south side of the King George V dock. The terminal is designed to handle 1.2 million passenger movements per year, this number relating to the constraints on numbers of aircraft movements imposed within the granted planning consent.

6. Dash 7 operations will focus principally within a range of 400 nautical miles, a circle of this radius containing a market of some 150 million persons, twice the number to be found within an equivalent circle centred on New York City. It is expected that London City services will be particularly useful to business travellers, and the design of the facility is based on this perceived market sector.

Case History

7. London City Airport is a development which has been created by, and at the time of writing is wholly owned by, John Mowlem & Co PLC.

8. The genesis of the idea was early in 1981 when Philip Beck, Chairman of Mowlem discussed with Reg Ward, Chief Executive of LDDC, the possibility of an airport for STOL aircraft as an element within the latter's concept of creating a transport interchange in the Royal Docks area. The centre quay between the Royal Albert and the King George V docks was identified as having many desirable characteristics

and detailed feasibility studies were set in hand. In these early days help was afforded by Bill Bryce of Brymon Airways, for example in organising a trial landing by a Dash 7 in Docklands for the purpose of educating public and politicians and assuaging their fears of the environmental impact of a STOLport in the East End.

9. A key feature of the site was that it was in east London in an area remote from the main airports and particularly close to the City. The perceived market was for business travellers to and from central London to domestic and shorthaul European destinations. There was also hope that Docklands itself would undergo a renaissance and become in its own right a thriving area generating business for the airport.

10. Although a greater runway length could have been accommodated on the site itself, the design had to take into account some tall mill buildings to the west and the intended future East London River Crossing bridge to the east. Allowing for these obstructions only aircraft with exceptional STOL characteristics would be able to use the airport, the Dash 7 being very much the candidate aircraft. Right from the start, therefore, the investor had to be aware not only of the innovation risk attached to such a novel venture but also the risk imposed by limitations of aircraft types. Nonetheless it seemed that there was a unique opportunity and that the inner city airport concept could be an idea whose time had come. An initial financial model indicated attractive returns; in December 1982 a planning application was submitted to the LDDC, the planning authority for the area.

11. The land was in the ownership of the Port of London Authority (PLA). Following confidential discussions with the Authority, Mowlem in 1982 agreed heads of terms for a long lease for

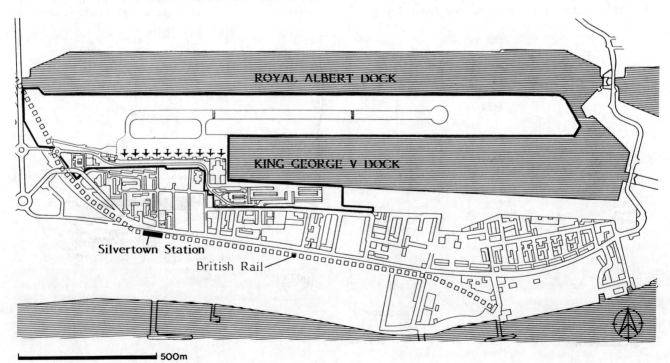

Silvertown Station
British Rail

500m

Fig. 2. General layout

use of the site as an airport. By March 1983, a formal "Agreement for Lease" was signed providing, in effect, an option on the land while the designs and the financial appraisal were developed up to the point of an investment decision.

12. In January 1983 notification was received that the planning application had been called in by the Secretary of State and that there would be a public inquiry. Mowlem appointed lawyers and experts to prepare the case. The hearing was scheduled to start at the beginning of June and was thought likely to last some five weeks. Two public opinion polls showed the local population to be strongly in favour. Naturally enough, some local people opposed the airport because of environmental concern; the major opposition, however, emerged from political bodies, namely the London Borough of Newham and the Greater London Council; the LDDC supported the application. Such was the range of evidence heard that the inquiry did not conclude until the end of October 1983, twenty-one weeks after it started.

13. It was a further nineteen months (May 1985) before outline planning consent was finally established, the planning process being taken right through to a judicial review of the Secretary of State's decision. Various conditions were attached to the consent: noise levels were specified; limits on the number of aircraft movements per day were set, effectively limiting annual passenger movements to just over one million; it was required that the application for detailed consent should incorporate displaced threshold runways; other points of detail were also covered.

14. As soon as the public inquiry hearings had finished, the developer had had to make a decision. Either expenditure would be stopped until the outcome regarding planning consent was known or alternatively the detailed design could be progressed but at the risk of considerable further sums. The decision had been to progress the design while awaiting the planning outcome and thus when the outline consent was finally granted the developer was virtually ready to submit for detailed consent.

15. Needless to say, in the period November 1983 to May 1985 it was not just design that was undertaken but a further financial update and appraisal. The full obligations of the lease would be undertaken by Mowlem upon issuing to the PLA a "Construction Notice"; accordingly, although the development would inherently remain a speculative one, the best possible financial appraisal had to be made before issuing that "Construction Notice". From May 1985 it was not only the application for detailed consent which had to be progressed. Detailed consent was granted in February but negotiations between LDDC and PLA about freehold ownership dragged on until April 1986, ultimately being the factor determining the start date.

16. Mowlem Management Ltd (the management contractor) began work on site in April, the first task being the demolition of massive dockside buildings across most of the 40-hectare site. Notwithstanding the scale of these clearance works, by Christmas 1986 the

concrete runway was complete and the terminal building was largely roofed over. At the time of writing, the target date for start of passenger carrying operations is October 1987.

The Investment Perspective

17. Before describing in detail the facility that is now being built it is well to consider the investment perspective in this whole undertaking, for design emerges in relation to perceived investment possibility and chosen investment strategy - not vice versa.

18. Inevitably the first concept of an airport in Docklands was framed simply on the basis of its being "a good idea". More structured reasoning led to the conclusion that the principal market sector to benefit from an inner city airport would be the business sector - but would the passenger demand be quantitatively such as to justify the investment?

19. Prior to the public inquiry the LDDC had commissioned an analysis of potential passenger demand for such an airport. This was a sophisticated analysis incorporating complex appraisals of inter-modal transfer in passenger behaviour and it forecast a very strong demand for the airport. This was a comfort to Mowlem but the analysis which they themselves commissioned was of a simpler and more specific nature. It was based on a study only of existing air travellers, and was restricted to one category, terminating business passengers. By consideration of passenger origin and destination in the different London areas the numbers of passengers on different routes who would gain an overall journey time advantage was assessed. It was calculated that terminating business passengers alone would utilise the capacity available within the planning consent - which is of course a small number of passenger movements in terms of those at the major airports serving London.

20. As a private investment of an innovative nature and with imposed capacity limits, it was never perceived that London City Airport would be able to afford to offer cut-price landing and passenger charges nor was it expected that airlines using the airport would be able to offer cut-price fares. The airport will be selling "position" and selling it to those for whom convenience is ultimately more important than price, hence the emphasis on the business passenger in the feasibility analysis; there will of course be leisure passengers, but each one will be a bonus in terms of the basis of the investment. This conservative approach to passenger mixtures was applied because of the numerous other uncertainties inherent in the project.

21. The investment being predicated upon the business passenger, it has been felt important throughout the design process to ensure that the airport will provide the facilities and the service that the business passenger wants. Some of the most important of these characteristics are: lack of hassle; speedy check-in and other passenger processing; minimum of unscheduled delays; efficient baggage handling; good flight frequency; business quality and range of services; courteous and efficient

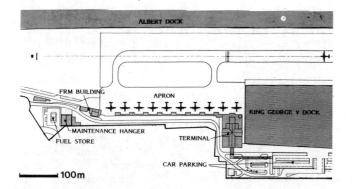

Fig. 3. Layout of airport facilities

staff.   In terms of such qualities it is intended that London City offer uniquely high standards, and the means of doing so will be described later in this paper.

22. During the long run-up to the award of the outline planning consent the Mowlem expectation was to bring in risk-sharing joint venture partners prior to issuing the "Construction Notice" and being totally committed to build and operate the airport. Accordingly heads of agreement were negotiated with two partners (40% and 10% investors) such that the Mowlem interest (and risk) would be reduced to 50% of the investment.

23. For reasons connected with his own business situation, not reasons related to the project itself, the 40% investor later withdrew. Not a particularly remarkable event, one might say, but the timing made it a very significant event, for this withdrawal occurred in the same week that the resolution of land ownership was achieved (para 15). After four years of effort, the project at last had a green light to proceed but was suddenly not in compliance with the promoter's previously determined investment criteria.

24. Detailed joint venture negotiations in respect of this sort of venture are laborious and time consuming; a decision to delay until replacement investor/investors had been found and a formal shareholders agreement concluded could have led to a long delay - which would of itself damage the credibility of the project. The Mowlem board decided to commit the project at its own risk without delay; this apparent departure from previous criteria was made possible by two factors:

1) There was by then evidence of real airline interest to operate from London City.

2) In the time since the planning application Mowlem had made acquisitions and had more than doubled in size, so the airport was no longer such a large project in terms of overall resources.

25. At the time of writing Mowlem still own 100% of London City Airport Ltd. Arrangements are just being finalised for the issue of shares to the 10% minority holder originally intending to participate. There are no immediate plans for selling off any more of the company.

The Airport

26. Fig. 3 shows in greater detail the layout

of the airport facilities. A new road layout west of the airport is currently being developed by LDDC and this will incorporate a new roundabout at the entrance to London City. Entering the airport one passes the fuel farm and an aircraft maintenance hangar to the south, the FRM buildings to the north. The main approach road then runs straight towards the terminal with the passenger pier on the left. This pier has a single pitched roof rising on its north face to a height of 9m above the airport apron.   This height (far greater than needed for a two-storey pier) has been constructed because the pier serves as a sound screen for residents south of the airport, adequate sound screening being a requirement of the planning consent.   The approach road is to be edged with lawns on either side, with a continuous line of trees on the south and grouped planting of trees and shrubs to the north, against the face of the pier.

27. The road passes the terminal via a narrow neck of land, illustrative of the disciplined design that has been necessary to "shoehorn" the airport on to the site. Space immediately south of the terminal affords drop-off facilities and metered car parking. Adjacent to this is the main car park. Parking initially will be at ground level, but as and when demand justifies the expenditure, it is expected that a multi-storey car park will be constructed to ensure that all passengers are parked conveniently close to the terminal rather than spreading further and further along the

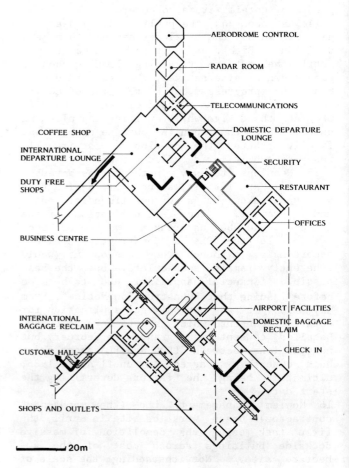

Fig. 4. Passenger flow through terminal

dockside. Access for emergency vehicles is provided between the east face of the terminal building and the western edge of the King George V dock. Entrance to the terminal is through the main doors in its south elevation.

28. Passenger flow through the terminal is illustrated in Fig. 4. The departing passenger will check in immediately to the right of the entrance door and, if departing without making use of any landside concession facilities, will proceed by escalator, stairs or lift to the departure lounges on the first floor, passing through a security check serving both domestic and international departures. Domestic passengers will, on flight call, progress directly to the domestic gate lounge; international passengers will pass along the upper level of the departure pier to the respective international gate lounges. No substantial dwell time in the gate lounges is intended.

29. Arriving domestic passengers will pass directly from the apron into the domestic baggage collection hall; arriving international passengers will progress to the international baggage collection hall via the ground level of the pier.

30. Other areas of the building are given over to operational use, to regulatory authorities, or to concessions as indicated. The nature of concessions available to the passengers is described in a later paragraph. The terminal has been sized to afford, at capacity of 1.2 million movements, a reasonably spacious environment without excessive crowd densities; in other words it has been designed to accord with the business traveller's desired ambience and lack of hassle. It can be seen from the flow direction arrows that passage through the terminal is extremely direct. While it is recognised that not all businessmen are in quite such a hurry as they think they are, and that many will have time to spare and will wish to make use of the concession and business opportunities in the terminal, the staffing levels will be set to ensure that the potential of very direct transit through the terminal is not lost and that quick times can be achieved by both arriving and departing passengers.

31. This lack of "imposed delay" will also apply in relation to the aircraft themselves. Times for embarking and alighting will be much less than would apply for larger aircraft. A

further saving will be that there will be little time spent in taxiing around the airport. Indeed there is hardly an opportunity to spend time so doing - a typical taxiing foray at Heathrow if applied from the end of the London City runway would get one halfway to the Bank of England!

Concession Facilities

32. Use of the title "concession facilities" does not necessarily imply that every activity will be let as a concession; it is a convenient and generally understood term for ancillary facilities available to the passenger. In the case of London City the aim has been to provide all the normal facilities, plus any others that the business passenger might want, and to provide them at a level of quality suited to this sector of the market.

33. The landside concessions available directly from the concourse will comprise banking and exchange facilities, confectionery/tobacco/newsagent and a flower shop, together with desks for car hire and hotel reservations. On the first floor, on the west side of the terminal, will be a telecommunications and business centre, while the landside bar, cafeteria and restaurant find themselves on the east side. At this point it is worth commenting that the bar and the restaurant, and also the domestic departure lounge, will command a magnificient view along the length of the King George V dock, a view which will also take in the runway itself and afford the opportunity to see the aircraft demonstrating their unusual STOL performance in landing and take-off.

34. As it is expected that three quarters of the traffic will be international, the international lounge and its concessions have been the focus of much attention during the design process. There will be a pleasant airside bar, and well presented retailing of high quality duty free and tax free goods.

External & Internal Appearance

35. Subject to the necessary cost constraints in a private development of this sort, every effort is being made in the design of the facility to ensure that its external appearance makes it a pleasing and worthy building to take its place as the first new investment in the Royal Docks redevelopment, and that the interiors are such that the users will take pleasure from them and be able to enjoy the overall ambience.

36. An artist's impression of the finished terminal viewed from the runway is given in Fig. 5. The general treatment of the cladding and glazing is such that if the reproduction were in colour it would be seen to be in a range of blue tones.

37. The chief feature of the interior design is the concourse itself, which has a clear height of 11m with clerestory glazing at its uppermost level ensuring a light and airy feel. This feel will be further enhanced by the full height glazing of the central portals to west and east, the latter of which opens up the view of the dock.

38. Without the facility for colour reproduction, and prior to the actual completion of

Fig. 5. Artist's impression of terminal

Fig. 6. Artist's impression of concourse

Fig. 7. Artist's impression of international departure lounge

the building it is difficult to convey any real picture of the interior design of particular areas, but Figs. 6 and 7 give a preliminary impression of the concourse itself and of the international departure lounge. Those wishing to know what the airport really looks like must come and use it.

Access to and from London City

39. It is anticipated that the majority of passengers will use cars or taxis to come to and from the airport, which lies within the central London taxi area. Even from day one, however, this will not be the only available means, for British Rail's North London Line serves this area and there is a station (currently named Silvertown) within 400m of the terminal. This will be useful to those travelling to or from the crescent of north inner London through which the line passes but it will not materially assist travellers aiming for the City itself.

40. While it is expected that road travel on

a door-to-door basis will always be favourite for the target market sector of business travellers, it is anticipated that London City will within about three years be able to offer a highly efficient rail alternative for those making the short journey to or from the City. The Docklands Light Railway is a rapid transit system currently being built for the London Transport Executive and LDDC by Mowlem in joint venture with GEC. The initial contract, due to come into service in July 1987 was for a link from Tower Hill to the southern tip of the Isle of Dogs Enterprise Zone (with a spur north to Stratford) as shown on Fig 1. At the time of writing, a parliamentary bill has been enacted authorising the extension of the Docklands Light Railway westwards to the Bank of England underground interchange, the heart of the City. It is hoped that the contract for this work will have been awarded by the time the World Airports Conference takes place. Very recently a parliamentary bill has been deposited in respect of an eastward extension to Beckton and

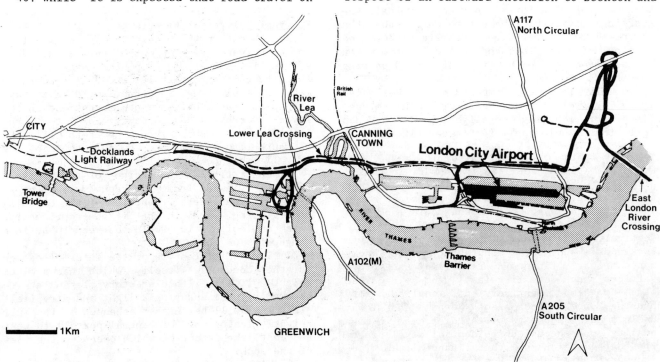

Fig. 8. Programmed improvements to road and rail infrastructure

the Royal Docks, as indicated on Fig. 8. When this part of the line is built it will not come directly to the airport terminal, but the station north of the Connaught Crossing will be not much more than one kilometre from the door of the terminal and a shuttle bus will offer passengers a high frequency service linking to the Docklands Light Railway. Overall journey time to the Bank of England will be extremely short even during rush hours.

41. At present, road access between the City and the airport is trouble free at most times of the day but there is congestion at rush hours, particularly at the Canning Town round-about where Silvertown Way (the normal road to use coming to or from the airport) joins the A13 main eastern road.

42. With the rapid growth of activity in the area as Docklands is redeveloped, it would have to be expected that traffic conditions would get much worse if no road improvements were made. Fortunately LDDC has a comprehensive plan for new road construction which is intended to keep ahead of the growth of demand and should ensure progressive improvement in journey times to London City. The new roads planned for construction are shown on Fig. 8 and they include a new crossing of the river Lea, by-passing the whole of the Canning Town road complex. There are also plans for a new Thames crossing just east of the airport site which, if granted planning consent following its recent public inquiry, will greatly improve the passenger catchment zone south of the river. It can be seen that, in toto, the outlook for excellent access to the airport is bright.

The Renaissance of Docklands

43. The above description of forthcoming infrastructure improvements in the vicinity of London City Airport calls for a more detailed reference to the burgeoning nature of develop-ment in the area as a whole. This does not claim to be a major national airport; it is a neighbourhood airport, a community airport. It will serve the neighbourhood of central and east London, and it will serve the business and financial community. The questions of whether it is needed, and of whether it is well sited to serve these specific markets, cannot be answered in isolation from study of the dynamics of those markets. Population and business locations are not eternally static.

44. By this criterion also, it can be seen that the timing of the investment in London City is propitious. Few people taking a tour of derelict east London six years ago could have dreamed what the scene would look like today. The newspaper industry has moved col-lectively eastwards into new premises in Docklands; hi-tech manufacturing, telecom-munications, finance, retailing and other services have done likewise; from being areas made up almost entirely of local authority housing, the boroughs of Newham and Tower Hamlets have become the focus of a boom in high quality owner-occupied residential development. The deregulation of the financial services industry (Big Bang) has generated a need for office accommodation. Much of this is being

provided in Docklands, some of the developments being on a spectacular scale.

45. In short, the centre of gravity of London is moving decisively eastwards after years of drifting towards the west. Although there are great areas still awaiting development, notably the Royal Docks area itself, the momentum of change is now unstoppable. London City Airport will both feed and feed upon this change. Clearly it will be good for the airport that it be centred upon a dynamic and flourishing neighbourhood; equally the promise of the availability of the airport is a further catalyst to businesses and individuals contem-plating relocation into the area. While it may be acceptable to make a long journey to or from an airport if one is going to or coming from San Francisco or Singapore, it is utterly tiresome to find a shorthaul European journey converted into a major obstacle race by problems of access to or from an airport. By resolving this problem for Docklands, and indeed for east London as a whole, London City has removed one of the disadvantages that were holding the neighbourhood down.

Airline Attitudes and Public Response

46. Before describing airline attitudes to the proposed London City development it is worth explaining that the project is perhaps even more unusual than is generally appre-ciated. The fact that a genuine inner city airport is novel, that an airport developed solely for STOL operations is novel, that a privately owned airport developed by a company with no previous history in the industry is novel - these aspects of London City are generally acknowledged. It is perhaps only those who stop and think about it, however, who realise that the creation of any new airport from scratch on a new site is in itself a rare event. The massive development of the airport industry in Britain since the war has been based almost without exception on the expansion of facilities which were already there, if only in the form of modest military airfields.

47. The various improbabilities summarised in the preceding paragraph possibly made interest-ed third parties such as airlines doubtful as to whether the enthusiastic promoter visiting them to establish market interest in the new airport would ever really get around to building it. Taking into account the fact that relationships between airlines and airports are not generally established as long term contract commitments, that there was accordingly no need for airlines to "commit" themselves to use of London City, and that successful existing businesses with high public profiles do not readily attach their names to ideas which could turn out to be castles in the air, it is perhaps not surprising that the response of airlines prior to actual commitment to build was interested and polite rather than positive and definite. It was necessary for the developer to commit the investment on the basis of faith in the concept and without any guarantee that any airline would ever fly from it.

48. Once that leap of faith had been made, however, reaction from the airline industry was

AIRPORTS FOR PEOPLE

extremely positive. Five UK airlines applied to the CAA for route licences and from among these it can, at the time of writing, be said that there are two strong and determined contenders - Brymon Airways and Eurocity Express. Brymon, as British operators of the Dash 7, have identified with the project since its inception (as referred to in paragraph 8) and have remained keen as the dream has approached reality. Eurocity Express is a new airline formed by the British Midland Group for the sole purpose of capitalising on the new opportunity offered by London City; this airline will be based at the airport. By the time the World Airports Conference takes place it should be known how route licences have been awarded between the contenders.

49. Since construction of the airport began there has also been a renewal of interest from continental airlines, both in seeking route licences from their own authorities and in seeking to reserve slots at London City.

50. Meanwhile it is fair to say that the new airport has attracted a considerable amount of media coverage and public interest. The Minister of State for Aviation, Mr Michael Spicer, kindly carried out a ground breaking ceremony at the start of construction, and HRH The Prince of Wales graciously laid the foundation stone; such a degree of interest in the project has naturally helped the development of public awareness.

51. This increased public awareness has in turn made it possible for candidate airlines to carry out detailed market research studies and customer attitude surveys such as would have been difficult before the project itself was known or understood. It is fair to say that such research has confirmed a strong demand among business travellers, and an enthusiasm for the service and facilities that London City will offer.

52. Finally it must be admitted that there is one problem that neither the developer nor the airport company management has, at the time of writing, solved. How does one allocate tickets for the first public flight from London City Airport? The number of people who have asked to be on that first flight is such that if they could all be miniaturised and put on board, the first year's target total would be at once achieved. Somehow an allocation has to be decided - but so many problems have been overcome that we can surely crack that one too!

Acknowledgements

53. John Mowlem and Company PLC and London City Airport Ltd wish to acknowledge the very considerable help and sympathetic forbearance of the Civil Aviation Authority in the resolution of the many issues upon which the completion and licencing of the airport has depended.

54. The project team has been:
Architect:
  R Seifert & Partners
Aviation Consultant:
  World Aviation Services Ltd
Civil and Structural Engineer:
  Donald Butler Associates
Services Engineer:
  Sir Frederick Snow & Partners
Cost Consultant & Quantity Surveyor:
  Axtell Yates Hallett
Interior Design and Concessions Consultant:
  Jenkins Group
Noise Consultant:
  Bickerdike Allen Partners
Airport Operations Consultant:
  Lockheed Air Terminal Inc

Discussion

INTRODUCTION TO DISCUSSION BY
J.S. McKENZIE, WIDERØE'S FLYVESELSKAP A/S,
BODØ, NORWAY

The Norwegian mainland is very long and narrow.
It spans from 58 N to more than 71 N and from
5 E to 30 E. While the length is more than 1800
km, it is, at its narrowest point, only 7 km
wide. The area is about 325 000 km2 and the
majority of the population live in the south.
The northern two-thirds of the country has a
population of less than 1/2 million people. The
majority of these live in small towns and
settlements. Since World War Two there has been
a tendency for the population to migrate towards
the larger cities in the south.

To prevent depopulation of the remote northern
and some western parts of the country, the
Norwegian government in the early 1960s
initiated construction of a number of STOL-ports
- i.e. miniature airports with 800 m runways -
to provide the necessary communications required
in a modern society. The idea was to establish
a secondary network of airline services which
could provide air service to the larger regional
centres as well as connection to the already
established domestic trunk carriers. Widerøe,
with its long tradition in Norwegian aviation,
was chosen to develop and operate this secondary
air transport system.

At the present time, Widerøe operates a fleet
of 12 DHC-6 Twin Otter and 8 DHC-7 aircraft.
Both aircraft types are ideally suited for this
kind of operation. The company route network
includes 35 destinations, out of which 20 are
STOL-ports. With the company's fleet of
aircraft, more than 270 route-sectors are flown
every day. More than 60% of the operation takes
place north of the Arctic circle - the
northernmost airfields being Honningsvag and
Mehamn at 71 N. In 1985, Widerøe transported in
excess of 900 000 passengers; in 1986, the total
number of passengers is expected to reach one
million.

It was only after World War Two that air
transport became a factor as a mode of
transportation in Norway; and it was military
demands which, within a few years, provided
major airports at the larger population centres
throughout the country.

The airline traffic started very modestly,
with 7000 passengers on Norwegian domestic
routes in 1946. In 1962, this figure had
increased to 390 000. In 1972, it had increased
to 1.99 million passengers. For the airlines,
this rapid growth in passenger numbers demanded

increased capacity and frequency, while the
growing cost spiral made it necessary to
increase efficiency and to rationalise the
operations. The answer was larger and faster
aircraft and more direct flights, giving
preference to the densely populated areas.
This, in turn, made it even less attractive to
live in thinly populated districts.

Lack of transportation was, therefore, one of
the major reasons why a general migration
towards the regional centres, and - even worse -
from the northern counties to the larger cities
in the south, started.

In the mid-1950s, there was a growing
political concern for the gradual depopulation
of the remote parts of the country. The
shifting of the population pattern from the
districts towards regional centres and the
already crowded cities was not encouraging.
Many of the traditional coastal settlements
became 'ghost' towns.

Modern society is characterised by an
extensive division of work. However, if this
system is to function, quick and reliable
communications are a necessity. In order to
reverse the population shift, a first step would
be to provide the entire country with a modern
communications system. It was in this situation
that a few, but influential, politicians claimed
that an extensive development of the domestic
air route network would be required; and in
1961, the Norwegian Storting (Parliament)
appointed a Committee to study the issue
further.

The Committee, which submitted its report in
1964, concluded with a proposal for the
construction of nine new major airports.
Bearing in mind the Norwegian topography, this
was a very ambitious programme which would drain
considerable resources from government funds.
Of even greater concern was the fact that even
if the required funds could be made available,
it would not solve the basic problem: that of
providing air transportation for the remote
districts.

The Committee's report provoked a heated
debate. There was considerable disagreement as
to whether this was the most cost-effective way
of spending government funds. Was it possible,
perhaps, to construct airfields in a different
way so that the remote parts of the country
could benefit from the massive public spending?
The Minister for Transport and Communication
provided the answer, namely 'STOL-ports'.

Through the building of STOL-ports, a much

larger number of airports could be constructed for the same amount of money spent. This would allow a relatively dense air traffic network to be established, and would cover most of the country. Because it was primarily the thinly populated districts which were to be served, there would be no need for large aircraft with the associated requirements for long runways and sophisticated airports. Smaller aircraft could be used.

As luck would have it, there was at that time an aircraft available which was ideally suited for the proposed operation. The aircraft was the de Havilland of Canada DHC-6 Twin Otter. This was an aircraft with a seating capacity of up to twenty passengers. It was dependable and well-proven in many climates - including the Arctic - and it required less than 800 m of runway for take-off and landing. Yet the aircraft was fully equipped for IFR-operations, and it met the standard requirements for commercial airline operations.

It was clear from the start that even with these small aircraft one could not hope to arrive at an economical break-even. However, it was felt that this question had to be seen in a wider context. The retention of the established patterns of settlement, with the preservation of values and lifestyles, was an overriding political goal. To this end, the government was willing to use a considerable amount of money in subsidising agriculture, modernising factories, building houses, schools, roads, bridges, harbours, etc., but first of all to provide faster and more reliable transportation.

The first regional air route was opened in 1968, connecting the two major airports in Trondheim and Bodø with four new STOL-ports. Widerøe's Flyveselskap A/S with its long tradition in Norwegian aviation was chosen as the operator. The trial period of one year was a great success, and the new airlink became more than a means to travel between two points. It gave the dormant communities new opportunites and new lives.

Phase II occurred with the building of five STOL-ports on the West Coast of Norway in 1971. Phase III was completed in 1972 and covered the all important fishing regions on the Lofoten islands - north-west of Bodø. Finally, Phase IV and perhaps the most challenging part was completed in 1974, linking the rest of the nation. The main objective had been achieved. Norway was linked through a network of air routes covering the country from Kirkenes on the Soviet border in the north-east down to Bergen and Oslo in the south.

In the period from operation start-up in 1968 to the end of 1985, a total of 5.8 million passengers have been flown on the secondary air traffic network. Looking at the statistics, traffic has increased by more than 10% each year. The total number of passengers transported in 1985 was about 730 000 on Widerøe routes, while we expect to carry more than 900 000 in 1986. In addition to the numbers quoted, Widerøe in 1985 transported 150 000-200 000 passengers for Scandinavian Airlines under a special charter contract, and a similar number is expected for 1986.

Today, Widerøe operates a fleet of 12 DHC-6 Twin Otters and eight DHC-8 aircraft. Both aircraft types are ideally suited for the task. The company route network includes 35 destinations, out of which 20 are STOL-ports. With the company's fleet of aircraft, more than 270 route-sectors are flown every working day. During weekends and holidays, the production is roughly halved. More than 60% of the operation takes place north of the Arctic circle - the northernmost airfields being Honningsvag and Mehamn at 71 N.

The STOL-port air service has won a reputation for being an efficient and well-run operation. The regularity was aimed at being 95%. Regularity in 1984 was 97.6%, and in 1985 was 98.2%. Turn around time at the STOL-ports is 10 minutes for the DHC-6 Twin Otter and 15 minutes for the DHC-7. From an operational point of view, it is fair to say that flying the Widerøe route network is a demanding task and requires a high degree of skill and professionalism. Obstructions are numerous. Winter storms with associated low visibility and cloud ceilings are frequent. Approach aids are limited. Surface and en route winds are constant problems. There are no fringes - and there is little room for error.

The company took a considerable step forward in technology with the introduction in 1981 of the DHC-7. This aircraft, which is designed to modern FAR25 standards, contains all the advanced systems necessary to operate a 20 ton aircraft in and out of 800 m airfields with as great safety and ease as the venerable Twin Otter.

It is naturally impossible to have this level of systems sophistication without a maintenance burden, but the aircraft has proven itself to be extremely safe and reliable even under the most demanding operations. During weekdays, the first DHC-7 take-off is at 04.45 hours and the last scheduled landing of the same aircraft is at 10 minutes past midnight. Twenty landings during the working day and an average technical dispatch reliability bordering on 99% are not possible unless both the aircraft and the maintenance framework are doing well.

Conclusion

The political move which made a regular air transport service available throughout Norway has been a formidable success. It has contributed decisively to the retention of values and lifestyles. These are important considerations for a small nation.

However, neither the politicians nor the operators intend to rest on their laurels. The STOL-port service in Norway has by no means seen the end of the line. We will therefore continue to see a considerable extension of the service over the next few years.

The STOL-port service has a potential to become much more than a means of bringing modern life to remote settlements, however important this may be. In 1987, Europe will have its first truly metropolitan STOL-port in the heart of the Royal Albert Docks, six miles from London City Centre.

Direct city-centre to city-centre air transportation will become a possibility - thereby saving time, which is the busy traveller's most valuable resource.

Dipl.-Ing. W. O. TOEPEL, Bayerisches
Staatsministerium für Wirtschaft und Verkehr,
Munich
Under what all-weather OPS Category (I, II or
III) are Norwegian STOL-ports operated? What
glidepath slope is maintained on Norwegian STOL-
ports?

MR J. S. McKENZIE
Norwegian STOL-ports were designed for non-
precision approaches. The normal
instrumentation consists of LLZ, DME and
VASI/PAPI (3.5-4.0). There is, however, one
exception. The airport in question has
installed a category I ILS SYS., with a glide
scope of 3.8.

It might be worthwhile to note that a number
of those airports using non-precision approaches
have a missed approach point situation 2-3 NM
from the threshold.

For further information, the Norwegian Civil
Aviation Authority in Oslo may be contacted.

MR L. K. HALVORSEN, Civil Aviation Authority,
Oslo
The communities running STOL-ports in Norway are
in deficit; therefore, subsidies are required to
keep them operational. Extended runways, larger
aeroplanes and so on would greatly increase the
cost of running the STOL-ports. This means
that, from a commercial point of view, it may
not be feasible to extend runways in order to
introduce larger aircraft.

MR J. S. McKENZIE
Mr Halvorsen's comments are based on the
economic realities in Norway at the present
time.

Without going into detail with regard to the
economies of operation of Norwegian STOL-ports,
I would assume that prospective planners and
operators of new development STOL-ports would
not necessarily depend on state subsidies to
make up operating deficits.

A potentially large traffic base combined with
a high number of aircraft movements and a
terminal building designed with the passenger in
mind would have the potential for operating at a
profit.

I think that the new London STOL-port will be
a good example to study in the future, from the
point of view of the STOL-port economies based
on the above-mentioned factors.

W1 The design of the new terminal complex: London's third airport at Stansted

S. DE GREY, Director, Foster Associates, London

'Airports should be tranquil places, simple to understand, and easy to use', stresses Norman Foster. 'Calm, clarity and convenience are the key words.' These words summarise the challenge to Foster Associates in their design for the new terminal at Stansted being developed to service London and the South East's future air traffic.

1. Now being constructed in Essex 32 miles north east of London, the new international airport facilities at Stansted will have capacity for seven to eight million passengers a year when it opens in late 1990. As part of BAA plc's network of airports in the United Kingdom, the Stansted development enjoys the two-fold advantage of BAA plc's expertise in the field of airport planning and starting with a green-field site. The site provided the opportunity to reconsider the configuration of an airport terminal from first principles, free from many constraints that face the majority of terminal buildings constructed today within existing terminal complexes.

2. As architects for the main passenger terminal and airside satellite buildings at Stansted, Foster Associates, together with Stansted Airport Management and BAA plc, identified two main objectives to be addressed in the design.

3. The first of these is flexibility - the ability to adapt easily to changing requirements over the life of the airport. This objective has been resolved by designing a demountable system for internal accommodation which can be reconfigured with minimum disruption to concourse operations. Overall, the masterplan permits the various elements - car parking, landside and airside coach stations, cargo and passenger stands, and satellites - to be enlarged or repeated independently as demanded by growth in various sections of the market.

4. Foster Associates' second objective for the new terminal, the subject of this paper, is simplicity - to provide an environment for the traveller that is clear, direct and as stress-free as possible. In attempting to simplify the scheme as far as possible, Foster Associates strove to recreate the clarity and convenience of the earliest flying era.

5. Before World War II, and the explosion in mass travel that followed it, the typical airport was a simple affair. The single-level concourse required only a short walk between car and aircraft (Diagram 1). This route was so clear and straightforward that directional signs were unnecessary : the traveller's destination, either road or aircraft, was clearly visible. This simplicty of the airport experience in the early days of air travel celebrated the enjoyment of air travel itself.

6. Today, however, the size and complexity of the typical international airport often produces a bewildering and stressful experience for the traveller. Foster Associates' attempt to return to the basics of an airport's function was aimed, therefore, at simplifying the experience of the airport for visitors and reinforcing the pleasure of flying.

7. In the first place, Foster Associates have tried to reduce circulation routes and spatial relationships to the simplest diagram. The configuration of the airport masterplan has orderly and clearly articulated zones for its various activities. The terminal building itself is organised with all passenger areas on one level to simplify circulation patterns and minimise walking distances (Diagram 4). Below this main concourse level, services plant and baggage

Diagram 1 *Dallas Airport 1931*

Airports for people. Thomas Telford Limited, London, 1988

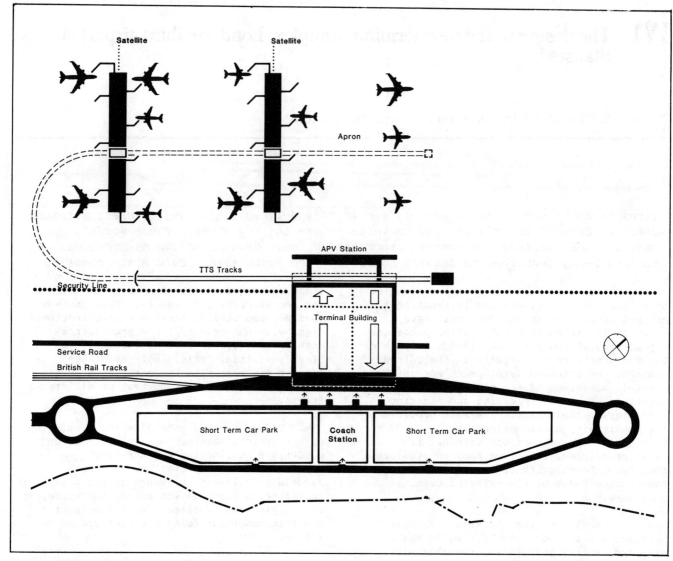

Diagram 2 *The terminal zone*

handling equipment occupy an undercroft level
that extends across the entire building.

8.   The terminal has been integrated as
closely as possible with all transport links
to Stansted (Diagram 2). The landside vehicle
forecourt and passenger set-down are
constructed at the same level as the main
concourse. The short term car park and coach
station are south of the forecourt, set at a
lower level to minimise their visual impact
and give easy access into the terminal from
below the forecourt. The British Rail station
is below the forecourt as an extension of an
undercroft which runs beneath the entire
concourse level. Lifts, escalators and ramps
bring passengers from the railway station,
coach station and car parks, directly up to
the concourse level within the building.

9.   Once inside the terminal, travellers
find all passenger processing areas and
amenities on a single level with arrivals and
departures facilities side by side. They progress from one to the next along a linear route
and in a logical sequence (Diagram 3). This
one level organisation avoids the disorient-
ation of major changes in level or direction.

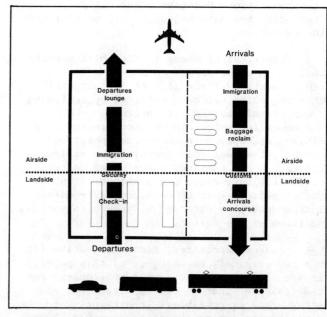

Diagram 3 *The strategic plan of the terminal*

10. The final connection to the aircraft is
by a rapid transit system to remote satellite
buildings. The transit system leaves the
terminal building at concourse level and then
drops below ground. At each of the satellites

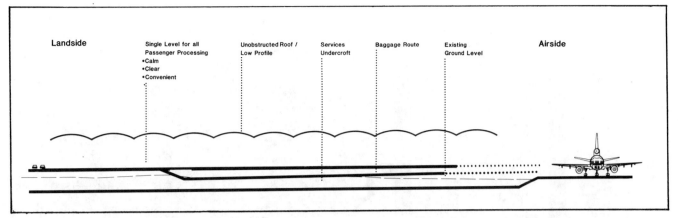

Landside — Single Level for all Passenger Processing •Calm •Clear •Convenient — Unobstructed Roof / Low Profile — Services Undercroft — Baggage Route — Existing Ground Level — Airside

Diagram 4 *The key cross-section through the terminal*

(two in the 8 mppa scheme, increasing to three or four when the the terminal expands to its final 15 mppa configuration), travellers arrive at a below-apron station linked to the satellite's main departure lounge level by escalators. From this level, they move directly onto the aircraft.

11. Working closely with the airport's own Development Team the design group has tried to reinforce the clarity and directness of the terminal building's organisation through the design of the services and structure. The design of the services minimises clutter in public areas and enhances the atmosphere of tranquility. Heating and cooling plant and baggage handling belts have been located discreetly out of sight below concourse level. No ducts, pipes or light fittings will intrude on the expansive ceiling area.

12. The terminal roof will be a series of gentle, partly glazed domes that admit natural light and act as reflectors for the indirect artificial lighting system. The result will be a calm and light space covered by gently glowing, umbrella-like roof panels.

13. Noise levels in the terminal will be kept low. There will be limited public address announcements with all flight information displayed on monitors throughout the concourse. Careful design of air distribution patterns will minimise mechanical sounds.

14. Just as the services strategy has been developed as part of the overall design objective of simplification, the building's structure has been designed to enhance spatial clarity and orientation for passengers (Diagram 5). The structural columns at concourse level are set on a 36 metre square grid, which was generated by the building's functional requirements and the need to preserve flexibility for future internal arrangements. The supports for the roof form tree-like structures composed of four interconnected tubular steel columns. These are angled at 4 metres above concourse level, to reduce the structural spacing at roof level to an 18 metre square grid.

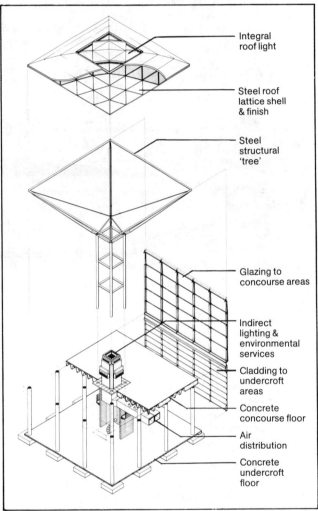

Integral roof light

Steel roof lattice shell & finish

Steel structural 'tree'

Glazing to concourse areas

Indirect lighting & environmental services

Cladding to undercroft areas

Concrete concourse floor

Air distribution

Concrete undercroft floor

Diagram 5 *Exploded axonometric showing the relationship between structure, cladding and services in the concourse and undercroft*

15. The roof is made up of lattice shell domes. Each dome rises 3 metres above eaves level to an overall height of 15 metres above the floor of the concourse. This height permits a clear view through the building and through the fully glazed walls of the airside and landside faces.

16. The centre of the structural trees provides the zone for distributing the heating, ventilation and air-conditioning to the concourse and is the location for the source of indirect lighting reflected off the

Diagram 6 *View through the terminal from the landside forecourt*

roof soffit. These trees are, therefore, the primary organiser of the services at concourse level.

17. In addition, the trees help to organise the space for travellers. Besides being the most prominent elements within the concourse, they become nodes where passengers will find flight information monitors, directional signs and public telephones.

18. The new Stansted terminal will be a busy place, with thousands of passengers passing through it every day. Despite this, however,

the inside of the terminal will be perceived as a single large space, airy and calm, with the landside and airside clearly visible from all points (Diagram 6).

19. The client for the terminal is BAA plc : Stansted Airport Limited and the consultant team is led by Foster Associates as Architects, with Ove Arup and Partners as Structural Engineers and British Airports Services as Mechnical and Electrical Engineers and also Quantity Surveyors. The consultant contractor is Laing Management Contracting Limited.

W2 Planning consideration and terminal design for Zagreb Airport

S. PAVLIN, Head, Organization, Development and Investment, Zagreb Airport, Yugoslavia

Zagreb Airport passenger terminal capacity has lagged behind the traffic needs for many years. This has been the reason to start terminal extension planning and designing. Expected standard busy rates of passenger flows as well as service quality standards (waiting time limits, waiting lounge area per passenger, etc.) have been established. Capacity calculation of the primary technological facilities has been made by queuing model method and computer simulation. Various terminal extension concepts have been studied, and a centralized, 1 1/2 level concept of passenger terminal with mixed configuration - open apron and linear concept - has been adopted.

INTRODUCTION

1. Ever since 1928 the city of Zagreb has been linked by air connection with other major towns in Yugoslavia, and since 1929 with the European ones.

2. Zagreb Airport, with an annual throughput in 1986 of 1.6 million passengers, 31,000 operations and 18,000 ton of cargo, is the second largest airport in Yugoslavia. The volume of traffic has fluctuated. However, the 1960s saw an increase in traffic by 60 or even 70% in respect of the preceding year. This increase in traffic was not met by an appropriate traffic facility development, e.g. passenger terminal, cargo warehouse, and apron.

3. The problem of shortage of capacity in relation to the passenger terminal has been a rather acute one for more than 15 years now.

4. This paper is aimed at presenting passenger terminal throughput and capacity development, planning considerations about its further development, and adoption of planning assumptions which globally determine the future passenger terminal design.

TRAFFIC DEVELOPMENT AT ZAGREB AIRPORT

5. Table 1. Annual passenger throughput in a 5-year sequence at Zagreb Airport

Year	Passenger throughput
1960	49,173
1965	172,712
1970	640,168
1975	1 484,964
1980	1 599,531
1985	1 558,864

6. The biggest passenger throughput at Zagreb Airport was recorded in 1979 - 1 917,197 passengers.

PAST DEVELOPMENT OF PASSENGER TERMINAL

7. A small, wooden passenger terminal was built for the opening of Pleso airport in 1959.

8. The ever-increasing traffic in those years soon outgrew the passenger terminal capacity, so that in 1966 a new passenger terminal was built and opened to traffic, measuring and area of 4,700 sqm and allowing a throughput of 500,000 passengers per year. That was a single-level, centralized building. The first floor was partly built with secondary facilities such as restaurant, buffet, VIP saloon, etc.

9. The capacity of the new passenger terminal sufficed until 1970. Due to shortage of capacity, an annex to the passenger terminal was built and opened to traffic in 1974. The annex measured 3,200 sqm in area (with the original building 7,900 sqm). Already at its opening its capacity figures proved to be below those required by the traffic - almost 1.5 million passengers per year.

10. In 1984 extension of passenger terminal was built and opened to traffic. It measured 3,600 sqm in area. Extension, annex and the original terminal form a single-level, centralized building measuring a total area of 11,500 sqm. Already as extension opened, the overall capacity of the terminal did not suffice - in 1984 the throughput was 1.5 million passengers.

11. From the technological point of view this is not the best solution as the technological conception of the passenger terminal changed with two extensions, and was adjusted to the dimensions of the building (Fig. 1).

12. Disposition of traffic facilities and surfaces at Zagreb Airport was determined in the late 1950s and is rather awkward from the point of view of planning further development. The distance from the runway, across taxiway, apron, and passenger terminal to the kerb, amounts to 400 m, which is a small figure. Such disposition has dictated extension of passenger and cargo terminals, and apron only in the direction parallel to the runway. Today the apron dimension ratio is 1 : 5 (ca 160 by 800 m). Likewise, by additional extension in one direction only the passenger terminal has become a prolonged building (ca 60 by 180 m).

13. In view of urbanization which has taken place on this location, it was the only possible direction of development of terminals and apron.

CHARACTERISTICS OF PASSENGER TRAFFIC AT ZAGREB AIRPORT

14. Zagreb Airport counts among those with a high proportion of transit and transfer traffic in relation to the overall traffic record. Transit passengers make one fourth, transfer passengers one third, and originating and terminating passengers five twelfth of the annual passenger throughput.

15. Transit passengers mainly travel by international flights originating from the inland part of Yugoslavia, most often with Belgrade as originating airport, via Zagreb, and vice versa.

16. Transfer passengers mainly transfer from the international to domestic flights usually bound for the seaside, and from the domestic flights, usually originating from the seaside airports, to the international ones. Most transfer passengers are tourists, and use the Yugoslav Airlines scheduled international and domestic flights. There are a lot more transfer passengers in the summer season.

17. Yugoslav Airlines, the national carrier, handles almost 4/5 of Zagreb Airport passenger traffic. It observes a flight schedule which allows running domestic arrival flights and the international departure ones in the morning, and international arrival and domestic departure flights in the afternoon. Within Yugoslav Airlines flight network Zagreb Airport serves as the major transit/transfer centre. In the morning hours it receives terminating, transit, and transfer passengers. A greater part of these aircraft change their flight No. in Zagreb from domestic to international and carries originating and transfer passengers to their destinations. The same fleet returns to Zagreb in the afternoon with the terminating, transit, and transfer passengers on board. A part of these flights change flight No. and in the late afternoon and evening hours they continue with the transit and transfer, as well as originating passengers on board to the final destinations.

18. Passenger flow figures at the 30th peak hour of the year (standard busy rate) have been as follows:

- International departure   600 pax
- International arrival   650 pax
- Domestic departure   450 pax
- Domestic arrival   400 pax

Within these flows there are also the following:

- Transfer, domestic-international   200 pax
- Transfer, international-domestic   250 pax
- Transit, International   250 pax

In total, the standard busy rate in the passenger terminal amounts to ca 900-1000 passengers in an hour and declines in the afternoon, when international arrivals and domestic departures take place.

19. Passengers in domestic traffic make 40% of the total annual passenger throughput, whereas those in international traffic 60%.

20. Passengers in scheduled traffic make 84% and those in charter traffic 16% of all the passengers.

TRAFFIC FORECASTS

21. Passenger traffic forecasts have been adopted in 1984.

Table 2. Passenger traffic forecasts

Year	Minimum	Maximum
1990	1 980,000	2 500,000
1995	2 400,000	3 350,000
2000	2 900,000	4 500,000
Average rate	4.3%	6.7%

PLANS FOR FURTHER DEVELOPMENT OF PASSENGER TERMINAL

22. A Working Group was set up in 1979 to define the concept of further development of passenger terminal. It was made up of experts in various fields, e.g. planners, architects, civil engineers, operators.

Concept of passenger terminal

23. At the early stage various terminal concepts have been considered, e.g. open apron, linear, finger, satellite, and combined ones. Because of space restrictions, requirements for the use of the existing facilities, and other reasons, the Working Group has made a decision that the passenger terminal should develop where space allows so, that is southwest, longitudinally between the kerb and apron.

24. Combined, open apron and linear concept has been adopted. Loading bridges, of which 3-4 are planned, will serve international traffic, especially wide-bodied aircraft. Open positions will predominate.

25. Combined concept appears to be the best solution according to the conclusion reached by the Working Group since peak periods - today 15 aircraft at the same time - are replaced by longer periods of only a few aircraft on the apron.

26. A 1 1/2 level passenger terminal has been adopted, that is, groundfloor and on the airside a part of the first floor.

27. It has been decided that the existing passenger terminal should be integrated into the future concept and serving only domestic traffic.

28. One of the reasons why a centralized passenger terminal has been adopted is a large proportion of transfer passengers in the overall passenger throughput, who transfer from the domestic to international flights, and vice versa, at peak periods.

Adopted standard busy rates and capacity calculation

29. The following standard busy rates per traffic categories have been adopted:

- International departure   1000 pax
- International arrival   1000 pax
- Domestic departure   700 pax
- Domestic arrival   700 pax

All flows contain transit and transfer passengers. Furthermore, flight schedule has been

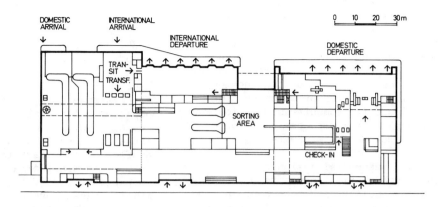

Fig. 1. Existing passenger terminal, layout of ground floor

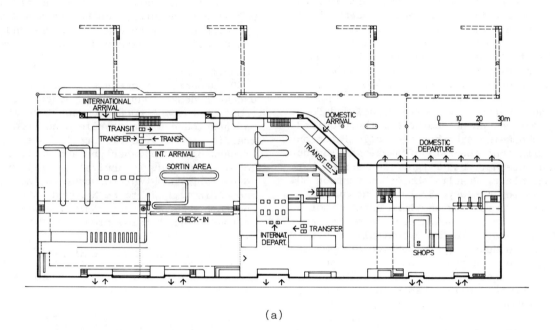

(a)

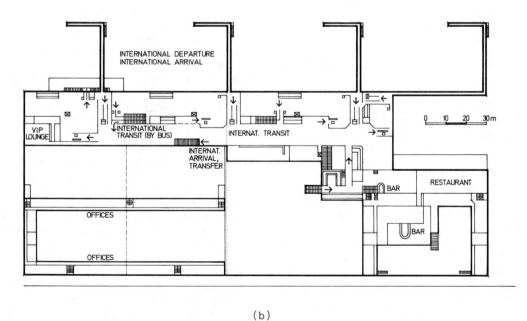

(b)

Fig. 2. Planned extension and refurbishing of existing passenger terminal: (a) layout of ground floor, (b) layout of first floor

109

drawn up and service time on the primary technological facilities specified. Queuing time limit
at the primary passenger handling facilities,
and the required waiting area per passenger have
been adopted according to the IATA recommendations (Ref. 1). Capacity calculation of the primary facilities has been made by queuing model
method (Ref. 2) and checked by computer simulation. Language used for computer simulation was
GPSS and the project had been assigned to the
University Computer Centre of Zagreb.

Centralization or decentralization?

30. Various technological concepts of passenger and baggage handling have been contemplated.
Capacity calculation has been made for the primary facilities in a centralized and decentralized system. This has showed that the centralized system requires ca 30% less check-in desks
than the decentralized one. As the current regulations stipulate that each check-in desk should
have a built-in X-ray unit, this allows, if
centralized system is applied, substantial cuts
in investments (number of check-in desks), as
well as in operational costs (smaller number of
operators, lower facility maintenance costs,
etc.)

31. As peak periods in international and domestic departures do not coincide, the required
number of check-in desks has been calculated on
the condition that check-in of passengers on domestic and international flights is carried out
in the same place. Results show that further 30%
can be saved in this way. So this concept has
been adopted. Overall expenditure cuts of the
maximum technological centralization are more
than 50% as compared to the decentralized system
at the check-in desks. By connection of domestic
and international passenger check-in, connection
of the sorting area has been made possible,
which will now be smaller than separate sorting
areas taken together.

32. Departure lounges have been analysed, too.
By dividing departure lounges in groups of 3 or
4 a lot of space can be saved, and also the
number of passenger and baggage control equipment can be cut down.

33. Apart from the decentralized system, use
of a common departure lounge in full centralization enables the largest savings.

Passenger terminal capacity calculation results

34. A required passenger terminal area of
22,500 sqm has been calculated.

35. This extension of the existing passenger
terminal of an area of 11,000 sqm, together with
the latest extension of an area of 3,600 sqm is
officially called the first stage of Terminal 2.

36. Double extension of passenger terminal necessarily results in modification to the passenger and baggage handling technology. Extensions
never achieve that technological niveau which
would have achieved if the whole structure had
been built according to the predetermined technology. For this reason project drawings (see Fig.
2), which are attached, might be viewed with
criticism. A lot of improvemnets could have been
made, which, however, would have required the
additional investments.

37. As underground water level is rather high

the terminal does not have a cellar, this resulting in various secondary facilities being
accommodated on the groundfloor.

38. A concept of passenger terminal has been
adopted whereby international arrival and passenger check-in in domestic departure are placed
side by side. This is because almost all transfer passengers in international arrival-domestic
departure flow claim their baggage, go through
the customs, and check it in again, whereas
those in domestic departure-international arrival flow do not claim their baggage.

39. A terminal capacity of 22,500 sqm in area
is expected to suffice a throughput of 2.5 - 3
million passengers a year.

40. Construction of the first stage of Terminal 2 was planned for the World University
Games 1987 to enable a provision of service
quality level comparable to the world standards.

41. Unfortunately, the shortage of funds has
not allowed construction before the Games. So,
the closing of financial structure and eventual
construction are expected after the Games.

Security aspect

42. Departing baggage will be controlled at
check-in desks, whereas body-check will be in
front of the entrances to departure lounges. Departure lounges are sterile areas. International
traffic on the first floor will see the mixing
of passengers in departure and arrival through
loading bridges. In arrival security is planned
to be carried out at the customs (all claimed
and cabin baggage to be X-rayed). Sorting area
and some passages to the airside will be covered
by the internal television.

Facilities for disabled passengers

43. Lifts, as well as facilities such as telephone, toilet, etc. for the disabled passengers
will also be provided.

Ultimate development on the site

44. The second stage of Terminal 2 would be a
further extension southwest of passenger terminal which will allow further 14,000 sqm or more
of terminal area to be created. Also, there is
a possibility of installation of the next two
loading bridges. If finger and further extension
should be built, at least 6 loading bridges will
be possible to install. Thus ultimate capacity
of the passenger terminal is expected to reach
6 million passengers per year.

VERIFICATION

45. The IATA Airport Consulting Commission has
evaluated planning attitudes, capacity calculation of terminal facilities and draft design of
Zagreb Airport passenger terminal. Most remarks
and recommendations have been accepted and will
be incorporated in the passenger terminal design.

REFERENCES:
1. Airport Terminal Reference Manual, IATA,
Montreal, Sixth Edition 1976
2. PIPER H.P. Design Principles for Primary
Facilities for Passenger Handling, Technische
Universität Hannover, 1975, May.

Report on Workshop 1

PROFESSOR N. ASHFORD, DEPARTMENT OF TRANSPORT
TECHNOLOGY, UNIVERSITY OF TECHNOLOGY,
LOUGHBOROUGH
The air mode differs from other public transport
modes in a number of significant ways.

1. There is long-term secular growth in demand
   which shows no sign of reaching saturation
   in the near or medium-term future.

2. The modal vehicles have recently undergone
   rapid and significant technological changes.
   Examples which may be cited are the
   widespread adoption of wide bodied vehicles,
   the advent of supersonic passenger vehicles
   accompanied by a sustained interest in this
   area by the manufacturers, and, lastly, the
   rapid advances in air traffic control
   technology.

3. The industry is undergoing rapid
   institutional changes by way of deregulation
   of airlines and privatisation of airports.

4. The industrial shake-up has brought in train
   significant operational changes. One
   example is the growth of hubbing in the
   United States which many view as a transfer
   of some of the economic costs of transport
   from the airline to the airport and the
   traveller. At some hubs, such as Atlanta,
   now the world's busiest airport, transfers
   and transits account for 75% of passenger
   traffic.

Although the passenger terminal is not the
airport, terminals are an extremely important
element of the totality; at the larger
facilities, they can make up three-quarters of
the total infrastructure investment.

In this workshop session, we heard about the
problems being faced at a number of airports:
Stansted, a greefield site; Zagreb, a major
refurbishment; Istanbul; Wichita; Baltimore;
Charlotte, a major new hub; Indianapolis;
Philadelphia; Phoenix; and Terminal 3 Heathrow,
also a major refurbishment.

Deregulation, in both its forms, de jure and
de facto, is causing very large changes in the
air transport market and in the type of aircraft
used.

(a) Deregulated major airlines have
    increasingly gone to hubbing to improve
    aircraft load factors. The higher load

factors, while seen as a gain in airline
efficiency, are achieved through increased
transiting operations at the hubbing
airport. The passenger enjoys a higher
frequency of service at the inconvenience
of a transfer or a transiting flight.

(b) In the more competitive atmosphere of
    deregulation, the major carriers have
    concentrated on the heavier densities of
    trunk routes. Many airports which
    previously had trunk carrier service have
    been abandoned by the major airlines. In
    this atmosphere, there has been a
    remarkable growth in feeder airlines using
    smaller commuter type aircraft.

(c) The growth of hubbing, and the subsequent
    major increase in feeder airline activity,
    has meant that many airports are now
    dealing with a greater range of aircraft
    mix. Small commuter aircraft in larger
    numbers require access to hubs which also
    carry large long distance wide bodied
    aircraft.

Refurbishment at airports is a continuing need.
Most terminals are built to require minor
changes within a five-year horizon and major
refurbishment within 15 to 20 years. This is
another aspect in which air transport differs
from other modes. Refurbishment, however, has a
number of identifiable difficulties which are
common across most schemes:

. operational problems: associated with trying
  to maintain an acceptable level of service
  during periods when there is dust, dirt,
  exposure to the heat, cold or wet, noise and
  a general deterioration of the internal
  terminal environment.

. security problems: associated with
  maintaining the airside secure during
  construction changes, and ensuring that the
  construction staff and their vehicles are not
  used as a cover for terrorist penetration.

. the narrow windows of time allowed for
  refurbishing relate to the small periods of
  decreased demand during off peak seasons or
  to those limited periods of time when excess
  terminal capacity is available, usually
  through some recently completed projects on
  the same site.

Airports for people. Thomas Telford Limited, London, 1988

Other operational aspects which were discussed related once again to hubbing. Terminals adopted as airline hubs are subjected to high crossflows of transfer passengers between gates. In some designs, such as the gate arrival design at Kansas City, this type of flow was never envisaged by the original designers and it is difficult to accommodate in the terminal as constructed. Equally as difficult to accommodate as the unforeseen type of demand, is the unpredictable level of demand. Deregulation has resulted in unforeseen levels of traffic growth in airports such as Tampa, Florida and Charlotte, N.C. Other airports have been unnerved by the potential of very rapid decreases in traffic which could accompany the failure or financial take-over of one of their major airline operators.

An aspect of uncertainty hangs over the head of some European airport operators. Economic Community regulations on cross border controls and duty free allowances seem imminent, by 1992. The former could substantially modify immigration requirements; the latter will have serious effects upon the commercial operations and, consequently, the profitability of the whole airport operation.

Designs which were considered during the workshop session were varied in their concepts. There were, however, a number of common threads in the concepts displayed.

Flexibility
Experiences of the last few years have confirmed the requirement that successful designs must be flexible to permit ease of change in a rapidly shifting economic and operating environment.

Openness
Closed, fixed designs are unattractive and not easily adaptable. They are less easily expanded or conceivably contracted to respond to demand.

Security
It is now quite certain that the security problem in air travel is permanent. Designs must reflect security needs by permitting easy isolation of sterile areas from non-sterile areas, and by reducing the requirements of security staff while maintaining the highest levels of security.

Interior environment
More attention is now being given to the internal design of airports. Many designers of older airports forgot the importance of human scale, while striving to achieve symmetry of design of the master plan. Airports are of such a vast scale that aerial symmetry of design is simply not apparent to the traveller. Design of the internal environment is much more important to the traveller, the visitor and the airport worker.

People movers
The continual growth of air traffic at all hubs means that terminals continue to grow. Twenty years ago very few airports handled above 15 million passengers. Now terminals and terminal complexes are being designed to capacities of 80 million, and some terminals are already handling over 40 million. Terminals on this scale required automatic people movers. The seemingly eccentric designs of automatic people movers of twenty years ago are now widely used and can be expected to become commonplace in another twenty years' time. Without them, the huge terminal complexes will become unusable.

This brings us to a question posed but not necessarily answered. How big should an airport terminal be? We know that the old finger pier arrangements of Atlanta and O'Hare handled approximately 45 million passengers in the late 1970s, but the serivce levels left much to be desired. Abraham Lincoln, when asked by a lady admirer how tall a man should be, replied that he should be just tall enough that his feet should reach the ground. Unfettered growth of terminals, however, leads to unnecessary wear and tear on the passenger. Many designers feel that international terminals should be limited to about 20 million passengers. Airports with two independent runways are likely to be able to carry at least 60 million passengers in the near future. We may envisage these as having at least three terminals with interconnecting and even internal people movers.

In summary, I would add that we found this workshop of great variety and of great interest. Terminal construction and terminal reconstruction currently present some of the greatest challenges to airport designers. This is likely to remain true for at least the next decade.

W3 Airport commercial development — giving the customers what they want

P.G.E. HAMON, Director, International Civil Airports Association, European Community Bureau, Brussels

1. The key to success in any business is to identify what the customer wants and then to find a way of providing it at a profit.

2. An airport's primary function is to provide a point of interchange between modes of transport. Indeed some airport operators restrict themselves to this activity and face the financial consequences, which often leave them loss making and a financial burden on their community. However, many airport owners believe that they should derive benefit from the very substantial number of people who pass through their airports or who visit them or work on them. All are potential customers. Such airports pursue the commercial exploitation of their assets to turn losses into profits with benefits to passengers, to airlines and usually to local or national tax-payers. Indeed, no less a body than the International Civil Aviation Organisation (ICAO) encourages the full use of non-aeronautical revenues to minimise airport charges and therefore direct costs to airlines.

3. I believe that a pre-requisite to success in the development of non-aeronautical revenues is to put on your payroll a marketing expert or experts with flair and at a sufficiently senior level to make things happen. Such a senior manager must be fully accountable for results. He must be given full executive responsibility to maximise commercial profits and to do that he will need the necessary capital and revenue expense budgets. Do not expect the average airport manager, however competent, to perform this role. He may come from such diciplines as engineering, planning, accountancy, aviation or even politics, but he is unlikely to have either the experience or the time to devote to the highly specialised commercial area. He will in any event be too involved in the demanding priorities of ensuring the smooth passage of people, freight and aircraft through the airport. Mainstream airport managers should, nevertheless, be encouraged to have a keen interest in the commercial development of their assets and indeed the specialists will need their full support if they are to succeed.

4. The basis of success in any business is to identify the market, its needs and the propensity of customers to buy; then to develop a strategy to meet these needs and take advantage of the opportunities. Airports them-selves differ considerably in their ability to exploit commercial opportunities. There are differences in passenger throughput levels, differences in passenger profiles in socio-economic terms, in the business/leisure ratio and in destinations. There are differences in an airport's proximity to population centres, surface access and therefore its catchment area. There are wide variations in space available on the airport estate and particularly within terminals. Finally, there are statutory constraints, political, social and religious differences affecting the freedom of airport owners to engage in certain activities. Before setting out to develop non-aeronautical revenues it is vital to know your airport and to know your customers: this may mean carrying out some consumer research, using of course a professional research team.

5. Many airport operators tend to be instinctively conservative, sticking to traditional non-aeronautical revenue-earning services and methods, without developing and evolving this important side of their business. This reluctance to change is manifest in both profitable and unprofitable airports, stemming possibly from a lack of specialised management in the commercial area or even unwillingness at the top of the organisation to make changes and take risks. Historically, there has been resistance by airport authorities to acknowledge the importance of non-aeronautical revenues; a feeling perhaps that such a sideline should not be allowed to gain importance or even a smug belief in the captive market.

6. It may be helpful to consider non-aero-nautical revenues as being traditionally derived from such principal sources as trading activities (eg, shops, bars, restaurants, banks, car rental, car parks, advertising, insurance etc), services (eg, energy handling, cleaning, fuel supply, licences to firms to operate on the airfield, etc), and rents (the straightforward letting to tenants of ground, buildings or other accommodation on the airport).

7. Successful commercial development must be marketed. I firmly believe that airport management should look downtown for their commercial inspiration. I suggest that the best retailing and catering ideas are not to be found in other airports, but rather in the most advanced city centre developments in the world. The same could be said of car parking, property development and many other activities. We should talk about customers rather than passengers and we should try to stand back and look at airports from the customer's point of view. Why re-invent the wheel, when the new business ideas abound in our cities. How many airport managers were busy installing lounge bars and traditional restaurants when the downtown trend was into wine bars, pubs and fast food. How many airports use the well proven high street retail promotional techniques? I submit that we cannot afford to indulge our professional complexes or our middle-class values; history has proved that successful businesses are market driven.

8. I would like to deal briefly with rents and services. Services provided on airports or the licences granted to other organisations to provide services should be reviewed frequently in order to maximise revenue. Wherever possible, long contracts should be avoided and charges should be reviewable as frequently as possible. An annual audit should be made of any activities being carried out on the airport estate, both landside and airside, to assess where and at what level charges could be levied. Even buses, taxis, firms delivering to aircraft, private ambulance services and so on should be considered as possible contributors; they do after all use expensive airport facilities.

9. Likewise rents should be reviewed regularly and leases drafted with this in mind: regular comparisons should be made with the downtown real-estate market. I know one regional airport, where a local real estate agent has been hired to handle the property portfolio and the results are very satisfactory indeed. Only in very large airports can one justify hiring a specialist manager, yet specialist advice is certainly needed.

10. In short, airport owners should endeavour to function as successful commercial enterprises, constantly reviewing their opportunities to charge fair prices for rents and services in order to maintain an adequate return on assets. Needless to say, the customers may well complain, but this is not an insurmountable problem if the charging policy is demonstrably fair and market orientated, while being the means of avoiding or reducing public subsidy. An airport should be managed on the same basis as any successful business.

11. Now let us turn to trading activities where the greatest potential lies. I believe that there is a very strong case for using specialist companies to run these highly specialised operations on airports as concessionaires or contractors to the airport operators. I do not favour trading activities being engaged in by airport staff. Almost certainly the culture will be wrong. Such concessions can be let by competitive tendering or by negotiation as best suits the culture of the airport authority. Some airports do operate their own shops and catering, but I believe they could be even more successful using concessionaires.

12. However, it is important that the financial deal between the airport and the concessionaire should not act as a disincentive to the shopkeeper or caterer but rather as a powerful incentive to maximise sales. We have certainly experienced problems in this respect due to the pressures of competitive tendering and you may care to explore these matters during the question time.

13. Here again contracts should not be for periods in excess of say seven years and for new ventures, trial periods of several months may be the answer. There are many formulae for trading concessions. I recommend that the concession fees paid to the airport should be turnover related either with or without a fixed rental element. The contracts must be so drafted as to give the airport owners full powers to protect their revenue and their reputation for service to the passengers.

14. Concessionaires may be required to provide the capital investment in fixtures and fittings, in which case the concession fees will be lower than if the airport owners provided them. Such decisions will be influenced by the availability of funds to the airport operator and the tenancy laws of the country. This is a very complex area and we have proved that it is the foundation of the whole business.

15. Under no circumstances should airport operators appoint a concessionaire and then leave it all to them. Very close liaison and performance monitoring should be established from the outset and both parties should work together in partnership. I would urge any airport authority to seek specialist advice before formulating a concession policy.

16. It is well known that shops and food outlets in downtown locations require considerable attention as to the precise size, location, trading formula and visual treatment of each unit. These considerations are the very essence of every successful business venture. The shops, restaurants and bars at airports must be sited and designed to attract and tempt busy travellers with much on their minds. We have proved conclusively within the last few years that such criteria, when applied to airports, produce staggeringly

successful financial results as well as giving great pleasure to the customers, whether passengers, visitors, or workers or airlines. When I was responsible for commercial development at the British Airports Authority, we started a programme of improvements and enlargement of all our trading units coupled with the branding of certain chains of shops and the characterisation of all food and drink units to attract our customers. We also analysed each business to improve the range and quality of products: we than set about promoting the new-look with strong in-store promotional activities and some advertising designed to convert passengers into customers. This dynamic process continues.

17. Downtown traders consider it vital to re-assess their trading formula constantly and often to express their selling proposition with different shop fronts and decor every couple of years or so. They also find it necessary to promote their businesses very strongly. All these techniques are doubly essential in airports, where customers come to fly rather than to buy and yet that old enemy the captive-market philosophy prevails in many airports.

18. Passengers are often in the frame of mind to spend money and give themselves or their loved-ones a treat, but they are equally often harassed by queueing for check-in and the various controls; they are probably in a hurry, perhaps excited, apprehensive, jet lagged, disorientated and unfamiliar with the language and customs of the airport.

19. We must, therefore, do even more than the downtown trader to tempt them into our shops, restaurants and bars and then provide the relaxing environment in which they can enjoy spending their money and find entertainment. OUR SELLING PROPOSITION MUST BE LARGER THAN LIFE.

20. Some airport managers still believe that there is conflict between trading activities and passenger service. I am confident that this is a completely wrong uninformed view. If you get the commercial formula right, the total airport product is improved and the customers are happy. The commercial units in a terminal must be conveniently sited: do not expect passengers to deviate far from their route to the aircraft. The larger airports provide satellite shops and catering units in forward passenger holding areas (eg near gaterooms): in these, customers can browse without fear of missing their flights so sales of luxury gifts increase. The trading outlets must be attractive, entertaining and enjoyable places to visit and conducive to spending money. To provide an enjoyable experience for passengers, during the hassle of travelling by air, is surely to improve passenger services, while maximising revenue.

21. Let us look for a moment at the potential customers. They fall into four distinct markets.
- passengers
- people meeting or seeing off passengers
- people employed on the airport
- airport neighbours (people and firms based near the airport)

22. I would not wish to give you a tiresome list of suggestions, but I would propose that brain-storming sessions should be held among varying levels of management to identify business opportunities in each market. These may range from the creation of a sports and leisure centre or a hypermarket for employees and airport neighbours to the provision of photocopying, telex and telefax service for business passengers in the departure lounge; from the creation of a duty and tax free high technology manufacturing zone (ie Freeports) to the marketing of airport-branded merchandise in your shops or even downtown; or from the provision of a real estate shop or a dry cleaning and laundry service for all airport employees to the provision of special facilities and equipment for aviation enthusiasts. The list is endless but the discipline is well worth the effort.

23. The next step is to develop a business plan for the airport dealing with both aero-nautical and non-aeronautical revenue earning proposals. And whatever you do, remember to provide funds every three years or so for the re-appraisal and refurbishing of commercial facilities, keeping a sharp lookout for new ideas and developments downtown. An annual marketing plan for airport trading activities must also be produced.

24. The enormous revenue-earning potential at every airport must be exploited with innovation and expertise and certainly not as a sideline to the serious business of operating the airport.

25. What does the future hold for us? The provision of airport facilities will continue to make heavy demands for investment capital. While on the one hand governments increasingly impose additional costs on airports, such as those for anti-terrorist measures; on the other hand they seek powers to regulate charges and to reduce the cost of air travel. In the European Community there is even an intention to abolish in 1992 duty free and tax free allowances for travel between the twelve member states and there is always the risk that other political or economic groups of states in other parts of the world may follow suit. As you probably know, sales of duty free and tax free goods represent perhaps the largest single source of non-aeronautical airport revenue. The European Commission, the bureaucrats of the European Community, have demonstrated time and time again that they are fundamentally opposed to the existence of duty free and tax free allowances for passengers travelling between member states of the European .Community (the

so-called intra-Community passengers). There have, indeed been many mischevious attempts to abolish duty free/tax free allowances, but so far we have managed to rebuff these.

26. We accept, in principal that when the long awaited Common Market is completed, that is to say when all Excise Duties and Value Added Taxes are harmonised in the European Community member states and when the last customs officer has been removed from the arrivals channels of travellers from one European Community country to another, then duty free and tax free allowances may no longer be justifiable. However, until that happy state is achieved, on current progress probably long after 1992, we must insist that there is no discrimination against intra-Community travellers, which would deprive them of a much appreciated right which is not only enjoyable, but without which air and sea travel costs would rise. To combat this regulatory fervour, to protect our customers and to present the facts of life to the legislators are important objectives of the International Civil Airports Association.

W4   Airports are for people: the importance of people to commercial enterprise

D.J. ALTOBELLO, Executive Vice President, Marriott Corporation, Washington DC

The topic 'Airports are for people: commercial applications' will be discussed in the context of the Marriott Corporation philosophy of the importance of people to its own commercial enterprises. Before my general comments on the topic, let me discuss our company, briefly.

MARRIOTT CORPORATION

The explicit mission of the Marriott Corporation is 'to be the best lodging and food service company in the world'. We are the world's premier company today in the hospitality industry, providing quality products and services to major segments of the population in the United States and internationally.

Marriott is the leading provider of contract food services. Our airline catering division, with 94 flight kitchens world-wide in 14 countries, serves more than 150 airlines in excess of one million meals a day.

Airport food and beverage and merchandise facilities serve over 250 million passengers annually in 53 airports, mostly in the United States, with a recent entry into the United Kingdom. Other non-airport food service management contracts at schools and colleges, corporate offices, and health care facilities account for more than 2000 different places of business.

Marriott is one of the world's leading operators of hotel properties, with more than 175 lodging operations around the world, with 40 at airports and 135 additional hotel and resort operations offering luxury, moderate range and economy facilities, with a total in excess of 77 000 rooms.

In the United States, we are the tenth largest employer, with 200 000 people, serving five million meals a day, developing 1 billion dollars of new real estate and facilities a year, and with turnover in excess of 6 billion dollars.

In airport related businesses, we believe ours is the largest private investment by any non-airline company in the world. Therefore, we were delighted to be able to present a Paper on the topic of creating airport environments which better serve people's needs.

Our deep commitment to the travelling public, for 60 years at the Marriott Corporation and for 90 years at our Host International subsidiary, has given our company a unique perspective on this important question. We have the broad based presence to enable us to see and know what is happening, and we spend millions of dollars

each year performing market research to keep our data base current and to keep in touch with the travelling public.

Marriott is proud of its commitment to its customers. We take pride in our company's responsiveness, our ability to serve our customers well, our marketing orientation, our consumer research, and the friendly people who work for us serving busy travellers.

WHAT OUR CUSTOMERS THINK

What I would like to discuss is not what I think, but it is an interpretation of what our customers have told us about the current air travel and airport service environments and about their needs. I would like to cover three specific areas: firstly, the airport environment elements and concerns; secondly, the role of airports as tourism centres; and thirdly, the impact of airports on regional economies. Let me establish the premise that we need to design airports for people, not just for airplanes.

An abiding principle of the Marriott Corporation is that we all need to listen carefully to our customers; and our customers are telling us that airports today are not serving their needs. The problem is that airports do not have the built-in input from their customers at the moment of their creation – that is, at the point of their design. Furthermore, the airports do not consider their customers' needs at later times either, with a view to trying to overcome any obvious design deficiencies.

Now I recognize that it is very expensive to make massive overhauls after the event, in order to correct design problems or adapt to new needs; however, even small changes can have large paybacks as long as our orientation is changed to focus on the customer, the travelling public. We need to listen and we need to understand the public's problems.

DESIGN IGNORES PEOPLE

Traditional airport design by very competent professionals has been oriented towards meeting the needs of airplanes and airlines, and not necessarily to meet the needs, comforts and convenience of people. Most airport designers have failed to put themselves in the traveller's shoes. Airports must become more than a conveyor system which takes people from the parking lot to the aircraft. Airports are not places where the individual only catches a plane; they are places where a myriad of human

Airports for people. Thomas Telford Limited, London, 1988

117

services need to be provided along the way:
food, beverage, duty free and tax paid
merchandise, barber shops, banks, conference
rooms, car rentals, multi-lingual travellers'
aids, medical clinics, nurseries, telephones,
exercise rooms, shoe shine, parking, showers and
sleeping compartments. Although none of these
services are essential to flight, and, in fact,
all are secondary to the trip itself, they are
just as important in determining the overall
pleasantness of the trip for the individual
passenger.

The ability of airports to serve their
clientele is becoming increasingly important
world-wide. Today, the business world is
shrinking internationally. Communications are
almost instantaneous, and executives think
nothing of hopping on to a plane to conduct
business on the other side of the world. Modern
air travel is a key element in this advancement,
and airports are increasingly being relied upon
to meet these needs.

Air travel is increasingly replacing other
forms of travel (e.g. trains, buses and cars) in
the case of a majority of the population, and
people are consequently spending more and more
time in airplanes and at airports, or as meeters
and greeters at airports, waiting for arriving
loved ones.

AIRLINE PASSENGERS ARE CHANGING
The demographic make-up of the air passenger
market is changing: younger passengers, more
females and families are travelling, and there
are more pleasure travellers, thus creating the
need for more diverse services. As an example,
in the United States in the preregulation era,
55% of air travel was for business purposes and
the balance for pleasure and other purposes.
Today, the exact opposite is true, merely eight
years later. There is a whole new generation of
travellers out there, and we need to be
servicing them. Today, in fact, the average
traveller arrives at the airport almost two
hours before flight time, and this on average in
the US where much travel is domestic, not
international. It may even be that in the major
hubs for international travel, the passengers
arrive even more in advance of the departure
time. We need to give them things to do and to
meet their needs.

Now while our research shows that passengers'
needs are woefully underachieved and under met
by airports and airlines, everyone will
understand that economic and space limitations
constrain many airports in their ability to
provide services. However, many passengers are
just not being served by the airlines either.
Some airports have made the commitment to their
clientele by building larger and more innovative
facilities. Today in Tampa in the United
States, our company is proud to manage a 12000
square foot merchandise mall of specialty shops
that satisfies a variety of human needs for the
traveller and provides a bit of entertainment as
well. Not only are native Florida products
sold, but there is a little gallery from which
one can select paintings and objects of art;
there is a Cuban cigar maker practising his art,
from whom you can buy either his instantly made
product or products made in the factory with

which he is associated. There are fresh food
and specialty items as well as clothing,
apparel, toys and the like. It is a beautiful
experience and one in which a passenger, whether
he or she purchases or not, can enjoy the
anxious waiting time in an atmosphere of beauty,
tranquillity and peace.

THE PASSENGER IS A CUSTOMER
In the past, concessionaires and airports had
often treated passengers as a captive clientele.
Indeed, passengers are no longer such. Among
the important choices available to passengers
are the choice of doing without a service or
delaying the receipt of that service, or using
an alternative on the route from home to the
airport or from the airport to their
destination. We need to create the airport of
the future with environmental services conducive
to meeting customer's needs at prices that they
can afford, and the convenience that make it a
pleasant and memorable experience.

Together with the shrinking of the world
economy through instant communication and rapid
jet travel, deregulation and competitiveness
have also witnessed an increasing availability
of international air travel to people of all
types. To a large degree, this has been the
result of increasingly efficient cost
performance by airlines. In relative terms, air
fares across the world have decreased. For
example, in 1982, the Heathrow-New York APEX
fare was $770. Today, fares are in the $688
range, an 11% reduction. World-wide air travel
has increased by 5% over the last five years.
Individuals and families on business and
pleasure trips are travelling more, and are more
price sensitive. There is a growing market
demand for products with prices geared towards
this market segment. There is a requirement
that airport services should offer
competitiveness with off-airport facilities.
Budget market demands in the airline, hotel, car
rental and other industries have more recently
been satisfied with lower fare and price
structures; similar needs are being expressed
and met in the airport services market as well.
Airport concessionaires are frequently operating
under a cost disadvantage against the off-
airport facilites (up to 25% differential
against off-airport), owing largely to the cost
of building within an airport structure and the
cost of rentals paid to airport authorities.

NEW SERVICE CONCEPTS ESSENTIAL
Our company and others like us are developing
new and successful fast food concepts and price
promotions to bring widely desired products to
our budget minded traveller. Increased
passenger traffic, broad exposure and high
volume are enabling the concessionaire to offset
some, but not all, of the cost disadvantage
which we face.

Food concept ideas to meet a wide range of
tastes - food courts, juice counters, specialty
restaurants, sit-down restaurants, walk-up
counters, fruit and nut stands, menu varieties,
pasta bars, pizza parlors, etc. - all offer us
opportunities to serve passengers and are
responsive to their needs.

Merchandise of every variety - flower shops,

book stores, toy shops, clothing, candy and other specialty stores; mall concepts; overall diverse product offerings - are helping to meet the needs of the travelling public. Lounges designed to attract single travelling women and the younger adult crowds, where fun is part of the experience, are helping to ease the monotony of the increasing waiting time that is a result of the burgeoning hub and spoke system that has followed deregulation in the United States.

MORE SPACE NEEDED

While we want to meet the needs of budget travellers, the former must be balanced against the important needs of business and first-class travellers who require and are willing to pay for unique services: full service restaurants and bars, VIP lounges, private jet facilities, helicopter shuttles, high quality merchandise and service. The most compelling and limiting factor in serving all of these diverse needs is the commitment of space within huge airports to the concessions. The airport designers and builders and managers of the future need to decide how they view themselves: as providers of space; a people mover for airlines; a virtual ground shuttle; or do they provide, in addition to that basic service, an exciting and high quality opportunity to satisfy many of the human needs of the travelling public who find themselves abandoned in the airport, sometimes for many hours, with little to do and little to excite the imagination.

WHAT DOES THE AIRPORT WANT FROM THE CONCESSIONAIRE?

The second thing that every airport authority must do to promote the human side of travel is to determine whether it desires its concessionaire to be a source of maximum rental or as a provider of a wide variety of goods and services at fair prices in first-rate facilities. This latter approach would not provide the maximum dollars attainable in rental. Those questions need to be carefully answered in respect of new facilities and need to be faced by every existing airport in the world.

PARTNERSHIP NEEDED

While we are listening to our customers and passengers, one thing is absolutely certain: their tastes are constantly changing. From my perspective at least, a partnership must exist between airports, airlines and concessionaires to begin to satisfy passenger needs. Customer research and responsiveness are needed to provide the correct types, levels and prices of service. This type of input is needed before we design and build our facilities and on an on-going basis to help us meet the changing tastes and needs of our clientele. The guiding principle needs to be: 'Ask the customer'. Focus groups make an interesting and informative way to determine what is going on in the passenger's mind. Airport intercepts and other similar questionnaire techniques can also be useful in redesigning our airport products. Broad experience, such as we have gained at our Host division and in the breadth of concessionaire's operations in a variety of

airport locations, is an important consideration because it is an invaluable way of broadening information and enabling cross-testing and cross-utilization of new ideas economically.

BETTER DESIGN

We, as concessionaires, need to make a better job of design, building flexibility into our food, beverage and retail facilities. Not only do we need to be willing to invest the initial capital and the continuing capital to meet the current needs, but we need to be able to redesign facilities at a lower cost than we now experience, in order to make them current with the traveller's changing needs.

STRESS RELIEVERS

We need to make our airports stress relievers rather than stress promoters. The fast paced environment in which we all live, and the limited space resources of airports, make the provision of a 'stress relieving' service all the more challenging. The use of larger aircraft and the banking of flights at certain times of the day, resulting in peak concentrations of large numbers of people in small blocks of time in the concourses and terminals, is overtaxing the facilities and the patience of the travelling public. The multiple bookings and timing of flights on many different carriers is also contributing to delays which keep people in the terminal longer.

Both concessionaires and airport operators and managers could find better ways of improving the physical design to create a more comfortable and relaxing atmosphere; the selection of colours and furnishings, lighting and noise levels, the planning of pedestrian flow, and the use of effective, quickly comprehended signs, exhibits and advertising will help to make airports stress relieving instead of stress producing.

EMPLOYEE SELECTION IS CRITICAL

The quality of service is very important and is dependent on the selection and abilities of the work force. Operators must ensure that their employees are courteous as well as competent, and that the overall impression left with the traveller is that of a friendly, caring, well-wishing, person-to-person, customer contact and atmosphere. Training, effective human resources, 'mystery shoppers', and close supervision by management are key elements for attaining high quality service.

MORE SERVICES NEEDED

High traffic loads, over capacity airports, weather and operating problems are all causing increased numbers of delayed flights. The situation of airline delays makes more time available to passengers in the terminals (however involuntary that arrangement might be) and creates the need for a more personalized, broader range of services. Delayed passengers are looking for consoling service, to help offset the inconvenience that the delayed flight may be causing. Concessionaires need sufficient square footage in proper locations to provide facilities to meet this growing market demand. Inattention to delayed passengers may yield poor airport public image. A direct relationship exists between passenger levels of service and the space devoted to various types of passenger service.

SECURITY A CONCERN

Security needs in this crazy world in which we live need to be very carefully balanced with passenger desires and needs. Security procedures need to be created and current ones improved, not only from the viewpoint of eliminating the threats by the threatening few, but also with the goal of minimizing the anxieties of the majority of passengers. To an international traveller, the problems resulting from procedures of allowing only ticketed passengers past security checkpoints, is causing significant anxiety and inconvenience to passengers and to the meeters and greeters themselves.

REDISTRIBUTION OF CONCESSIONS

A redistribution of airport concession space from the main terminal to the sterile area would also help to meet the needs of passengers. Too frequently a passenger has remained in line, gone through security, walked into an area of the terminal in which there are no concessions, experienced a delay but has not wanted to return to the main terminal, as this would have meant another long delay going through security. Adequate equipment and friendly, courteous people who have helpful smiles on their faces at security stations would contribute a great deal towards making our airports 'people places' rather than 'thing places'.

CUSTOMS AS A SERVICE

Customs areas need to be redesigned to be adequate and spacious, to meet the needs of the 747 passenger. Physical amenities need to be provided: information centres, rest rooms, instant currency exchange, perhaps food and beverages, telephones, baggage carts and the like. The availability of free baggage carts throughout the airports and train stations of Switzerland and most of Europe, needs to be imitated in airports in the United States. The congestion of baggage handling areas is causing more and more business travellers and pleasure travellers alike to keep hold of their personal possessions through the entire flight. Our customers are behaving this way and our airports are not finding the facilities and services to make their lives easy. Older people are seen lugging or tugging suitcases in apparent distress because no convenient carts are available. American travellers in the United States would be overwhelmed if adequate carts were available for use, without fee, throughout our major US stations. Enough, perhaps, on the things we need to do to make our airports people and user friendly. Let me turn to the role of an airport as a tourism centre.

THE AIRPORT AS TOURISM CENTRE

First impressions are quite enduring. Travellers' recollections are frequently affected by what they first see and what they last view. The moment of truth for many international passengers is the feeling they get when they first arrive at the gateway city.

Therefore, the sum total of the airport's experience has a major impact in promoting (or discouraging) future tourism in a region. Whether planned for or not, a region's airport makes a community statement to travellers about the flavour and allure of a region, about the community and its people, about its friendliness or coldness. Our airports should be showplaces to all the world, reflecting regional foods and products, industry and crafts, architecture and style, and simple hospitality. The friendliness or unfriendliness of service in the airport reflects positively or negatively on the city and the region.

Stop-over or hubbing passengers frequently form an opinion of an area that they have never visited, strictly from the airport itself, a particular concourse, an individual restaurant in which they ate, or a retail shop where they purchased a particular item.

Twenty percent of the concession business is generated by meeters and greeters who are in the airport not to travel but to meet, assist, and welcome those who are travelling. We know they are there, yet airports are rarely designed to recognize and provide for these people. They crowd and clog the passageways, as passengers exit planes or exit customs areas, because there are no adequately sized and comfortable arrival areas to take care of their needs. It is an annoyance to the arriving passenger and a frustration to the meeter and greeter. The ability of an airport to be a tourist attraction itself can add to the drawing power of a region. Services needed in airports to meet the demands of the modern international tourist market are tourist information centres, multilingual language centres, business facilities, and greatly improved custom handling systems and procedures. Airports in the US have been found to be particularly deficient with respect to these types of foreign travellers' aid service.

Ground transportation planners need to do a better job, as so many of the great European airports have done, in marrying effective, efficient, ground service transportation for the arriving airline passenger. I know of very few cities in the United States that have come close to solving the problem in the way Gatwick and Heathrow have done in Europe, or such as might be experienced at Zurich, where one can go immediately from airplane to train with a free luggage cart, pass some attractive services and go throughout Europe on a network of efficiently operating railroad trains.

Customs people should be taught, trained and retaught on a regular basis that they are more than government functionaries, providing a control service: they are also part of the hospitality of the welcoming nation, and, as such, they need to be schooled in hospitality as much as in their skilled arts of inspection; they need to welcome people, rather than being appliers of rubber stamps to little passports. This will take some effort, but those who represent governmental agencies should think in terms of their being official greeters and symbols of the hospitality of the receiving nation.

IMPACT ON REGIONAL ECONOMIES
Finally, I want to comment on the impact of airports on regional economies. Airports are important to regional economies not only because they process passengers and freight into and out of the region, but because they represent important engines for growth by providing jobs and by stimulating activity beyond the basic flight services. Airlines employ pilots, stewardesses, baggage handlers, maintenance people, reservations and ticketing personnel. The airport itself employs security, air traffic controllers, cleaning and maintenance people, administrators and managers. Concessionaires provide people who involve themselves in food handling, retail clerks, production, inflight kitchen employees, and they create large boosters for the economy of a local region. They are an important source of employment in the community by direct, on-premises people working for airlines, airports and concessionaires, and by direct, off-premises people that support businesses that surround an airport, such as hotels, rental car companies, maintenance companies, freight forwarding, training offices, inflight catering kitchens, travel agancies, stores, shops, and the like. They are also a secondary generator of revenue through convention and business travel: hotels, meeting and banquet rooms, fun places, theme parks, entertainment centres, centres of business and commerce in and of themselves, where offices are located and where meetings take place.

Our observation of our airport operations group at the Marriott Corporation is that it is an exciting place to be. Growth seems to be exponential, people find good jobs and keep them for long periods of time. The combined economic effect of a major airport and even a medium-sized one, are measured in billions of dollars. In general, the tourists and travellers who pass through an airport buy products and services that create additional jobs and income for the region. Airport employees represent a sizeable workforce and they are an important contributor to the economic cycle, to the local economy, and to the tax base. Airport construction stimulated from growing passenger levels creates more jobs for local workers, and it generates demand for local construction materials and equipment. The local transportation requirements of travellers (taxis, rental cars, limousines, subways, buses, mass transport) all contribute essential elements of the economic impact of the airport.

In many areas, and indeed this is our own company policy, a large number of hotels are located at or near airports to provide opportunities for business travellers from different destinations to meet, to work, and to engage in world-wide commerce. The airport is the gateway, and today the gateway of preference, through which people come and view cities. There is so much more we need to do, but we need first to think of airports as places for people; if we do this, and if we listen to what those people are telling us, this mighty engine of the economy can continue to grow stronger and better for all of our benefits.

W5 Can a busy air carrier airport really be compatible with its neighbours?

R.H. DOYLE, Principal Consultant, Peat, Marwick, Mitchell & Co., San Francisco, USA

As may be true elsewhere, the primary problem between airports and their neighbors in the United States is aircraft noise. Although some communities have not been very successful in resolving their airport/environs problems, a number of airport operators have developed very successful compatibility programs. These "success stories" typically involve an enlightened approach by airport management to treat the aircraft noise problem in an open, fair, and objective manner, and also to be willing to commit both dollars and manpower in support of comprehensive plans designed to improve conditions in the surrounding area.

ONE. INTRODUCTION

1. The title of this paper poses the question, "Can a busy air carrier airport really be compatible* with its neighbors?" Based on the experience record of the past 20 years or so, airport operators in the United States would probably answer "no" as often as "yes" in response to such a question. However, because the achievement of maximum compatibility between an airport and its environs is universally considered to be a very desirable goal, the paper's focus is on those cases where positive rather than negative results have been obtained, how, and by whom.

Scope of Presentation

2. Characteristics of the airport-oriented environmental situations most often encountered in the United States are described in Section Two. Some of the underlying or historical factors responsible in part for these situations are also discussed.

3. Section Three provides a general indication of the nature and range of environmental problems that may be associated with the operation and presence of a busy commercial airport. In addition, this section outlines some of the opportunities and benefits derived by the surrounding community as a direct or indirect result of the airport's existence.

4. A variety of "success stories" are featured in Section Four. These include the compatibility efforts, plans, and programs that have evolved in connection with public air carrier airports serving Seattle, Washington; Tucson, Arizona; St. Louis, Missouri; and Honolulu International and Lihue Airports, Hawaii.

---

*Compatible: capable of living together harmoniously (Oxford American Dictionary, Oxford University Press, 1980).

5. The final section of the paper offers a number of conclusions and recommendations for consideration, if and as appropriate. Some current trends, new concerns, and future directions are also noted.

Meaning of Terms

6. This paper contains a number of terms that are frequently used in the United States relative to airport-oriented environmental matters. The meanings of these terms are provided below for ready reference.

AIR CARRIER. An individual or group who undertakes directly by lease, or other arrangement, to engage in the transporting of people and/or goods from one point to another by means of aircraft.

AIR CARRIER AIRPORT. An airport designated by design and/or use for air carrier operations.

AIRPORT ENVIRONS. The area surrounding a given airport that is most directly affected (beneficially/adversely) by the presence and operation of that airport.

AIRPORT OPERATOR. An individual, group, or public body (such as an authority) responsible through ownership or official designation for the operation of a specified airport. As recognized by the Federal Aviation Administration (FAA), such an operator may also be referred to as an airport sponsor.

AIRPORT NOISE. Unwanted sound emanating from an operating aircraft engine while on the ground or in the air during flight.

DAY-NIGHT SOUND LEVEL (Ldn). The noise measurement system (noise metric) commonly accepted and used in the United States to indicate the extent and level of aircraft noise exposure associated with a particular airport. In the Ldn procedure, the noise energy in decibels (A-weighted sound meter scale) that is produced by individual aircraft landings and takeoffs at a particular airport is calculated for each separate operation. (Note: The mathematical formula used in the calculations reflects a 10 times "weighting penalty" for those operations that take place between the hours of 10 p.m. and 7 a.m.) These individual noise energy figures are then aggregated for an average or typical 24-hour period during a specified year so as to yield single-number noise exposure values, such as Ldn 65 or Ldn 78. The respective Ldn values for a given condition (e.g., the average day) can be readily mapped in the form of noise contours or noise grids, and compared to other operational conditions--actual vs. hypothetical, present vs. future, before and after an air traffic control (ATC) procedural change, etc.

NOISE ABATEMENT. The reduction of aircraft noise in degree, intensity, or frequency. Modification in the noise source (e.g., the engine) as well as in aircraft operational procedures is representative of "on-airport" abatement actions that are or may be employed by operators, air traffic controllers, airline companies, and aircraft pilots.

NOISE MITIGATION. The alleviation of aircraft noise impacts that human receivers of such noise are or may be exposed to. Off-airport mitigation measures often include the sound insulation of homes and schools, the acquisition and subsequent conversion of noise-sensitive properties, and the development of airport-compatible land use arrangements.

NOISE REMEDY. An action, measure, or program undertaken by responsible parties of interest to (a) abate the aircraft noise associated with a given airport, or (b) mitigate the adverse effects of any such noise that cannot be entirely eliminated--at present or over time.

TWO. PREVAILING AIRPORT/ENVIRONS CONDITIONS

7. What characteristics, if any, are common to those situations where an airport is currently or potentially incompatible with its environs? Also, what scenarios are likely to result in confrontation between an airport and its neighbors? This section of the paper provides some answers to these important questions that have emerged as a result of recent American experience. They may or may not be fully applicable to similar situations in other parts of the world.

Typical Airport Locale

8. Just prior to and after World War II, most of the public airports that served large as well as small cities in the United States were located in undeveloped suburban or rural settings. As a consequence, these pioneering "air age" facilities were then largely compatible with their surroundings.

9. However, as the national interstate highway system permitted a growing population to move readily into the nearby countryside, the formerly remote airfields were gradually

encroached upon by residential and other developments not always in harmony with the operation of an airport. The situation was further aggravated by the introduction of jet-powered commercial aircraft in many locations around 1960.

10. Even a relatively new airport such as the 18,000-acre Dallas/Fort Worth International Airport (DFW) in Texas--which wasn't opened until 1973--has now been virtually surrounded by suburban residential homeowners who do not want to "put up with" noisy aircraft activity. With few exceptions, then, the typical airport in much of the United States may be characterized as having a fully urbanized (or rapidly urbanizing) land use pattern with numerous incompatibilities that require attention and positive action by the airport operator and other parties of interest.

Multijurisdictional Factors

11. If the airport environs is made up of several political jurisdictions (cities, counties, states), the compatibility situation can be much more difficult to cope with. Under the American system, which tends to favor strong local rather than central governmental control, the airport operator may have to deal with many diverse interests if a compatibility program exists.

12. For instance, resolution of the incompatible condition will require a cooperative effort to (a) define the problem, (b) pose and analyze optional solutions, (c) develop consensus as to what should be done and by whom, and (d) implement the program of improvement that is ultimately agreed upon. Needless to say, this process requires a great deal of time, patience, and old-fashioned "give and take."

13. To emphasize the point further, some 13 municipalities, including the Cities of Dallas and Fort Worth, who own and operate DFW via a special Airport Board, and three separate counties may need to be consulted relative to an Airport/Environs Problem. Then, too, the St. Louis International Airport (STL) Environs Plan described in Section Four involved participation by 20 separate cities (8 of which adjoin the Airport boundary), St. Louis County, and the State of Missouri. More than 150 public meetings were held over a 40-month period to develop a workable compatibility plan for this airport.

Airport Image Considerations

14. The degree to which a busy commercial airport is viewed as a community asset has changed radically in the 40 or so years that have elapsed since World War II. A brief decade by decade review will highlight this point.

• Late 1940s. The five-year period after the War was primarily devoted to the conversion of numerous airfields from military to civilian ownership and operation, and to the establishment of staff, funding, and management capability needed at the local level to accommodate what seemed to be an exciting future for air transportation. This optimism was fueled by the growing ability of manufacturers and airline companies to capitalize on the aircraft technology developed as part of the wartime effort.

• 1950s and 1960s. Like many other enterprises in the United States, air carrier airport facilities experienced major growth and improvement over the 20-year period beginning in 1950. Planned in response to the widespread introduction of jet-powered aircraft such as the B-707, DC-8, B-727, DC-9, and BAC-111, major new airports were opened in the Washington, D.C., area (Dulles International); Jacksonville, Florida; Sacramento, California; and Houston, Texas (Intercontinental). In addition, extensive new terminal facilities were placed into operation at John F. Kennedy International in New York, at Los Angeles International, at Hartsfield Atlanta International, and at Chicago's O'Hare International. Of course, dozens of similar provisions were also being added in city after city in every one of the 50 states.

As might be expected during this heady period of expansion, a modern new airport was often considered to be the local community status symbol. Airport management could do little wrong, financing for improvements was relatively easy to come by, and only a few locales had what we now refer to as a "noise problem."

Indeed, the 1950-1970 period represented an era in which outside influences on the planning and management of airports tended to be super-supportive rather than super-critical of facility expansion or improvement.

• 1970s. Passage of the National Environmental Policy Act of 1969 (or NEPA) heralded a time of environmental and economic stalemate that followed two decades of virtually unfettered growth. Apart from the new airports of DFW and Kansas City (Missouri) International, and new terminals at Tampa, Florida, and Newark, New Jersey, no major facilities came into existence between 1970 and 1980.

This situation was not the result of a lack of effort, however. Ambitious ventures were initiated in Atlanta, Boston, Chicago, Cleveland, Los Angeles, Miami, Minneapolis-Saint Paul, New Orleans, New York, St. Louis, San Diego, and Seattle (among others) to develop replacement or additional air carrier airports. With few exceptions, these ventures were sidetracked for environmental and/or cost reasons.

• 1980s. Figure 1 provides a graphical representation of how the planning and development of airports has changed--at least in the United States--over the past 30 years or so. Whereas technology, engineering, and design prevailed in the 1960s, and environmentally oriented public concerns dominated the 1970s, sophisticated management and financial techniques have come to the forefront in the current decade.

The necessity for airport sponsors to draw from and rely upon such techniques stems from the need to consider environmental costs (primarily noise) on a co-equal basis with the more traditional financing requirements of new terminals, airfields, ground access, and cargo-handling provisions. In short, airport management is now obliged to fairly and equally consider all of its constituents-- close neighbors as well as key airport users.

A Litigious Society

15. Yet another factor that has precipitated confrontation between airport operators and the occupants of airport environs in recent years is the fact that America has become a litigious society. Whether the reason for this trend is a liberal U.S. Supreme Court (as some would say), an overabundance of lawyers (as contended by others), or simply a reaction against what is perceived as a "don't care" attitude on the part of airport management is immaterial. What is important is the reality that litigation against an airport sponsor now occurs quite frequently and must be treated seriously. Indeed, the entire approach to the planning process may have to be altered because of this nationwide "phobia" to use the Courts to right real or alleged wrongs.

16. The current situation facing the City of New Orleans in its capacity as owner and operator of New Orleans International Airport is a classic case in point. A Louisiana Court recently decided that all 6,500(±) property owners who lived within the Ldn 65 and above noise exposure area, as indicated on a map showing Ldn contours generated by 1980 aircraft operational levels at the airport, would have to be either a plaintiff or a defendant in separate cases involving the City. If this ruling holds up, New Orleans may have to litigate up to 6,500 individual cases involving some 20,000 or so occupants of a court-prescribed airport environs! To say the least, an enormous amount of time, energy, and dollars will need to be devoted by all sides in this particular "neighborhood dispute."

THREE. PROBLEMS & OPPORTUNITIES

17. The New Orleans litigational situation outlined in the preceding section is ostensibly related to the problem of airport noise. It should be noted, however, that an underlying issue may actually be of greater relevance to what has occurred to date. That issue is the continuing fear of an out-of-control aircraft falling into one or more homes in a residential neighborhood with the subsequent loss of life, as occurred in Kenner, Louisiana (adjacent to New Orleans International Airport on the east) on July 9, 1982.

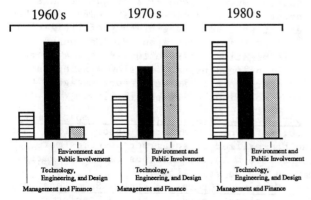

Fig 1. The changing importance of key influences of airport planning and development

18. While an even greater noise problem existed at the airport prior to the 1982 tragedy, there was little in the way of lawsuits against the City of New Orleans up to that time. Since then, however, there has been an almost continuous stream of legal activity which shows little sign of abating, at least in the near future.

Types of Airport-Oriented Environmental Problems

19. Excessive or annoying noise exposure generated by aircraft operations (with or without the related safety issue) is clearly the number one problem for airport operators and environs occupants alike. And it promises to remain so for many years to come in a number of locations throughout the United States. However, there are other environmental factors that can be a source of airport/environs disputes or concerns. They include:

• Air Quality. The most common air quality problem associated with airports involves the build-up of automobile-polluted air in terminal curbside or parking garage locations. Special ventilation provisions are sometimes needed to improve such conditions. In off-airport locations, homeowners used to complain of exterior damage to their residences caused by fuel "droplets" stemming from overflying aircraft. Fortunately, the influx of newer, more fuel-efficient, and cleaner equipment has tended to eliminate this type of observation.

• Water Quality. From an environmental standpoint, aircraft fuel spillage accidents that might contaminate surface or subsurface water supply sources is of occasional concern. Most major airports have installed specially designed on-site systems in recent years that have greatly reduced the possibility.

• Flora and Fauna. Every now and then, a proposed airport improvement program must take into account specialized wildlife and/or plantlife conditions. In some cases, such as those involving the Honolulu International and Oakland International Airports, expensive new habitats have been required by the FAA or the courts to accommodate an endangered bird (Honolulu) and a diminishing supply of undeveloped wetland acreage (Oakland). The latter is needed to permit the continued propagation of certain bird, fish, or animal species.

• Surface Traffic Congestion. Vehicular ground traffic to and from a large airport complex can be a source of major aggravation for both the residents and merchants of some airport environs. In San Francisco, for example, many of the 30,000 or so persons who work at the International Airport in San Mateo County used to create (and be victims of) intolerable morning and evening traffic tie-ups in such neighboring communities as San Bruno and Millbrae. This particular problem was largely resolved by the establishment of a multilane, limited access freeway--a very costly but necessary solution that has been used in several other U.S. situations in addition to San Francisco.

• Growth Inducing Role of Airport. A "bone of contention" in certain locales is the role played by an airport in inducing additional urban development. On the one hand, area-wide business and political interests often rely upon a given airport to be a reason for and catalyst of new job opportunities, new construction activity, and new tax sources. Localized environmental and property owner interests, however, may be adamantly opposed to any influx of new people, new traffic, and new pollution to their communities. Due to its complexities, this type of problem can be very difficult to deal with in a free society such as we have in the United States. Nonetheless, the Lihue Airport (Hawaii) case described in Section Four is an example of how such a problem can be worked out to the general satisfaction of most of the contending interests.

• Uncontrolled Urban Encroachment. As mentioned in the Introduction, most American airports have gradually become surrounded by urban development not always compatible with an air transportation facility. All too often, expansion or improvement of an airport--even if needed for purposes of greater compatibility--may not be possible due to such encroachment. While this type of problem sounds very similar to the preceding one on growth inducement, a different set of positions is held by the protagonists. Airport management is typically unhappy that affected local units of government do not (or will not) properly consider future airport needs in their process of approving new noise-sensitive developments. These governmental units, however, are often more beholden to their local developers and taxpayers than they are to the airport sponsor--particularly if that sponsor is a "big city" neighbor who may have "bullied" them on other matters in past years.

• Airport Management Attitudes. A negative attitude on the part of airport management toward any real or perceived noise issue in the environs has acted as a prime deterrent to the satisfactory resolution of a local compatibility problem in too many U.S. situations. Such an attitude is characterized by the view that "most of those people knew about the airport when they moved into the neighborhood--why should we do anything special in response to their noise complaints?" Of course, where a general attitude of this nature has prevailed in past years, one should expect to find a long history of litigation against the airport sponsor. Fortunately, this negative attitude towards the airport environs (and beyond) is slowly dying out as younger, more positive airport managers take over positions of responsibility.

Opportunities By Way of Greater Compatibility

20. A few of the numerous opportunities that can be realized if an airport becomes more compatible with its environs (and vice versa) may be listed as follows:

• Continued Operation at the Same Location. It is almost certain that the Sea-Tac International and St. Louis International

Airports would not have been able to function much longer in their present locations if workable compatibility plans had not been developed and carried out (see next section). Instead of costs on the order of billions of dollars that would have been needed to construct new replacement facilities elsewhere, both of these important facilities have been "saved" via the expenditure of millions of dollars for noise mitigation programs involving such techniques as property acquisition (including avigation easements) and the sound insulation of noise-sensitive homes and schools.

• Regional Economic Stability and Growth. The preservation and continuance of St. Louis International Airport at its close-in urban site has had, and will continue to have, enormous implications for the metropolitan area and the State of Missouri, in addition to the City of St. Louis. Although it was not the only factor involved, the St. Louis Airport Environs Plan must be given primary credit for this extraordinary "salvage" operation. Similarly successful compatibility efforts could be cited in other U.S. locations that have likewise preserved and capitalized on the economic power generated by the operation of a large public airport.

• Litigation Avoidance. A carefully constructed compatibility program that does result in an improved airport environs situation over time will definitely result in far fewer suits against the airport proprietor, the airlines, and perhaps even the FAA. This contention can be verified by the "track record" over the past 10 years of such airports as Tucson International in Arizona, Portland International in Oregon, and Kansas City International in Missouri, among others.

• Positive Management Attitudes. Where noise-related compatibility problems are in existence, a helpful rather than hostile attitude by airport management can result in greatly improved relationships with neighboring communities. In turn, these bettered relationships can often lead to needed on-airport improvements that might otherwise have never been achieved. Verification of this type of opportunity can be furnished by the current managers of Sea-Tac International Airport in Washington, Burbank-Glendale-Pasadena Airport in California, and Tucson International Airport in Arizona.

• Demonstration Projects. Yet another opportunity that can grow out of an enlightened airport/environs compatibility effort is the ability to demonstrate noise abatement and noise mitigation measures for the benefit of skeptical or uncertain human receivers of aircraft noise. Specially designed projects (some successful and some not) to demonstrate such things as different flight patterns, night-time operational limitations, residential soundproofing, and property transaction assistance procedures have been and are being carried out by a host of airport sponsors in all parts of the United States.

FOUR. RECENT SUCCESS STORIES

21. Five very different airport/environs compatibility efforts are discussed in this section. Large, medium, and small airports are represented by these examples, as are varying local jurisdictional situations. Each story reflects success in dealing with the difficult problem of how to make an airport more compatible with its neighbors. Each story also indicates to some extent how opportunities can arise from and be capitalized on as a result of compatibility issues.

Sea-Tac International Airport

22. In 1973, the Port of Seattle and King County, Washington initiated an FAA-assisted $642,000 study to develop a plan for the improvement of Sea-Tac International Airport and its surrounding communities. The study area included about 60 square miles and 137,000 residents. The overall goal of this undertaking was to "make the Airport and Community better neighbors."

23. Completed in 1976, the Sea-Tac Communities Plan proved to be a model for dozens of similar efforts that have followed its pioneering lead. Among other things, the FAA patterned its Advisory Circular (AC) 150/5050-6, "Airport Land Use Compatibility Planning" on the process used in Seattle, and the American Institute of Planners (now American Institute of Certified Planners or AICP) conferred a Meritorious Program Award on the Plan.

24. Subsequently updated in 1983, the original Sea-Tac Communities Plan fulfilled four specific objectives according to almost every participant in, or observer of, this landmark effort. These objectives were as follows:

• To develop a comprehensive Airport and Communities Master Plan that will improve relationships between Sea-Tac International Airport and its Environs.

• To incorporate detailed environmental inventories into the study such that all relevant environmental factors are assured full and careful consideration.

• To proceed in a manner that (a) fully addresses the advantages and disadvantages associated with each viable plan alternative, and (b) provides for adequate public involvement in all such deliberations.

• To develop final recommendations that are soundly based on all pertinent technical, economic, social, environmental, and financial factors, and which provide for the adoption of specific implementation policies by the Port of Seattle, King County, and other appropriate agencies, including the Federal Aviation Administration.

25. More than $60 million has been spent by the Port of Seattle and the FAA to carry out Plan recommendations to date. Close to 1,000 families have been relocated away from high noise areas and an extensive sound insulation program has been initiated based on the results of a special demonstration project. All in all, the Sea-Tac Communities Plan effort is representative of how well an airport sponsor can work with occupants of the airport environs to improve conditions to the general satisfaction of all parties of interest.

St. Louis International Airport

26. Following unsuccessful attempts to build a new airport in Illinois to serve the St. Louis Metropolitan Area, local, state, and federal officials decided to make the existing Lambert-St. Louis International Airport more compatible with its complex set of neighboring communities. The resultant "St. Louis Airport Environs Plan," which covers a 60 square mile area inhabited by some 183,000 full time residents, was completed in 1981. Since that time, close to $100 million has been spent and/or authorized to implement various Plan recommendations such as property acquisition, purchase assurance, acoustical treatment of noise-sensitive structures, and the acquisition of avigation easements. Perhaps the most noteworthy point to be made about the St. Louis story is the fact that agreement can be reached and improvements facilitated even when nearly 30 different political jurisdictions must be consulted at every important point in the planning process.

Honolulu International Airport

27. A coordinated airport and environs plan was also completed in 1981 for Honolulu International Airport. As the principal entry point for the millions of visitors who come to this island state every year, the Honolulu terminal is designed to capture the open-air, tropical atmosphere associated with Hawaii. Also, since nearly as many visitors come from Japan and the far East as from the U.S. mainland, the terminal area often takes on the character of an international bazaar or meeting place. The Overseas Terminal is particularly successful in helping the arriving passenger to make the transition from his or her originating point to the island environment.

28. With regard to the area immediately surrounding the airport, a compatible land use pattern is and has been in place since the $80 million "Reef Runway" became operational in the early 1970s. Located so as to permit the ocean-spanning jumbo jet aircraft (B-747, L-1011, DC-10) to approach and depart the airport via overwater routes rather than over Downtown Honolulu (as was formerly necessary), the Reef Runway could not be built until a satisfactory replacement habitat for the endangered Hawaiian Stilt was provided by the State Department of Transportation, owner and operator of all civil airports, including Honolulu International Airport. Because of this previous action, the 1981 Environs Plan focused on how to prevent incompatible uses from coming into existence in the undeveloped agricultural areas situated west of the Airport. The preventive nature of the 1981 Plan thus contrasted highly with its remedially oriented St. Louis counterpart.

Tucson International Airport

29. Another airport/environs planning project was completed in the early 1980s for the City of Tucson and Pima County, Arizona. Involving just the two political jurisdictions and the Tucson Airport Authority, this effort resulted in a unanimously approved plan that encompassed both remedial and preventive land use compatibility measures. Features of the plan included an extension of the primary NW-SE runway so as to reduce noise exposure over the City of Tucson to the northwest, and the acquisition of more than 4,000 acres of additional land to protect the airport from future urban encroachment to the east, southeast, and south. As with the other "success stories" in this section, the Tucson Environs Plan was developed in concert with citizen and airline interests as well as the respective local governmental bodies.

Lihue Airport

30. A 1975 master plan for the Lihue Airport on the Island of Kauai in Hawaii is included here because of its many environmental ramifications. Now constructed and in operation essentially as planned, this smaller airport facility would not have been improved if the environmental concerns had not been properly identified and addressed. These concerns included:

  • the growth-inducing impacts of terminal improvements,
  • the role played by the addition of a runway in reducing aircraft noise exposure, and
  • the potentially damaging effects on shoreline bird, animal, and fish life if the airport were to be expanded seaward.

31. Local environmental interests argued that expansion and modernization of terminal facilities would encourage more unwanted development on this "Garden Island." The argument proved to be unfounded, however, when the planning team pointed out the fact that substantial growth had taken place even though the terminal had not been improved in any way for almost 30 years! As noted by the team, Lihue Airport exists solely as a service facility to accommodate the traveling public. If that public is growing too much or too fast, resolution of such a problem (real or perceived) rests with the elected Kauai County Commission, who decide whether or not additional destination resorts are to be permitted on the Island.

32. In the case of Lihue Airport, the addition of an entirely new runway permitted overwater approaches as well as departures from the facility. The new airfield configuration thus eliminated noise exposure problems for occupants of the environs, including the nearby Town of Lihue.

33. Evolution of a workable, environmentally sensitive master plan for the airport resulted in there being no need to expand in such a way as to create new flora or fauna problems. Careful consideration of such possibilities as part of the required environmental impact assessment was carried out by well-qualified professionals who carefully considered the implications of each and every airport development option posed by the planning team.

FIVE. CONCLUSIONS AND RECOMMENDATIONS

34. It is possible to make an airport more compatible with its neighbors provided that certain guidelines are followed in the process. This section contains findings and recommendations as to successful programs of improvement that can be and have been implemented in the United States.

Approaches to Achieve Compatibility

35. It seems evident that airport management must have the right attitude in order to commit the time, personnel, and fiscal resources needed to achieve maximum compatibility between their facility and its environs. Characteristics of such an attitude might include:

• A belief that a problem does exist and can be resolved.

• A belief that occupants of the environs are constituents of management on an equal footing with users of the airport.

• An approach to the situation that is open, fair, and objective.

• A willingness to consider any and all possible options.

• The necessary patience to "hear out" all sides of a controversy.

• The ability to compromise toward a consensus solution, if necessary.

Compatibility Plans and Programs

36. Although an airport environs land use compatibility effort can be mounted as part of a master plan project, the most common procedure is to undertake the development of an acceptable program under the FAA's FAR Part 150 guidelines. These guidelines deal with the airport noise compatibility planning process that is most likely to produce acceptable results and thereby qualify for all or part of the funds needed to carry out noise remedy measures.

37. An FAR Part 150 project covers both noise abatement (on-airport) and noise mitigation (off-airport) options. Although it is not perfect, a Part 150 effort can and does deal with real issues, it permits and encourages full participation by all parties of interest, and it does serve as a prerequisite to the ultimate funding of agreed-upon implementation actions.

Current Trends and New Concerns

38. Many airport sponsors have recently completed or initiated a Part 150 program. As a consequence, the $80 million or so that is annually available from the Airport Trust Fund is typically used up very rapidly. Several bills are now before the U.S. Congress that would increase this noise set-aside up to as much as $350 million per year. However, noise-oriented litigation also seems to be growing in both frequency and intensity. As a consequence, those sponsors who still refuse to address their noise problems are falling farther behind and also risking the possibility of spending several years in court.

39. One of the newest concerns that has surfaced in the United States might be termed the "airfield capacity versus noise abatement" confrontation. Airline groups such as the Air Transport Association (ATA) contend that the proliferation of locally determined noise abatement procedures now in effect at airports in all parts of the country will result in air traffic control problems, intolerable delays, and a loss of badly needed airfield capacity. The present head of the FAA, Donald Engen, seems to agree with this view.

40. The Airport Operators Council International (AOCI) and the American Association of Airport Executives (AAAE), however, argue that local airport sponsors need and must have the ability to promulgate noise reduction measures of benefit to their respective environs constituents. While this potentially volatile issue is just now heating up, it seems certain that noise compatibility planning that works will be in even greater demand in the future than it has been in the immediate past.

W6 Airport and environment: the British experience

G.P. YOUNGMAN, Landscape Architect, Kings Langley, UK

This paper is entirely concerned with British experience. It describes the statutory arrangements for consultation between airport authorities and both the local planning authorities and representatives of local communities: it lists the main elements of neighbourhood nuisance caused by airports and describes ways in which these are mitigated: and it describes three examples of ways in which airports can produce positive local benefits. At the conference the talk will be illustrated by slides.

INTRODUCTION

1. This paper derives mostly from my work as the main (but not the only) landscape consultant to British Airports Authority since 1972, when I was first called in to advise on developments then being planned in the eastern sector at Gatwick. This authority managed the major airports of England and Scotland from its formation in 1966 until its privatisation last year. There are, however, some forty airports owned and managed by local authorities. Of these the largest are Manchester, Birmingham and Luton. The two former I have visited and investigated for the purposes of this paper; and have found that their polices and actions correspond very closely with those of British Airports Authority.

2. On the face of it, the title of this workshop is self-contradictory. Nothing could be less friendly than to establish a new airport or greatly expand an existing one close to where people are living. Yet for many people in its hinterland an airport does bring one great benefit. It boosts the local economy, providing jobs and paying substantial rates (in Britain the local tax levied for local purposes). So, for example, at Gatwick this year some 35,000 jobs directly or indirectly derive from the existence of the airport; and some £7,000,000 is paid in rates by the British Airports Authority alone. In less quantifiable ways also an airport must stimulate commerce and industry in the surrounding region. This factor, undoubtedly, for an appreciable number of people does outweigh the drawbacks. Thus at the Stansted public inquiry to offset the understandably vociferous objections of those whose enjoyment of a quiet rural way of life would be upset were those who welcomed the job opportunities the expanded airport would create. Also the plea was made, most strongly by Manchester (which has plans to more than double its present capacity) that the deprived areas of the midlands and the north should be given the benefits of airport expansion rather than the prosperous south-east.

3. Nevertheless there are too many people for whom the nuisance of an airport is only too audible and visible and the benefits too diffused and ill-perceived; and it is to their concerns that this paper is addressed.

CONSULTATIONS

4. In Britain all changes of land and building use, other than for farming and forestry, require the consent of the local authorities who have the duty to prepare plans and powers to exercise control: and airports are no exception. Where developers and authority cannot agree, the developer has the right of appeal to central government; and if the issue is sufficiently important a local and public inquiry may be held. In contentious issues of national importance central government may pre-empt the normal process and initiate a public inquiry under an independent inspector. At such an inquiry the two parties make their cases; but anyone affected by the proposals, whether as a group or as an individual or as a public body, can have hearing to register objection or support. So, for example, the new terminals at Gatwick and Heathrow and the whole expansion of Stansted were the subject of public inquiries (the latter, until Sizewell B nuclear power station, being the most protracted that had ever been). A major inquiry of this kind and the government decision to which it leads will set the main pattern for development; but many detailed matters will remain for discussion with the local planning authorities. Thus for the new terminal development at Gatwick there have so far been nine applications of this sort, which have included the various landscape proposals for the perimeter areas.

5. In this there is a legally established procedure for a local community, to a small extent individually but largely through its elected representatives, to have, without over-riding operational and functional necessities, some influence on the specifics of an airport's development. There is also another channel of influence. This is through the airport consultative committees, which exist for both the British Airports Authority and the local authority airports. For Gatwick (and I presume much the same applies elsewhere) this committee is composed of members appointed by the parish, district and county councils and by semi-official organisations like the local Chamber of Commerce and the Tourist Board. It is chaired by an official of the Department of Transport and meets in public four times a year. It has a direct channel of communication to central government to which it reports annually. It is regarded as highly

important by British Airports Authority; and all its meetings are attended by the airport director and senior managers, who are fully open to questioning by members of the committee. The recent Airports Act that privatised the airports (local authority as well as British Airports Authority) provides for the continuance of these consultative committees

MITIGATION OF AIRPORT NUISANCE

6.   Noise.   This obviously is by far the worst nuisance. As the greatest noise comes from aircraft in flight nothing that can be done at ground level at the airport can minimise that: but airports do contribute towards the costs of sound insulation for the worst affected properties and are required by the recent Airports Act to purchase, if owners so demand, properties that have demonstrably dropped in value. Planes once airborne come under the control of the Civil Aviation Authority, which imposes restrictions on night flying and directs flight paths away from the most densely populated areas.

7.   Ground level noise is another matter: and solid barriers such as earth mounds, walls and fences can do something to lessen this. How much I find it difficult to judge; and may be the improvement is as much psychological as physical. For British Airports Authority noise barriers have been required as a result of public inquiries and in consultation with local planning authorities; and in these matters it has had the advice of Professor John Large of Southampton University. At Gatwick, as part of the new north terminal development, is a mound 13m high and over 1km long. Space is cramped; and the slope, at 1m $2\frac{1}{4}$, is kept as steep as will be stable. But even so the mound occupies over $6\frac{1}{2}$ hectares. At Stansted there will be similar but much shorter mounds. At Heathrow terminal 4 a long mound helps to shield houses from the traffic noise of the new access road: but elsewhere there is no available space and the aprons are screened by concrete walls 7m high and in total $1\frac{1}{2}$km long. At Birmingham there are two mounds, one close to the aprons and the other between the runway and nearby houses. Construction of the latter produced an immediate complaint from a householder objecting to his loss of view of taxi-ing aircraft. That is a good example of the familiar truisms that, however well intentioned our endeavours, we can never please everybody and that it is always the complainants (often a minority) who make their views known.

8.   Scenery.   An airport wipes out the familiar features of the countryside, replacing the fields, hedges, small woods and streams with huge hangars and terminal buildings and multi-storey car parks, with vast areas of concrete and tarmac, all at night brightly lit. This is the next most common cause of complaint. But unlike that of noise, much can be done, at any rate where the surrounding terrain is lowlying (as it usually is) and given time, quite simply by mounding and planting around the airport perimeter at the outset and within each sector as it is developed.

9.   Mounding (and noise barriers can contribute scenically) is immediate in its effect; but often must wait until a site is being developed. At that stage, however, it may well become one of the functional requirements of a landscape scheme, to accommodate the huge quantities of surplus soil; thus avoiding the cost and the traffic nuisance to the local

community of heavy lorries trundling the material to distant tips. Creative use of surplus muck is a characteristic of contemporary landscape design. Both Gatwick and Heathrow provide current examples; so do the Edinburgh and Aberdeen projects of the past; so will Stansted in the near future.

10.   Planting, of course, does need time. How much depends on many variables: but trees and shrubs as woodland, though needing eighty years or more to reach full stature, should make an appreciable effect within ten years. Therefore airport development plans should allocate perimeter areas for what in our fashionable professional jargon (which I much dislike) is called structure planting, to be carried out long in advance of any construction. This should be woodland in character, of species that suit the local ecology and in belts at least 25m wide and preferably 50m. Only woodland can match the vast scale of an airport on the one side and echo the rural landscape on the other; and at the same time, even though predominantly deciduous, provide enough of a screen in winter. Such planting was carried out at Gatwick twelve years ago, primarily along the northern boundary, and small areas at Edinburgh and Aberdeen, though with varying success. Substantial areas are included in the proposals for Stansted and in the development strategy for Manchester.

11.   Planting of this kind has to be planned with awareness of its possible encouragement to birds that might be a hazard to aircraft in flight. Though the grassland feeding birds, especially gulls and lapwings, are the main cause of air strikes, there is always a possible risk from woodland nesting and roosting birds like rooks, pigeons and, above all, starlings. These latter can gather at roosting time in flocks of many thousands, swooping and swirling in flight directions that take no account of passing aircraft. But there is no certainty or predictability; and most British airports have existing woods and hedgerows close to their runways and flight paths but beyond their boundaries which cause no problems. A complete embargo on new planting is not called for. British Airports Authority has a policy directive, now nine years old, which relies mainly on shooting, nest destruction or scaring to disperse any colonies of birds that do materialise. At Gatwick, for the first time since extensive new planting began in 1974, there was last year a large gathering of starlings in one small area; which were dispersed after three days intensive scaring.

12.   Traffic.   Large airports generate much traffic. In Britain the provision of new approach roads and the upgrading of existing ones is the responsibility of central government. Interchanges between airport roads and local roads have to be designed to avoid interruption and congestion of local traffic. Road proposals have to be agreed with the Department of Transport or the County Councils acting as its agent. For the recent new terminal at Heathrow the first proposals were rejected; and only after a protracted period of discussion was a scheme agreed.

13.   More worrying to local residents is the construction traffic that for many years may crowd the local lanes and minor roads with large, noisy, dirty and dangerous vehicles. As far as British Airports Authority is concerned the least harmful routes are selected in consultation with the local planning authorities; and contractors, even though they may charge more for longer or more inconvenient routes, are required to use only these.

14. <u>River flooding and pollution</u>. In Britain all the river systems, to their smallest backwaters, come under the jurisdiction of a number of regional authorities which have the tasks, among other things, of controlling floods and preventing pollution. Airport rooves, roads, surface car parks, aprons, taxiways and runways generate at times of heavy rain far greater volumes of surface water than the small, sluggish local streams can absorb directly: and the water may be polluted with oil and chemicals. So, to the satisfaction of the river authorities, there have to be balancing and aerating ponds (Gatwick has already five and a sixth planned) and settling tanks (the largest and latest at Gatwick is part of the new north terminal development).

15. <u>Ecological destruction</u>. This is the most recent factor, reflecting growing public concern, to influence airport planning. Though the vast scale and stringent functional requirements must inevitably annihilate most of the previous fields, ditches, streams, hedges and woods, there is still some scope, in the outlying areas and among the more flexible ancillary uses, to preserve habitats and vegetation that have some special value. Landscape plans also may create new areas of interest in substitution for those lost. At Gatwick in the development of the eastern sector woodland, copse and hedgerow trees were preserved (though more for scenic than ecological reasons): and in the present plans for the north-western sectors, after a recent study by a professional ecologist, two woods are to be preserved and measures taken to establish a more varied grassland flora. At Stansted, in preparation for the proposals submitted at the public inquiry, a comprehensive ecological study was made not only of the airport site but the adjoining land also. On the airport the main interest was found to be among the scrub and in the grassland. During the past year action has been taken to transfer herbage, both in turves and rotovated topsoil, from areas doomed to disappear.

POSITIVE CONTRIBUTIONS

16. <u>Spectators</u>. Many people are attracted to an airport merely to watch the coming and going and manoeuvring of planes: and Manchester Airport Authority has noted "an increasing public demand for aircraft viewing". Most airports have made special arrangements for spectators (who can be a nuisance, especially with their parked cars clogging airport roads, where they are not wanted). British Airports Authority have viewing terraces on the rooves of terminal buildings; and at Heathrow have provided a separate car park from which, at weekends and on public holidays, there is a free bus service to and from the terminal area. Birmingham has a grass picnic area with a full view over aprons and aircraft stands close by. Manchester's development plan includes a spectators area close to the west end of the runway, to be connected by footpath to a nearby country park.

17. <u>Footpaths and public open space</u>. Airports developing in rural areas will progressively disrupt an existing pattern of footpaths and bridleways. In Britain for those that have been mapped, recorded and given statutory status, an alternative diversion has to be provided. Local ramblers associations are jealous of their rights and active in securing them. So new footpaths become an element in the landscape plan. At Stansted they will be associated with perimeter woodland; and for one bridleway a bridge is being provided across the new dual carriageway access road. At Gatwick in places the paths pass through the new urbanised landscape of the built-up area; but in the northern zone the path follows, along the inner edge of the boundary woodland, the line of the diverted river Mole. Here the local people are being given the use of new riverside park, narrow but, when complete, 4km long. Manchester's development plan provides for interim diversion of existing paths and ultimately for new statutory paths to maintain connection between existing paths beyond the airport boundary.

CONCLUSION

18. Airports have to function efficiently and operate profitably (or at least without loss). Passenger safety and convenience take precedence. But within these limits airport authorities, in so far as I have experience of their working, are genuinely concerned to do what they can for their neighbours. Local authorities on the whole are satisfied. How far the individual residents are satisfied I do not know.

Report on Workshop 3 and Discussion

PROFESSOR W. F. SHEA, CENTER FOR AEROSPACE
SCIENCES, AVIATION DEPARTMENT, UNIVERSITY OF
NORTH DAKOTA
The importance of airports to nations is most
profound, for they are a precious international
commodity. An airport is viewed by airport
neighbours differently today than it was thirty
years ago. The importance of airports is
understood completely by everyone, although the
question of aircraft noise remains a real issue
with airport neighbours.

Some airports have made great progress with
their neighbours, while others have not. It was
noted at the environmental session that the more
sucessful compatibility programmes have been
accomplished when the airport
management/operator treated the programme with a
forthright approach, discussing issues openly
and objectively. Furthermore, where possible,
the airport established a programme to find ways
of mitigating noise. Residents for and against
the airport noise issues had an opportunity to
participate in the hearing process as well as
participating in the mitigating programmes
themselves.

It was noted at this environmental session
that US airports have not always had success in
resolving airport noise issues. However, many
US airports have worked diligently in mitigating
airport noise. Although noise is caused by
aircraft, the airport management teams work on
noise resolution.

Fortunately, technology is developing quieter
engines on new aircraft. In the USA, some
significant environmental laws are in place that
affect airport development and operations. Some
nations are reviewing the environmental laws of
the USA and other world airports. Further,
litigation against US airport operators is being
monitored as to the impact of this activity on
the air transportation system.

Mr R. H. Doyle (Paper W5) noted that the
achievement of maximum compatibility between an
airport and its environs is universally
considered to be a very desirable goal. He
noted the current situation facing the city of
New Orleans in its capacity as owner and
operator of the International Airport. A
Louisiana Court decided recently that all 6500
property owners who lived within the Ldn 65
noise contour and above noise exposure area, as
indicated on a map showing Ldn contours
generated by 1980 aircraft operational levels at
the airport, would have to be either the
plaintiff or a defendant in separate cases

involving the city. If this ruling holds up,
New Orleans may have to litigate up to 6500
individual cases involving 20 000 or so court-
prescribed airport environs.

Mr P. Youngman (Paper W6) described what is
being done in certain UK airports to move
towards an improved compatibility programme with
airport neighbours. He demonstrated the use of
earth mounds and tree planting to screen and
baffle noise. It was abundantly clear that
landscaping can be complementary to and
compatible with airport operations. Further, if
planned properly and in consultation with the
local community planners, the development of
woodland and surrounding area could result in
the airport's becoming an asset to the
community.

Types of airport environmental concern were:
noise, air quality, water quality, flora and
fauna, surface traffic congestion, growth
inducement caused by airport, uncontrolled urban
encroachment, etc. Noise was, however, the
dominant environmental issue.

It was noted that airport management teams
with positive attitudes have had the most
success with the resolution of airport
environmental problems; some airport management
teams have had negative attitudes which have not
always resolved the environmental concern with
airport neighbours. Actions that may help some
airport operators are

(a) keeping the public informed as to the
    airport development; airport neighbours are
    constituents of the airport

(b) keeping neighbours informed on new or
    deleted air carrier services

(c) developing noise mitigation programmes
    involving both airport management and
    airport neighbours in order openly to
    discuss the options available for
    addressing the airport noise issue

(d) continually upgrading the noise
    compatibility programme to include
    identifying noise abatement measures when
    possible

(e) assurance that the airport is committing
    time, effort and funds to developing a
    meaningful Airport Environs Plan or
    reasonable facsimile

(f) positive airport management attitude

(g) demonstration projects.

It was agreed by all that it was essential to have good planning. Professor N. Lichfield (Nathaniel Lichfield & Partners, London) noted the importance of the need for amelioration of noise in the planning systems of various nations. He noted that the UK and the US are working towards amelioration and compatibility. He noted the need for good design planning, taking into account the many variabilities in the planning options developed.

With regard to noise mitigation, Mr R. C. Lambert (Birmingham International Airport) noted that it was important for airport operators to continue to work with air carriers in constantly reviewing flight paths, which may assist in reducing noise, as long as it was a safe procedure. He underlined the importance of trying to resolve the noise issue.

Mr W. O. Toepel (Paper 5) noted that in the Federal Republic of Germany, the German Federal Parliament passed an aircraft noise abatement plan in 1971, establishing noise contours, noise monitoring systems within the airport vicinity, and the establishment of aircraft noise abatement commissions. These commissions have been very successful.

Aircraft noise was the dominant environmental subject discussed. Most large cities in many nations are very much aware of this problem. Although not all noise issues can be totally resolved, the important fact is that every effort has to be made, and continue to be made, by the airport operator and the airport neighbours to achieve a degree of success and understanding. It appears that an open, up-front approach is encouraged and this approach has been successful. Good planning, communication and community involvement are required to develop successful compatibility programmes.

MR R. C. LAMBERT, Birmingham International Airport plc
Following considerable earlier discussion on major UK and US airports, it may be useful to consider the question of approaches and resources in the context of Birmingham Airport, a smaller scale airport.

Birmingham is a UK regional airport, located in Central England, some 120 miles north of London. In 1986, it was the fifth busiest UK airport with a passenger throughput of some 2.2 million passengers, and it had the highest growth rate in the UK of over 27%. Traffic growth estimates are of 3 million passengers by the end of the decade, and of 7 to 8 million by the end of the century.

Part of my management responsibilities cover environmental matters. Therefore, I would like to take this opportunity to review a number of the issues under discussion in today's workshop, based on my experience at Birmingham.

In the past, the effects of an airport's operation have been treated by some airport staff as 'none of our business' or 'outside our fence'. This was, and to some extent still is,

a view expressed by operations staff and by airlines in particular. Indeed, for those living in East Anglia under the flight paths of a local NATO base which operates Phantoms, an F5 Aggressor Squadron, and accommodates other military aircraft including the SR71, this sort of view was prevalent until recently. However, what I call the 'Rambo' approach to aircraft noise - the distribution of bumper stickers proclaiming 'Jet noise - the sound of freedom' - is not an adequate response. Proper compensatory measures are now finally underway by the authorities concerned.

AIRPORT COMMITMENT
I certainly must endorse the view that fundamental to developing any solutions to environmental issues is the resolve of Airport Management to treat the problem seriously. It must positively decide to commit both effort and resources to easing environmental impact.

LIMITS TO ACTION
Airport Management must, however, be realistic. It should be aware of what actions it can, itself, take, and must temper the enthusiasms and ambitions of community groups or politicians on what is practical. Measures available can be grouped under three classifications.

Those directly under the airport's control
- Noise prevention facilities and layout
- Operational procedures - flight paths, reverse thrust usage
- Financial incentives - incentives for quiet aircraft, night curfews, except for Stage 3 aircraft, etc.
- Reduction measures: house insulation; noise monitoring; compensation; overall design, visual matters, surface access.
- Community liaison - 'Sell to public'
- Consultative Committees/Public Relations/ Sensible and honest complaints process
- Reduction measures: house insulation; noise monitoring; compensation; overall design, visual matters, surface access.
- Community Liaison - "Sell to public"
- Consultative Committees/Public Relations/Sensible and honest complaints process

Those which the airport can influence
- Land use planning: monitoring development in vicinity; assisting with zoning advice to local planning bodies.
- Issues influenced by airport organisations: legislation; national/international noise standards; air carrier operation and equipment use
- Comprehensive planning assessment: UK Public Inquiry, or EIS type procedure

Those dependent on the aerospace industries
- Engine/airframe noise improvements
- Operational performance gains, reducing need for runway lengthening and so on
- ATC and airspace systems to navigate etc. at minimum ground noise

For example, while there has been considerable discussion on improvements to passenger aircraft, recent experience at Birmingham can show how technology can help new freight initiatives.

In the last two years, Birmingham has experienced considerable growth in overnight freighters on parcels services. Starting with small piston and turboprop operations, resident operators such as TNT and Federal Express have expansion plans needing larger aircraft. TNT initially used a 737-200 QC freighter, but have now brought into operation the first of a number of BAe 146 freighters, known as the QT - 'The Quiet Trader'. Noise impact is significantly reduced, to the extent that such operations do not register on the Airport's noise monitor system. To give some idea of the difference, George Doughty at Stapleton Airport, Denver (Paper 2) has introduced a slot allocation based on noise. Using a 727-200/JT8D-9 as a base measure, the BAe is allocated 70 movements for every 727-200 movement. A performance only beaten by some light turboprop commuters.

MEASURES AT BIRMINGHAM

Specific measures to reduce noise have been taken at Birmingham, and these are as follows.

Noise bunds

The noise bunds consist of two bunds: average height 12 m, total length 1.75 km with 675 000 m3 earth used in construction.

These bunds shield houses from ground noise caused by: parallel taxiway - main bund (where movement is also banned at night by planning conditions); the domestic apron, where there is noise from ground operations (fixed ground power was also installed on this 'sensitive face' first).

Estimates at the Public Inquiry were a 10 dBA reduction from ground noise in closest residential area. Tests by an independent local environmental health department showed actual effect to be some 15 to 17 dBA reduction.

In addition, substantial landscaping is gradually establishing a screen on the landside face seen from the houses.

During construction, there were some complaints from residents about dust. Since construction, complaints have varied. There has been one from a keen aviation resident who 'could not see the planes'. Some residents have complained that the bund 'made the sun set earlier'; others that the headlights of police security patrols reflected off the bund and shone into their bedrooms at night. These complaints have all been responded to and, where necessary, satisfactorily resolved.

Noise insulation grants

The Airport had to gain powers to implement the scheme by means of a Private Parliamentary Bill. By 1990, some £4m will have been spent, over a ten-year period, on insulating 4020 dwellings in the eligible noise contour. There is a resource decision to be made each year: that is, whether to spend £0.25m on the next phase of insulation, or whether to spend the limited budget on an airbridge or new crash vehicle, for example. These are the competing choices that occur.

Land Compensation Act 1973

The Land Compensation Act (1973) runs for six years from 12 months after the use of the project has started. Eligibility is due to major works. The houseowner must prove loss of property value on account of airport expansion. Potentially, 30-40 000 houses are eligible. An expenditure cost of around £0.75m is immediately likely, and perhaps £2.0m ultimately.

Noise monitor system

The noise monitor system was installed at £100 000 cost to cover both ends of the main runway. It was used as a scientific tool for answering complaints, as a means to monitor airlines performance, and as a public relations tool proving commitment by the Airport.

CONCLUSION

No one measure can solve the environmental problems. Rather, management must organise contributions by direct and indirect processes to give an Environmental Management Package. However, this is at a cost.

Measures are internally funded, not generated by external grants or special government funds. This is illustrated by the fact that in a £62m development represented by Birmingham's new terminal facilities, some £5.5m of extra spending is being devoted to easing environmental impact and to demonstrating a responsible attitude to the communities in the airport's location.

Reference

LAMBERT R. C. The airport's response to environmental issues. Proceedings of the Institute of Acoustics, 1986, Vol. 8: part 4. (Also other papers in 10A Journal, 1986, Vol. 8: part 4.

DR D. COUSSIOS, Commission of the European Communities, Brussels

With regard to the points made by Mr R. H. Doyle (Paper W5), I would like to quote a sentence from his conclusions: 'It is possible to make an airport more compatible with its neighbours provided that certain guidelines are followed in the process ...' On the basis of this sentence, the following statement on the European Community Noise Policy is made.

The European Economic Community (EEC) is one of the smallest organisations currently involved with noise policy, representing only 12 European member states. There is also the European Civil Aviation Conference (ECAC) located in Paris, which represents 22 European member states. Although these states are working towards a common noise policy, they have not yet managed to achieve this. In addition, there is the International Civil Aviation Organisation (ICAO), which embraces more than 150 states, including almost all European nations. However, its proposal falls short of a detailed noise policy because a level cannot be found which is sufficient for, and thus acceptable to, each individual member state.

What we are attempting at the moment within the EEC is to establish these 'certain guidelines' referred to by Mr Doyle. As a first step - one which is being strongly pushed by the environmentalists and frequently being opposed by the big air carriers - we are simply trying to eliminate the use of Chapter 2 aircraft (as specified by ICAO), i.e. the most noisy aircraft still in existence, and to encourage the widespread introduction of Chapter 3 aircraft operation, as these aircraft are, to a certain extent, quieter.

It has already been stated that a new directive, following the previous one of 1983, is now under discussion within the EEC. We hope that one will eventually be passed, but are realistic enough to know that a great deal more needs to be done to ensure 'compatibility plans and programmes' for all member states of the EEC. However, we are prepared to make the maximum effort in order that a viable directive, acceptable to all EEC states, may be realised, and its terms duly implemented by these states.

W7 The use of automation in the airport environment

J.M. WINEBERG, International Air Transport Association, Cointrin-Geneva, Switzerland

From the moment a passenger enters the environs of a modern airport he will likely perceive that he is no longer in control of his own destiny. Rather, he will rely on the airport operator, the airlines and a variety of service providers to ensure that he has a safe and pleasant journey. These entities in turn rely on automation to give them the tools necessary to provide the passenger with the service he expects at a competitive price. Airport planners, operators and the airlines face the challenge of accommodating and exploiting automation in order to better manage the airport environment.

1. Huge amounts of information flow through a typical airport every working hour; the equivalent of 20,000 pages from a novel, thousands of telephone conversations, hundreds of radio contacts and more. Imagine the effect on an airport if automated information flow ceased. Predictably, air traffic would come to a complete halt, but other essential services would likewise be affected including security, ground services and ground transportation.

2. In spite of the already sizable quantity of information processed or flowing through an airport, the use of automation in the airport will continue to increase. This is due to a variety of factors whose origins are commercial, technical and regulatory in nature.

Factors Leading to Greater Use of Automation

3. Deregulation in the U.S. has permitted airlines to adjust routes and prices freely. Since 1978 the number of U.S. passengers has increased 60%. Last year nearly 950 million passengers flew worldwide while nearly 200 million passengers flew internation. Each of these passengers required a reservation, ticket and boarding pass, with many needing a hotel and rental car as well. Most paid with credit cards which required verification due to lower floor limits. (The limits are which the merchant is required to verify the transaction with the card company.)

4. Conjointly airlines have embraced the hub and spoke concept resulting in scores of simultaneous or near simultaneous aircraft arrivals and departures. Hub and spoke operations are particularly dependent on automation in the areas of crew management, flight operations, equipment planning, boarding control, baggage handling and security. As deregulation (or liberalisation as it is sometimes called) becomes more widespread so too will the need to automate these functions. Even the smallest carriers are beginning to automate such functions using PC's which will generally be located at the airport.

5. The largest airlines are frequently near the point of capacity constraints of one form or another on their large centralised passenger service systems. This phenomena, along with the need to exchange more information with other businesses and to be more responsive to local user requirements, is encouraging migration to distributed processing. Once again this will result in more automation at the airport facility.

6. One of the few remaining areas in which airlines can reduce costs is labour. Automation represents a tool to achieve greater labour productivity. Automation is the essential ingredient in the recipe for the two man crew which has resulted in enormous savings to the airlines and therefore the passenger. Similarly the airlines can be expected to push more work onto the passenger in return for a lower fare. The self ticketing features of airline shuttle operations and flight information displays are examples. More such automated systems will be used in the future to reduce labour costs.

7. The ruling in the International Civil Aviation Organisation (ICAO) Annex 17 requiring, for security reasons, the passenger and his baggage be reconciled before departure will almost certainly require automation for effective implementation.

8. A wide variety of decision support systems are being considered for implementation by the airlines and some airport managers. Such systems will likely involve or centre on the airports. (The National Airspace plan in the US effectively involves implementing a large decision support system.)

9. Other airport users as well as the airports themselves are becoming significant users of automation. The systems implemented by these users often require links to other users, e.g. cargo agents, customs, the postal service and so forth, resulting in still more automation.

Systems and Services

10. A variety of systems and services have been implemented in response to the factors mentioned above. Still more are being envisioned and yet others remain to be discovered. Some of the major developments fall into the following areas :

11. Passenger Services Systems. Systems and architectures which allow (and require) the customer to do more of the work of making a reservation, paying for and receiving his ticket and obtaining a boarding pass are likely to become increasingly popular in the future. Self ticketing machines are an obvious and important aspect of this scenario. However there is more to it than just issuing a ticket. On-line credit verification is required and seat selection certainly becomes feasible. Again the hub and spoke system of on-line connection favours such developments. Self ticketing machines provide the side benefit of moving passengers away from crowded ticket counters.

12. Automated Check-In and Departure Control. A great deal of speculation has occurred regarding the feasibility of fully automating the ticketing/boarding process. In such a process the self ticketed passenger checks himself in and passes his ticket/ boarding pass over/through a sensor which activates a turn stile allowing him to pass onto the airplane. Such a scene takes place daily in a number of subway stations worldwide. While the problem is much more complicated for air travel there is no technical reason that the same thing or something very like it cannot be implemented at the world's major airports. Such a system could use a "smart" credit card to eliminate paper completely.

13. There is at least one major technical reason why totally automated passenger boarding systems are not in commercial use; that is the lack of a distributed architecture consistant with airline passenger service systems along with the underlying service definitions and standards necessary to support it. Work is currently underway within IATA groups as well as in other organisations to overcome this technical hurdle; though not with the explicit purpose of implementing such a system.

14. There are other, non-technical factors as well including : interlineling the passenger to another airlines; capital investment; ownership and sharing of the equipment and permanence of route structures. Again while the hub and spoke may lend itself to automated boarding control, the other issues are basically economic and hence may be addressed when a carrier is seeking a way to be more price competitive.

15. Baggage Handling. While the ICAO Annex 17 directive will impact more than just airport automation, adherence to the directive will almost certainly involve automation. Work is presently underway within an IATA strategy group to define industry accepted standards for bar coding of baggage tags. It is envisioned that the proposed baggage tags will be readable by laser scanner.

16. Security. Security is a very complicated and complex area which from the airlines point of view involves both passenger check-in and boarding and baggage handling. One can envision systems whereby the passenger (or more precisely his boarding pass or "smart card") is electronically tracked as he moves through special "gateways" within the airport such as check-in, security and jetway or boarding lounge. Below, and on the airside, the movement of his baggage would be tied to his timely progress through the gateways.

17. Aside from the unease which might be felt by the passenger in knowing that his every move is being tracked; there are an enormous number of technical problems associated with such a scheme. Its implementation almost certainly would be difficult to justify commercially. However, achievement of automated ticketing, automated check-in and automated boarding control for commercial reasons tied with increased automation in baggage handling may provide much of the necessary foundation for improved security. It is unreasonable to expect that even vast (and unaffordable) amounts of automation applied at the end of a process can ensure security. The threat created by terrorism must be dealt with at its source.

18. In addition to the physical aspects of security the airlines are addressing the commercial aspects as well. Working cooperatively with the credit card companies and issuers, airlines are using real time credit verification with the intent of reducing fraud and accidental misuse of credit. Credit verification transactions involving hundreds of millions of dollars are routinely handled every month. IATA member carriers have recently agreed a plan which will increase using of existing automation to intercept fraudulent use of lost and stolen tickets.

19. It is important to recall that the time a passenger spends in a ticket or check-in line is critical to the airline and the airport. Anything which adds to that time is enormously expensive to both parties. Hence it is imperative that additional security features not delay the passenger's progress through the ticketing check-in and boarding processes.

20. Customs and Cargo. The various customs agencies worldwide are seeking to automate their activities utilising a worldwide electronic data interchange standard. Activities are currently underway in the UN and ANSI to finalise that standard. Cargo agents and freight forwarders are seeking real-time information concerning incoming shipments and customs clearance. The resulting systems, often called Cargo Community Systems are typically unique to each airport and, as such, represent a real difficulty to airlines who must fly into a variety of airports.

21. IATA and other groups are involved in attempting to specify an automated solution

which will allow the airlines to communicate to the resulting systems in a standard manner, from the airlines point of view. At the same time the airline industry is following the standards activities of the UN, ANSI and others trying to determine if these standards can meet the needs of the airline industry and, if so, how best to migrate toward their use.

Airports and Automation

22. Most of the world's major airports have at least parts of their infrastructure which are relatively old and hence predate many of the new automation activities taking place in the airline industry. Furthermore these older airports were designed to meet the needs of the "landside" and the "airside", and to a varying extent they have succeeded. However, another "side" is emerging; the "automation side". To an increasing degree airport design and renovation must include the facilities to support large scale automation.

23. Airlines must work more closely with airport designers and operators to ensure that the automation needs of all the airports users can be met without expensive modifications later on. Airlines frequently spend scores of man-years developing new systems; they must be prepared to invest the few man-months necessary to include automation and communications knowledgeable technical staff on airport engineering teams. These individuals can advise the teams on the nature and support requirements of new and enhanced systems. Airport designers and engineers can then provide for facilities such as : adequate cable trays and ducts; sunken floored rooms suitable for computer flooring; satellite processing rooms along the concourses; specialised lighting; control of RF noise; improved cable access to ticket counters and check in points; etc, if they are needed.

24. In return airport planners and operators should bear in mind the far flung nature of the airlines' business and attempt to support the implementation of systems and services which are compatible with airline and other airport systems.

25. It has been said that transportation and automation are engaged in a race, the loser will be relegated to the status of second-best or even redundent. I prefer to think that the marketplace has spoken in favour of both and that both are in a race to meet the needs of the consumer. No better case can be made for my assertion than to observe the meeting of automation, transportation and the passenger in a modern airport.

W8 Maglev — a magnetically levitated people mover system for airports and other public transport requirements

R.W. STURLAND, Chief Engineer, GEC Transmission and Distribution Projects Ltd, Stafford, UK

This paper describes a magnetically levitated people mover system (Maglev), and discusses the benefits to airports from such a system. Comments and observations are made as to the suitability of Maglev for this purpose. Some detail is given about the first Maglev system to go into revenue service at Birmingham International Airport in order that the scope of such systems can be explained.

INTRODUCTION

The method of transporting people with their luggage, both air side and land side in an airport complex is of great interest to companies in the transport business.

A quick efficient service, attractive to passengers, with maximum availability and very low maintenance costs are the basic requirements. Consideration of capital and running costs must be taken into account when deciding upon the solution for any given airport's requirements.

One such transportation system, suitable for airports and worthy of consideration uses magnetically levitated vehicles. The system has the advantage of being a new high technology solution that is somewhat novel and captures the imagination of the public. This is borne out by the reaction of passengers at the link from Birmingham International Airport to the British Rail mainline station.

The only moving parts on the vehicle are the doors and a cooling fan for the propulsion motor which is only used during periods of peak load. Maintenance is therefore a very light-weight operation, mainly electronic in nature, with no turning-down of worn steel wheels or replacing running rails, as would be necessary with a steel wheel on steel rail solution. As a result the maintenance facility is greatly reduced.

The system is fully automatic and therefore does not need large numbers of staff in attendance, only a supervisor in the control room is required. This supervisor can observe all that takes place by way of Closed Circuit Television, and a supervisory data acquisition system.

By using an elevated guideway the system can be incorporated into the airport complex with little obtrusion, entering the buildings at the level required, leaving the ground below clear for roads and car parking as required. The stopping area or platform for a Maglev train can be within the airport buildings since the system is pollution free and very quiet. This keeps the distances, which passengers have to walk, to a minimum.

THE GUIDEWAY

The elevated guideway can be carried on vertical columns spaced at intervals of approximately 15 metres. A typical height for a guideway would be about 5 metres. The construction used at Birmingham employed reinforced concrete columns and a top section carrying the prefabricated dual trackwork. A walkway down the centre of the two tracks is provided.

The track work consists of two laminated support rails for the levitation system, with the reaction rail for the linear motor, which provides the propulsion, in the centre. The vehicle picks up its electrical power from aluminium conductors with a stainless steel facing which are carried on the structure. Since the brush gear contacts the stainless steel face, conductor wear is minimised, while the aluminium portion maintains good conductivity.

The vehicle sits down on the support rails when not in the flying position. Additionally there are cable loops laid along the track to form data links with the car for automatic operation and aluminium marker plates are provided for speed detection purposes (See Fig. 1). Having accommodated all these features it is necessary to ensure that the natural frequency of the track system is above 10 Hz to avoid any possible excitation and interaction with the vehicle suspension.

Finally, safety has to be built into every design aspect of a public transportation system. The structural design of the guideway, the track alignment, overrun distance and buffer specifications have to be co-ordinated with the vehicle dynamics and braking performance in order to meet the excellent safety record demonstrated by conventional railways and other types of guided transport systems.

POWER SUPPLY SYSTEM

The vehicle is powered through sliding collector shoes made of metalised carbon. These shoes run in an extruded channel in conductor rails, which are rated at typically 1000

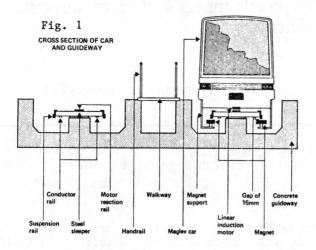

Fig. 1

CROSS SECTION OF CAR AND GUIDEWAY

Conductor rail | Motor reaction rail | Walkway | Magnet support | Gap of 15mm | Concrete guideway

Suspension rail | Steel sleeper | Handrail | Maglev car | Linear induction motor | Magnet

amperes, 750 volts d.c.

The d.c. current is provided from converters housed in a substation along with the necessary switchgear and transformers. The power supply for this substation would be obtained from the normal airport electrical supply facility at typically 11 kV. The substation design would be arranged to give the maximum security of supply to the cars in order that interruptions to service are kept to a minimum.

In order to prevent stray currents with associated corrosion and electrical interference problems, the 750V system is earthed at one point only at the substation. This ensures adequate safety for passengers on the vehicle or walkway while providing a convenient place to monitor the earth leakage current and de-energise the supply if an unacceptable level of leakage is reached.

Both positive and negative 750V conductor rails are well insulated and protected throughout their length making accidental contact or short-circuit virtually impossible. Nevertheless, all exposed steelwork is bonded together and connected to substation earth to minimise touch voltages should a system fault occur.

VEHICLE

The cars are 6.00 mm long, 2.25 m wide and 3.00 m high with a tare weight of 4.8 tonnes. The fire-retardant glass-fibre shell is carried on a welded aluminium chassis, with all electrical equipment under the floor or the seats. All equipment that may require replacement, checking or adjustment is mounted in modular form in easily accessible compartments. This is an essential system engineering requirement that ensures good serviceability, minimal mean time to repair, and thus high system availability.

A feature of this design is the ability to change the styling and colours to suit a particular airport or architectural requirement.

SUSPENSION AND GUIDANCE

The system comprises controlled d.c. attraction electromagnets, non-contacting

sensors, power transistor choppers and suspension control electronics.

Magnets

The vehicle has eight E-core axial flux magnets supplied by GEC Witton Kramer Ltd., mounted in pairs at each corner of the vehicle. The magnets of each pair are laterally offset by 10 mm on opposite sides of the support rail centre line, to provide guidance. They operate at a nominal gap of 15 mm and an airgap flux density of 0.8 Tesla. The magnetic flux paths are in the direction of motion of the vehicle, resulting in an economical 50 mm wide support rail, with vertical steel laminations. The magnet core is solid, electrical steel and it carries a winding made from anodised aluminium foil in which a number of temperature sensors are embedded to detect temperature and prevent the magnets from overheating. The magnet pairs are driven together by choppers to give vertical control and guidance, and differentially to introduce lateral damping. The average power for levitation and control is about 3 kW/tonne, with a lift weight ratio of 11.7 at 15 mm gap. Current density is $1A/mm^2$ per magnet.

Levitation

The naturally-cooled chopper module uses gate turn-off thyristors and freewheel diodes to form a pair of two-quadrant bridge circuits, each switching in antiphase at 1 kHz. The choppers have an efficiency of 97 per cent and transform the nominal 750V d.c. supply to a variable positive and negative voltage to provide a precisely controlled unidirectional magnet forcing current rated up to 25A continuous or 65A short time. The modules have a degree of local intelligence that interlocks the operation of the two halves of the switch pair such that the output becomes an electrical analogue of the input control signal.

PROPULSION AND BRAKING

The propulsion system employs an inverter driven linear induction motor. The LIM is of the single-sided, axial flux, short-stator type consisting of a three-phase, seven pole field winding embedded in slots of a laminated steel core mounted on resilient supports centrally under the vehicle. The reaction rail is formed by a steel T-beam capped by an aluminium plate. This is fixed longitudinally to the track between the suspension rails.

By using the linear motor it is possible to cope with steeper gradients than those associated with wheeled vehicles since tractive effort is not lost through slip as it is when transmitted through steel wheels to rails. Snow, ice or wet leaves are not a problem for this type of drive.

The configuration described can produce a tractive thrust of 4 kN from standstill to about 15 m/s while a nominal motor operational air gap (between motorface and reaction rail) of 20 mm is maintained. At this gap the motor has acceptable power factor at all but the lowest speeds which only account for a small proportion of running time.

The drive inverter is pulse width modulated using gate turn off power switching modules. The inverter rating is 240 kVA continuous or 325 kVA (450A) for 60 seconds. Frequency range is 0 to 45 Hz and power factor 0.5 to 0.9 lag or lead. Cooling is by natural air flow over fins presented to the outside of the vehicle. (See Fig. 2).

Waveform generation, system protection and inverter control are achieved by a microprocessor. The inverter responds to a thrust demand generated by the on-board, automatic train operation (ATO) computer. The inverter control then determines the correct voltage and frequency to apply to the motor taking into account the vehicle speed, line voltage, motor current and the instantaneous air gap of the motor.

During braking the motor acts as an induction generator and feeds energy back into the conductor rails. The regenerative energy is absorbed by the suspension system without an unacceptable rise in line voltage. The velocity profile is designed to suit the alignment of the track (vertical and horizontal) to give comfortable acceleration and braking rates.

In the case of a power failure or a major system malfunction the car settles down onto four brake pads and is brought to rest with an acceptable deceleration rate. The choice of brake pad material is critical for maintaining consistent braking performance in all weather conditions.

An auxiliary power unit is provided to charge an on board battery to support essential supplies when the main 750V d.c. supply has failed. The essential features maintained are communications and limited lighting. (See Fig. 3)

SYSTEM OPERATION

System operation can be selected by the operator to be either "continuous" (i.e. vehicles running backwards and forwards on one or both tracks with a preset dwell time between 0 and 99 seconds at each station) or "on demand" (i.e. vehicles only running in response to requests from passengers). Normally continuous operation would be used during busy periods, and on-demand operation during off peak periods.

The operator may choose either or both tracks from a "shut down" state, and cause the vehicle to run automatically, or hold it at a station docked (with its doors open) or parked (with its doors closed), despatching it manually by means of a button on the desk.

When the car is selected for "on demand" running, the passenger, on entering the station platform area, uses the system very much like a lift. He operates a "call car" button and when a vehicle is available for boarding, an illuminated sign indicates the boarding position. The passenger may also operate the "car start" button within the vehicle.

When the car is selected for "continuous" running, the vehicles are started from stations by means of the central or local scheduling logic (in accordance with traffic demand) and

the trains then run between stations under the control of the ATO computer on board one vehicle in each train. This computer controls the speed and stops the train at the next station. Then the trackside scheduling logic takes over to control the dwell-time at the station.

Vehicle starting is carried out under the control of the ATO system but all safety functions are interlocked by means of the Automatic Train Protection (ATP) circuitry. For instance, the doors must be proved to be closed before the vehicle may be levitated, and the vehicle must be proved to be levitated before propulsion power may be applied.

CONCLUSIONS

In conclusion attention must be drawn to the fact that further developments and improvements to the system are likely in the future. Materials such as super conductors with operating temperatures at or near room temperature will take magnetic levitation into a new era.

The development of longer articulated cars will increase the capacity without having to couple many small cars together to make a train. It is considered important to have access along the whole length of trains in these applications to get even loading and increase the safety of passengers from mugging or assault.

People mover systems will benefit from improvements in electronic components and control system techniques, enabling more efficient and lighter vehicles to be built. This will have beneficial effects on guideway requirements, possibly leading to advances in the civil engineering design.

MAGLEV - DATA SHEET FOR SYSTEM AT BIRMINGHAM INTERNATIONAL AIRPORT

SYSTEM:	
APPLICATION	People movers with capacity range up to 5,000 passengers per hour per direction.
PERFORMANCE	Maximum speed: 15 m/s = 54 km/h = 34 mph (typical journey) Curving capacity: 40m rad Maximum slope: 10% Acceleration/deceleration: up to 1m/s (typical)
POWER	750V dc for propulsion; suspension and auxiliaries; two trackside conductor rails; 48V d.c. on board battery/charger. Energy consumption: 0.165 kWh/passenger-km (typical journey)
OPERATION	Computer controlled; electronic fail safe speed and position monitoring; microprocessor local intelligence; automatic; driverless; bi-directional; on-demand or fixed

Fig. 2. Inverter fin for Maglev propulsion drive

Fig. 3. Auxiliary power unit

schedule; dedicated right-of-way; system monitoring from a remote control centre.

VEHICLE: Light-weight construction: welded aluminium chassis; GRP body shell; with coupling facilities for forming trains.

DIMENSIONS 6.00 m long; 2.25 m wide; 2.23 m high

WEIGHT 4,800 kg (tare), 8.000 kg (max total)

CAPACITY 34 standing, 6 seated passengers (typical)

DOORS Double-leaf on each side; doorway opening 1.6 m wide, 1.92 m high; independent electric operation.

PROPULSION Without wheels or moving parts; on board inverter supplying variable voltage and frequency; linear induction motor; 4.7 KN thrust at 15m/s providing traction and braking forces without mechanical contact with the track.

BRAKING Electrical (normal operation) regenerative, plugging, or d.c. injection using linear induction motor. Mechanical (emergency) by fail-safe brake pads.

SUSPENSION Without springs or moving parts. DC controlled attraction electromagnets mounted under two steel rails enabling the vehicle to float in air nominally 15 mm above the track.

ENVIRONMENTAL Noiseless (wind noise only); absence of vibration; pollution free. Design alternatives enable operation on elevated guideway, at grade or in tunnel. Compatible with modern urban infra-structure.

MAINTENANCE Practically maintenance-free; availability in excess of 99%; self checking and auto-diagnostic design features.

ACQUISITION COSTS Environmental acceptability permits maximum use of economical elevated guideway design. Vehicles employ standard industrial components.

OPERATING COSTS Low staffing requirement; high system reliability and absence of wear; no bearings; no transmission gears and no joints to lubricate. Straight forward maintenance by

automatic fault indication and module replacement. Low power consumption.

SAFETY Fail-safe automatic vehicle operation and protection based on conventional railway-engineering standards. Automatic over speed detection and braking initiation. Vehicle captive on guideway thus eliminating derailments. Redundant vital functions. Fire risk minimised due to absence of friction, moving parts, rubber tyres, lubricant, oil and fuel. Fire-retardant material employed throughout. Central control room monitoring, TV surveillance and two-way speech communications with vehicles.

REFERENCES
1. RHODES R G and MULHALL B E, Magnetic Levitation for Rail Transport, Clarendon Press, Oxford 1981.
2. JAYAWANT B V, Electromagnet Levitation and Suspension, Edward Arnold, London 1981.
3. MUSTOW S N, Maglev at Birmingham Airport, International conference on Maglev Transport Now and for the Future. I Mech E Conf Pubs. 1984-12., Mechanical Engineering Publications Ltd, London, Oct 1984 p.127.
4. BENUSSI J, CZECHOWSKI M K, HARBER J, and HUMPHREYS E M H. Birmingham Airport Maglev - system development, guideway design and construction. Ibid p.211.
5. NENADOVIC V, Maglev transit link for Birmingham Airport, Ibid P.169.
6. MCGEOUGH P A and SUTTON A, Birmingham Airport Maglev vehicle construction. Ibid P.177.
7. TAYLOR D R D, GOODALL R M and OATES C D M, Theoretical and practical considerations in the design of the suspension system for Birmingham Maglev. Ibid P.185.
8. POLLARD M G and SIMONS N J A, Passenger Comfort - the Role of Active Suspensions, Proc. Inst. Mech. Engs. Vol 198D, 1984.
9. LINACRE H, CHANAL J S, CRAWSHAW G, and RAWLINSON B, Birmingham Airport Maglev propulsion system. Ibid p.193.
10. BARNARD R E B, Birmingham Maglev - automatic control and communications. Ibid P.203.
11. JOHNSON W and NENADOVIC V, World's First Maglev Operation moves into Test Phase, Railway Gazette International, April 1983.
12. LILLEY M J. A Track Switch for Magnetically Levitated Vehicles, Track Technology for the next decade, Thomas Telford Ltd, London 1984.
13. Maglev at Birmingham Airport from System Concept to Successful Operation. V NENADOVIC and E RICHES. Gec Review Vol 1 No.1 1985.

Report on Workshop 4

MR J. M. KELLY, AVIATION PLANNING DIVISION, THE
PORT AUTHORITY OF NY & NJ, NEW YORK
The issues discussed during this workshop
session can be summarised as follows.

1. The need for special consideration early in
    design to be given to certain aspects, such
    as power requirements and computer rooms.

2. The need to broaden our thinking.

3. Consideration has to be given to the
    question of how technology (existing and
    future) is to be accommodated.

4. The fact that airlines change from
    simple/durable to complex/state-of-the-
    art/soon to be obsolete equipment.

5. It is important to place in proper
    perspective the requirement to move people
    and baggage: emphasis should be on
    reliability/safety features (all weather
    compatibility); life-cycle costs (simple
    controls/one operator) must be considered.

6. The need to serve the customer better -
    which should be the primary objective of
    technology: there is a current preference of
    customers for 'warm personal service'
    against high technology; and there is
    tremendous potential in baggage handling
    area for technology application, for two
    major reasons: $140 million per year cost to
    industry of lost bags; and the associated
    goodwill loss.

7. The role of Immigration Authorities: the
    need to collect information on passengers;
    the need to exploit technology (e.g. optical
    character recognition) - machine readable
    passports have already been issued in the
    USA, and will be issued in the UK during
    1988; different administrative needs of the
    Government have to be integrated.

8. There is a role for new technology in both
    the design of new facilities and in the
    refurbishment of existing facilities.

9. The design of facilities should be flexible
    and should anticipate future technology.

10. Maglev technology is readily implementable
    i.e. two years), dependent on the market.

11. Private sector financing/development
    opportunities exist, particularly for urban
    applications.

12. Competition among airlines should not be an
    impediment to introduction of new technology
    (IATA).

13. Government agencies, Immigration in
    particular, are committed to improving
    l.o.s., using technology where appropriate,
    within the real constraints of the priority
    needs dictated by security and political
    concerns. 'Procedural' options have been
    optimised. There is some potential for
    eventual privatization, although not much
    current optimism.

14. Airlines and airport operators are also
    committed to improving l.o.s., using
    technology where appropriate.

CONCLUSIONS
Given the substance of the issues discussed
herein, it would appear that new technology is
serving the air transport industry quite well.
However, it also became apparent during the
workshop that there is a pressing need
significantly to improve communications among
airport operators, airlines, government agencies
and the design professions, not only early on in
a particular project but on a continuing routine
basis.

It was also suggested that a single source
document (or perhaps several readily
identifiable documents) describing new
technologies and their applications for use by
all of the aforementioned parties, should be
made available and publicised.

At the conclusion of the workshop, some
specific lines of communication between
interested parties were developed. In addition,
continuing attention must be paid to improving
and expanding these communications on a regular
basis in order to ensure the best possible
product for the ultimate client - the air
passenger. The Conference has served as an
excellent catalyst towards this end.

Airports for people. Thomas Telford Limited, London, 1988

Closing Address

SIR PETER MASEFIELD, Director, British Caledonian Aviation Group

The theme of this Conference has been: 'Airports for people'. In this respect, I think that the most basic fact of all is that we are in a business which already provides a vital service for more than one billion airline passengers a year – that is, some three million a day; and we believe that this number of customers to be cared for will double during the next 13 years to the end of this century. So we are presented with formidable tasks indeed.

Against that background, there have been some memorable (and highly significant) points made at this Conference, starting from the opening speech given by Stanley Clinton Davis, the UK Commissioner for Transport at the EEC. Stanley Clinton Davis is, in fact, no stranger to the aviation business. He was Minister of State for Aviation – and one of the better Ministers – in an earlier British government. In opening the Conference, he made two statements which, I think, have not been said before – at least not in such precise or positive terms. They are highly significant to all of us.

Statement number one was that, from 1992, passengers flying in and out of all the 12 countries of the European Community would be considered as domestic passengers when passing through European airports. That means, in theory at least, no customs, no immigration and no extensive border controls: almost as in the USA. Of course, we will only believe it when we actually see it. However, there is no doubt that neither security nor some of the immigration laws will be relaxed, nor the search for drugs; nor should they be relaxed. But when so many flights (which are at present wholly international) become, at least in part, domestic, a very substantial change in all the arrangements will have to be made at Community airports – including those in the UK. Eventually, no doubt, the logical thing will be for this to lead on to 'European cabotage', where national airlines can fly freely between and within other national territories, with traffic rights. A whole new era for European air transport will then open up. Statement number one, therefore, has enormous implications.

Statement number two was that, from 1 January 1993, there would be no duty-free goods within the European Community. I believe that somewhere around half the total revenue which airports gain from duty-free goods in this part of the world comes from intra-European flights. Such a change would, therefore, have a very

substantial effect upon airport finances. We have a five-year warning of what may be in store.

Stanley Clinton Davis said one other important thing. He stated his belief that no United States type deregulation would come about within Europe – just a gentle move towards 'liberalisation' instead. I think that this is probably true, and I believe that the pendulum may well swing back to a less extreme form of deregulation in the United States, also. However, we are certainly in for a time of continued change; not least in more competition between airlines and airports.

Dr Gunter Eser of IATA reminded us that, in this year, the billion passengers who are being handled by World airports and World airlines – massive as that scale is – are going to increase steadily at, not less than, five or six percent per annum, and that this continued rate of growth will bring about a crisis, between demand and capacity, within the next decade. In some directions it has happened already and (in the United States alone) some 17 airports are approaching saturation – likewise, Heathrow and Gatwick in the UK.

The position is certainly made more difficult, particularly for long international flights, by rigid curfews, and Dr Eser called – quite properly – for a review of these curfews in the light of the much quieter aircraft which will be using the airports, to the exclusion of the noisier types, by 1991 or 1992.

Therefore, I think there can be doubt that – from this Conference – one of the subjects which must cause us all concern is the fact that, all round the world, we are heading for this 'crisis of capacity' at our major airports; and, in due course, at STOLports too. Certainly, that is well understood by all Airport and Air Carrier people, but there is nevertheless a great deal of complacency about it generally – and certainly on the part of politicians.

The problem which will confront us here in the London area is typical of elsewhere as well. This year about 52 million passengers will fly through the four London airports – Heathrow, Gatwick, Stansted and Luton, with 48 million of them (92 percent) through Heathrow and Gatwick. By the year 2000 (only 13 years ahead) – at only five percent average rate of increase a year – those 52 million will increase to 100 million; almost double today's numbers.

Experience shows that – taking into account the probable average sizes of aircraft using

Airports for people. Thomas Telford Limited, London, 1988

these airports - we cannot expect to get more than 20 million passengers a year through each runway; nor can we expect more than about 15 million passengers a year through any one terminal building. Hence - by the year 2000 - to cope with 100 million passengers a year in the London area, we shall need no fewer than five major runways, each fully up to capacity (each at about 160 000 transport aircraft movements a year), together with seven major terminal buildings at capacity also. At present, the four London airports have a total of five runways and eight terminals; not all of them capable of handling the full quotas of capacity.

At the best, therefore (and a 5% average growth rate is, perhaps, conservative), the London area airports will be chock-full by the year 2000 - or before. We know that - with the political and environmental problems which surround us - it takes fully 12 years on average to achieve any major new airport project from first proposition to first operational use. So we have just about one year in which to begin to put into action a plan with which to provide adequate airport capacity in the London area from the year 2000 onwards. We had better 'get weaving' - fast. And that applies to a great many other traffic centres as well. That is one of the basic facts to emerge from this Conference: there is no time to 'sit on our hands'.

Runways and terminals are not the only bottlenecks. Adequate ATC services and adequate access are vital too. Therefore, I suggest that two interrelated points arise from this Conference.

1. We must start to prepare right now, to be ready for the needs of 20 years hence
2. A question: How big should individual airports be designed to grow?

It has been said - and I am sure that it is true - that above and beyond a certain size, airport efficiency begins to break down: to break down on access, on parking, on transfers between terminals and aircraft, and on the number of gates available.

This raises another point - perhaps only touched on at this Conference. Should scheduled trunk and regional air services and airports be segregated from 'whole-plane' group charter services? There are persuasive arguments for this, but also some resistance. In this country, Stansted might become primarily a charter airport for leisure flights. Interlining between scheduled services would than be concentrated between Heathrow and Gatwick. There would then be room for regional airlines to feed in and out of these two hubs.

From that - in discussion at this Conference - comes the point that air transport services are beginning to develop into two quite distinct categories. The major air carriers are continuing to move into larger and larger aircraft flying over longer ranges at higher frequencies. Alongside, new regional and commuter airlines are developing, flying smaller aircraft into the major hubs - or, at least, wanting to do so, subject to slots. To what

extent can that develop in the face of the airport capacity problem?

At the end of this Conference we are left with as many questions as there are answers - or more questions still to be answered. But then it is better to debate a question without settling it than to settle a question without debating it.

There is one other point of great importance. Every 30 years or so since, in 1905, the Wright Brothers began really sustained flight there has been a major technical advance in aeronautics. In 1935 - with the DC-3 - we moved from the fabric covered biplane to the stressed-skin monoplane with retractable gear and controllable pitch propellers. Thirty years later, in 1965, we moved from the piston engine to the long-range jets, which represented another revolution. Now we have eight years to go to 1995 - a further 30 years on. What is on the horizon to come in then? I am sure: 'We ain't seen nuffin' yet'. I suggest that 1995 (and after) may be a profoundly interesting time for air transport and airports; although every year is an interesting year - which is why the airport business is such a great business. Behind all this everywhere (and inevitably) in spite of all that we do, one of the troubles is trying to get rapid, precise and favourable decisions out of politicians - not least of these being decisions on new airports to meet future needs.

In a different direction, when we heard the views presented to us by both airlines and airport authorities, one of the major points which became increasingly clear was that there is a fundamentally different approach to the task of an airport by the airport authorities, on the one hand, and by the airline operators on the other. We have all known this, of course, for many years, but it has been brought out especially strongly at this Conference.

An airport is, after all, first and foremost an interchange point between surface and air transport in an outward direction, and between air and surface transport in-bound; and one of the things we are all selling is 'Time'. Airlines look towards an airport to provide the least hassle, the shortest possible delays and the shortest possible 'time-in-transit' for the passengers whom they have attracted through their marketing efforts and whom they are contracted to fly from A to B.

Recently, I came upon an old Imperial Airways notice which had been put up at Croydon Airport in the early 1930s. It read: 'Passengers are asked to arrive at the airport counter a few minutes before departure time'. Today, airport authorities - quite understandably - look on the airlines' passengers (together, to a lesser extent, with the 'meeters and greeters') as fair game for generating additional commercial revenue. Therefore, the passenger, passing through the airport, is exposed, to a maximum extent, to attractive opportunities for the purchase of a great variety of retail goods.

All this was brought out very clearly by Colin Marshall (Paper 3), expressing the complaints from airline operators (with which I have a great deal of sympathy, having sat in both camps over many years) that too much space and too much effort is devoted to relieving passengers of substantial funds on their way through airports rather than devoting the maximum effort to smoothing and speeding their way.

These are, indeed, to some extent irreconcilable attitudes, but we have to understand that they exist now and will go on existing in the future. Even so, when delays do occur - as they do even in the best regulated (or deregulated) families - shops and other attractions are very welcome to bored, waiting travellers.

Early on in our Conference, an independent and knowledgeable voice, that of Michael Donne of the Financial Times (see Paper 1), had, in his own words: 'some harsh things to say about airport standards'. His theme was that both airlines and airports should try harder to provide a service to those who use both their amenities. He was particularly critical of some of the standards provided at some of the smaller airports devoted primarily to holiday traffic.

Michael Donne and Geoffrey Lipman (Papers 1 and 4), speaking for passengers, listed, in order, key factors in the task of providing 'Airports for people'. Prominent among them were seven or eight points and they are worth repeating. Passengers require: good access; quick check-in; fast baggage claims; good security; ease of interline transfers; fast customs and immigration services; enough trollies, with shorter walking distances and high frequency of services. That is: 'Everything for the best in the best of all possible Worlds'. One other passenger requirement is that, in the future, allowance should be made for more carry-on baggage than is generally permitted at present.

In a move towards meeting these, quite proper, perfectionist requirements, there has been the continual plea for more urgent long-term planning, looking ahead perhaps some 20 years, especially in making available sufficient land for developments - always a scarce and vital commodity.

All of us who have been in the business for many years are well aware of the environmental problems involved. We are also well aware of the difficulties of looking even two or three years ahead, let alone 20. However, longish time-scales will obviously apply to some of the interesting and important new airports which are now in prospect (see Papers 5-7) - namely, at Munich, Sao Paulo and Sydney - together with those under way already at Stansted and the STOLport in London Docklands.

What I thought was particularly interesting was the fact that the major new airports at Munich, Sao Paulo and Sydney are all planned with two major runways and the terminal complex in between them. An even more extensive airport at Denver, Colorado (see Paper 2) is being projected for the end of the century, with nine runways. A fascinating figure came to light there: out of 34 million passengers handled last year at Stapleton International Airport, Denver, no fewer than 20 million were in transit and never left Stapleton Airport - they flew in and then they flew out again - whereas the remaining 14 million came and went to Denver itself.

This brings out one of the main aspects of the current development of major hub airports in the United States, in which transit passengers tend to exceed those originating and terminating at the hub. Indeed, one of the important points for the future (discussed at this Conference) is the extent to which hubs will develop in future airport patterns throughout the world. There is no doubt that in the United States this is a highly significant development which - among other things - is leading to monopolistic practices. Hubs become the centre of operations for some of the relatively few mega-carriers and for any regional carrier associated with them. They get slots - all others are lucky to do so. Otherwise, as deregulation has shown in the United States, some smaller communities are worse off now, and into the future, than they have been in the past, in terms of direct airline services.

Perhaps more STOLports will be a solution - and we have heard some heartening things about STOLports at this Conference (see Papers 10 and 11, and subsequent Discussion). There is clearly an increasing demand for STOL- or semi-STOL- runways at the major hub airports - linked to such City-STOLports as can be contrived. Furthermore, it is not beyond the bounds of possibility to fit in STOL-runways at both Heathrow and Gatwick in this country.

This leads us to a significant point with respect to Gatwick Airport. It is the fact that here is a very busy international airport, which is - almost uniquely - confined to a single runway. That is already - and is going to be increasingly so in the future - a substantial embarrassment to the development of Gatwick which, almost from now on, will have to be restricted in additional passenger numbers by increases in the size of the aircraft which are using the existing runway. The decision to confine Gatwick to a single runway was taken on political and environmental grounds - possibly one of the most unfortunate appeasement actions since Munich.

Gatwick was, in fact (contrary to some statements made earlier), originally planned as - essentially - a two-runway airport. The second runway was abandoned only when yet another Public Inquiry became almost too much to bear. I say 'almost' because, clearly, it ought to have been faced.

Now to two heresies which have been propounded at this conference. One is that Gatwick is the third busiest international airport in the world. Gatwick is, in fact, the international airport which handles the third largest number of international passengers. But that is not at all the same as being the third busiest international airport. In fact, among the international airports of the world, Gatwick is either the eighteenth or nineteenth busiest. For example, Denver, Colorado, of which we have heard so many interesting things at this Conference (see Paper 2), is a much busier international airport than Gatwick - along with 17 others. However, it handles fewer international passengers.

Another heresy which, in my view, was perpetrated (this time by Michael Donne (Paper 1)) was that the problems of capacity in the London area would have been better served had the Maplin plan gone through some 15 years ago.

Maplin was a projected four-runway airport, off-shore, some 63 miles away from London on the East Coast near Southend. Michael Donne bemoaned the fact that Maplin was shelved and believes that it would have solved our problems without the restrictions we are running into at existing airports. The fact is that Maplin would have been an economic disaster - and an air transport disaster as well, I believe - for six cogent reasons.

Firstly, the costs of reclaiming the offshore sands, which would have been necessary to convert these sands into an airport, would have been astronomical - more than £400 million in 1970 terms. Secondly, an airport more than 60 miles away from the main centre it serves would have been further away than any other major international airport in the world from its chief traffic catchment area. Access costs would have been enormous. Thirdly, because the airport would have been off-shore, the actual catchment area for traffic would have been confined to one narrow sector instead of a surrounding area. Fourthly, from an environmental point of view, access from London through the Eastern suburbs and then on through Essex for more than 60 miles would have cut a swathe through the countryside which would have caused immense opposition. Fifthly, public opinion towards Maplin, had it ever existed, would have been divided equally between those who would be horrified by the potential hazards to aircraft from the thousands of Brent geese who have migrated into the Maplin Sands for countless years and would still have gone on coming, airport or no airport, and those good people who also would be horrified by the hazards to the Brent geese from the aircraft coming in. Finally, the economics of operating out of such a vastly expensive airport in a remote corner would have been disastrous to the air transport business.

Therefore, we are well rid of Maplin but we still have problems in finding enough airport capacity in the London area - a problem which faces so many major cities today and which is one of the great difficulties in our business for the future. This has been well underlined at this Conference. Therefore, we must devote our full attention to the problems, as Gunter Eser described them, resulting from the crisis between demand and capacity in the airports world between now and the end of this century - and, I am sure, after that as well.

The wide sweep of affairs at the Conference included, of course, the vital facts about access and the remarkable success which has been attained at Gatwick by the Gatwick Express (running every 15 minutes from Victoria Station in London right into the airport terminal complex) with a 30-minute journey, non-stop, each way. This is a good example for other airports to follow and is one of the success stories of Gatwick, as I am sure it will be of Stansted with a similar rail link in years to come.

The workshop sessions covered many interesting topics. We also heard new prospects for the STOLport in Docklands - a portent for the future already in action in Canada and Norway, so successfully and happily linked with that great name of de Havilland.

From the aircraft manufacturers we have heard the latest thoughts on aircraft and engine developments, especially in the directions of bigger and longer-range aircraft, offering more amenities to the travelling public, although some additional problems to airport designers, constructors and operators.

Therefore, this Conference leaves us with the clear impression of a continually expanding business, still beset with problems but now a vital element in the economic prosperity of the world. Fortunately, one of the bugbears of earlier years - noise - is not so loudly acclaimed these days. And thanks to great technical success, aircraft noise will get steadily less as time goes by.

In a business such as this, everyone must face some criticism in striving to improve standards and, or course, airports are criticised for charges in many directions. However, we must maintain a sense of perspective on this. As one who has been deeply involved in airports as well as in air transport, I can take a strictly neutral viewpoint. There are many generous and kindly spirits even among airport operators. After all, airports allow free take-offs. They only charge for landing, so one could say it is a 50-50 business.

In conclusion may I say that, whatever our prayers for the future, one of the lessons of this Conference is that, although we must continue to pray for things to go the way we hope for, they will come about only if we work hard for them and never let up. Then, in due course, everything will work out for the best. At least, we hope so. In the meantime, we can offer up prayers that things will continue to be 'all for the best in the best of all possible worlds' in the tasks which confront us in the years ahead.